Injustice Is Served

Injustice Is Served

By Lynn Moller

Mill City Press

Mill City Press, Inc.
2301 Lucien Way #415
Maitland, FL 32751
407.339.4217
www.millcitypress.net

Printed in the United States of America

Edited by Mill City Press.

ISBN-13: 9781545602584

Table of Contents

*T*he story you are about to read is true. Credit for that quote goes to *Dragnet*, but I modify the remainder of its opening line — *some* of the names have been changed. The children referenced in my story were unwitting participants, dragged into this matter by their parents, the police, and the prosecutors. Their names have been changed to protect their privacy.

Although I believe that the parents of the children should be held accountable for their deceitful, hurtful, and frenetic behavior, I have changed their names to avoid identification of their children.

Actual names of all other key players have been maintained.

Court records and transcripts provide documentation of details rendered in my story. Conversations that have been seared into my mind are accurately disclosed. The substance of all other dialogues is described to the best of my recollection.

Penning my story has been painful, forcing me to relive the nightmare. I was often tempted to ditch the writing attempt. The desire to publicize my story and help others avoid what I experienced motivated me to continue. Regrettably, my tale is not an isolated occurrence. As long as allegations of child abuse are met with hysteria and lack of common sense, anyone working with children runs an inherent risk. If it happened to me, it can happen to anyone.

"I do not think that you can get a fair child abuse trial before a jury anywhere in the country...I do not care how sophisticated or law smart jurors are, when they hear that a child has been abused, a piece of their mind closes up, and this goes for the judge, the jurors, and all of us."

– Abner Mivka, U.S. Court of Appeals, D.C. Circuit 1990

Chapter 1

A Good Life

*P*ainfully shy. Meek as a mouse. Reticent. Reserved. Those were accurate descriptions of me as a child and young adult. Social situations were uncomfortable and awkward for me. With age and maturity, I came out of my shell, but I've always remained an introvert. However, there's one group of people with whom I shine—young children. I've always enjoyed being with kids, and my normal inhibitions and shyness disappear in my interactions with them. From an early age, I knew I wanted a career working with children. My sister was born when I was thirteen, and I played a key role in raising her. In high school, while my friends struggled with college and career decisions, I already knew the direction in which I was headed.

I attended the University of Wisconsin-Stout and earned BS degrees in Early Childhood Education and Child Development. I graduated in May 1984, and by August I had relocated and settled in Madison, Wisconsin, to start my job as preschool teacher at

1

University Avenue Day Care, right on the edge of the University of Wisconsin campus.

In early 1992, my husband Ki and I learned we were expecting our first baby. I decided to open up my own family child care business, allowing me to both care for my own child and maintain my career. We lived in a small duplex at the time, so I thought it would be best to start with infant care. Quality infant care was scarce, and I was excited to provide such care. I obtained a state license for family child care, and had no problem finding my first clients. In August 1992, I received a wonderful goodbye party from the staff and families at University Avenue Day Care, and welcomed Daniel, Eric, and Jack to Lynn's Day Care. Our son Evan was born a few months later, completing what I lovingly referred to as my "Boys Club."

Our second son Aaron arrived in December 1994, just as we began the process of buying our first house. It was small, but it was ours, and we were thrilled to have it. I continued my child care business there; I had no trouble getting families, mostly through referrals and having second children from previous families.

In 2002, we had the opportunity to build a house. I looked forward to designing it with a dedicated space for my child care business. We chose a site to allow a walkout lower level, which would be the day care space. In order to save costs on our new, larger mortgage, we did not initially finish the basement, so I ran the day care from the main level, but by 2006 we were able to complete the lower level.

I happily moved my child care program down there, with its own entrance, bathroom, kitchenette, large play area, and storage. I was thrilled with this new area. It was my dream space for the day care. I had fun planning and carrying out activities for the kids I loved. At the end of the day, I just walked upstairs to go "home."

In 2008, Ki and I started planning a trip to Hawaii for our upcoming twentieth anniversary. We were looking to make an addition onto our house and possibly buy some land for a cabin. Life was good.

Until it wasn't. The unthinkable happened, and my whole world came crashing down. I lost my career, my dignity, my savings, and, perhaps worst of all, my respect for the justice system.

Chapter 2

The Cast of Characters —
Day Care Families

*I*n 2008, seven children were enrolled in my day care program: Miles, Cody, Tommy, Emma, David, Eddie, and Max (again, names have been changed). Background information on certain children and their families is included here, some of which contributed to the events that shattered my life.

Jeter Family

The Jeter Family—Holly, Marty, and Annie—lived in my neighborhood. Annie Jeter started with me when she turned two years old in September 2003.

As a fellow teacher, Holly was supportive of my program. She presented gifts and tokens of appreciation throughout Annie's time with me. When my kitchen was painted and wallpapered and I had limited access to the facilities, Holly even brought lunch for everyone. I was appreciative of the gestures and was happy to have such an accommodating family in my care.

On August 26, 2004, one of the other parents told me that Annie arrived to day care riding on the lap of her dad in the car. I was shocked to hear that. The next day I made sure to watch for Annie's arrival, and, sure enough, Annie was sitting on Marty Jeter's lap, helping him "drive." It was only a few blocks from their house to mine, but accidents can happen anywhere. As it was rather hectic when Annie and Marty came in that day, I didn't get a chance to confront him about this situation. However, during the day, I wrote him a note explaining that Annie needed to be properly transported in a car seat. The next morning when he arrived (again with Annie on his lap), I presented him with the note, along with a copy of the Wisconsin child seat rules. I even spoke to my licensor about it when she came for an inspection visit, and I noted the occurrence in my day care log book. Holly called me later that evening, stating that Annie had informed her about riding on Marty's lap. She assured me that Marty wouldn't do that anymore, but did ask me to keep an eye on the situation. I did, and from then on Annie was properly restrained for her transport to my house.

Later that fall, Holly told me that she was pregnant. I was happy for their family. The baby boy was due in April 2005, and Holly asked if I would be able to enroll him in my child care starting in the fall. However, my program was full, so I could only offer part-time care. Holly was disappointed, but agreed to that, and said she would find someone else to take the baby on the days I couldn't. I expressed that maybe it would be better to find someone who could take the baby full-time, but she said she wanted him with me and would take whatever days I had available. I was pleased that this family wanted to stay with me, even under less-than-ideal circumstances.

Miles was born April 5, 2005. Holly had the rest of that school year off for maternity leave, but Annie stayed with me until the end of May. She would graduate to preschool in the fall. As I did when any child left my care after an extended period, I cried on her last day. I had no inkling that one day in the near future, I would meet my Waterloo because of that little girl.

Miles started with me at age five months on September 1, 2005. Miles was a happy, normally developing baby. He was in my care on Mondays and Thursdays and was with his grandma for the other weekdays.

On Monday, October 10, 2005, Holly picked Miles up early for a doctor appointment. At this visit, he received a clean bill of health and his six-month series of immunizations, including DTP, polio, and PCV. The next morning, Holly called me to ask if Miles had been okay the day before, in terms of physical abilities. Upon waking Tuesday morning, he was limp, floppy, and unable to support himself. He had been able to sit up on his own, roll over, and stand with assistance, but seemed to have lost these milestones overnight. I told her that he was fine and active on Monday and I had not noticed anything unusual concerning his motor abilities; in fact, he had been bouncy and active in the "Johnny Jump Up" doorway bouncer. She said she would call their pediatrician, Dr. Conrad Andringa.

Dr. Andringa was not able to give any diagnosis, and recommended a wait-and-see approach. Miles did not improve throughout the day, so Holly took him to the emergency room in the evening. The ER doctor could not find anything either, and recommended that he go back to his primary doctor. Holly went back to Dr. Andringa on October 12, who noted that all Miles' extremities were flaccid. A neurologist consult was obtained, and Miles was admitted to the hospital for tests.

Holly called me later that week and said that, although she suspected that his six-month vaccines caused the problem, an MRI had shown a Chiari I malformation and possibly a presyrinx in the spinal column. I was not familiar with these conditions. Holly indicated that there was a family connection for the Chiari. She explained a bit about the condition, and I did some research to get a sense of what Miles was experiencing.

The National Institute of Neurological Disorders and Stroke describes Chiari malformations (CMs) as structural defects in the cerebellum, the part of the brain that controls balance. Normally the cerebellum and parts of the brain stem sit in an indented space at the lower rear of the skull, above the foramen magnum (a funnel-like opening to the spinal canal). When part of the cerebellum is located below the foramen magnum, it is called a Chiari malformation.

CMs may develop when the bony space is smaller than normal, causing the cerebellum and brain stem to be pushed downward into the foramen magnum and into the upper spinal canal. The resulting pressure on the cerebellum and brain stem may affect functions controlled by these areas and block the flow of cerebrospinal fluid — the clear liquid that surrounds and cushions the brain and spinal cord — to and from the brain.

Holly kept me updated with Miles' condition and the newly discovered diagnoses. I gave the Jeters a non-paid leave of absence for the remainder of 2005, stating that I would hold a spot for Miles whenever he was ready to return. Miles had decompression surgery in November.

Holly called me in mid-December of 2005, stating that Miles would return to child care after Christmas. I would then be able to take him full-time, and she said that was the best present I could give her.

It didn't take Miles long to adjust to being back in my care in January 2006, and he was the same happy little boy he had been before his absence. He was not physically at the level of other kids his age, but he could sit up. Little by little, he gained some primitive crawling skills. He was not immobile. I was impressed by his ability to compensate for what he couldn't do in his movement attempts. His legs were strong enough to enable him to stand up against something sturdy. I also made sure to move him to different spots around the room if he couldn't get there on his own.

During this time, Miles started the oral medication Neurontin (Gabapentin); I'm not sure of the reasoning. I gave him 1.5 ml each morning. A rare side effect of Neurontin is unusual bleeding or bruising, and it is not generally a medication given to children under age three.

Holly's neighbor called me in the spring of 2006 in search of summer-only child care for her son. She knew Holly was a teacher and might want to have Miles home with her, so she was requesting Miles' spot. However, Holly did not want to give up the spot, even though it meant she would not have to pay for summer child care. She wanted Miles to remain in my care during the summer, if only on a part-time basis.

Fall of 2006 was when I moved my child care program down to the lower level. I purchased a push toy/walker for Miles to use, and he was able to walk behind it. He had a physical therapist, Arianna, who came weekly and worked with him for an hour while he was at my house.

One morning in spring 2007, upon Miles' arrival at day care, another parent stated to Marty that he liked how Miles drove the car with him. I'm sure my mouth dropped open. I said to Marty, "Oh no—you're not doing that again?" Marty sheepishly looked at me and said to the other parent, "Yeah, Lynn doesn't like it when

I do that." Since my child care area was now in the lower level facing the back of the house, I was unable to see when or how the parents and children arrived. How long had Marty been doing this again? My concern for Miles' safety trumped my unease of being a tattletale, so I emailed Holly about the situation. She expressed gratitude for letting her know, and said she would speak to Marty about it. I never heard of the issue again.

Miles started walking independently toward the end of 2007. His gait was clearly side-to-side and he used surrounding furniture or stable items to help him navigate. He would tire easily, and his usual length of walking on his own was less than six steps, after which he would resort to crawling or using his walking toys.

In 2008, Holly submitted a claim to the National Vaccine Injury Compensation Program (NVICP), alleging that Miles suffered neurological injuries because of the receipt of his vaccinations on October 10, 2005. The 2012 decision from the U.S. Court of Federal Claims determined that she failed to establish causation; therefore, compensation was denied.

Marshall Family

Steven was born in August 1998. His mother, Maria, was referred to me by her coworker. I had an immediate connection with the family, which included Maria's husband, Joe. Steven was a first child, and Maria was protective and vigilant. Steven started with me in November 1998, and Maria called me every day to see how he was doing. Her calls were so frequent that I would pick up the phone and say, "Hi Maria," before I even had caller ID. Steven graduated from my care to preschool in the fall of 2002, but I still kept in touch with the family. Steven would come a few times for drop-in care over the next few years. He always asked me if I remembered his birthday. I would say, "Of course! August 27."

The Marshall's second child, Cody, was born in February 2006. In spring 2007, Maria learned that I had one day care opening, and asked if I could take Cody. I was thrilled to have the family return. Cody was just over a year old at this point, and had no trouble adjusting to his new setting. I fully expected to start the daily phone calls with Maria again, but was surprised when there no calls. I know parents are often much more relaxed with a second or subsequent child, but this was such a drastic change from daily calls for Steven to none for Cody.

Cody usually arrived at my home by seven a.m. I didn't officially open until 7:15 but I allowed the early arrival. Therefore, Cody and I were alone for a while before other kids arrived. This was our bonding time, and he helped me get things ready for the day. Although not talking, he seemed to understand anything I said. By the time the other children arrived, he was ready to start playing with them. He happily greeted his friends and their parents. Cody was an active, healthy, happy little boy.

However, by late spring of 2008, when he was a little over two years old, I started to notice some troubling changes. Upon arrival, he was whiny and clung to his dad. It didn't last long after Joe left (typical of how many kids act), but it was new behavior. He would continue to help me in the morning before other kids arrived, but he followed and clung to me as he had not done before. I often turned around and ran into him, not aware that he was right on my heels. So focused was he on remaining close to me that he didn't watch where he was going, resulting in him occasionally bumping into something. Once the other children arrived, he ceased his routine of greeting them and the parents; he remained attached to me. I had to direct him to find something to play with. He seemed dependent on me telling him what to do, he wouldn't approach or join the other kids to play, and he would stay at one activity. When I suggested he move to another activity, he would start to cry in a whiny manner, and it didn't stop until I said, "Shush now, Cody," or "Time to stop crying." Outside, Cody would get on one of the riding toys and ride around the patio in a circle. He would spend the whole outside time doing that unless I encouraged him to do something else.

Cody liked and participated in our circle times where we sang, played games, read stories, or did art projects. However, these times were led by me and not self-directed.

Even upon getting up from naptime, Cody needed a direct prompt from me. I would open the blinds and all the other kids would excitedly hop up from their cots. Cody would remain on his cot, observing the other kids arising, until I physically went over to him and told him it was time to get up.

This puzzling behavior continued all summer. He was a barnacle on me. When he was directly with me or if I was leading a group or activity, he was fine. Left to his own devices, though, he sat quietly looking at books or riding around in circles outside.

When a toddler has a regression of skills or behaviors, I worry about autism. I didn't want to needlessly concern Joe or Maria, so I decided to monitor the behavior for a while. Cody's attendance at day care was down that summer, so I speculated that he was enjoying his extra time at home and not thrilled about being at day care. We all know how it is going back to work or school after a vacation.

During the summer, Cody also started spitting up at meal or snack times. He would eat something, and then a short while later regurgitate it. I didn't think much of it the first few times, but I became concerned the more it happened. He wasn't throwing up as in being sick; it was just after consuming some food. I wondered if he was having a gag reflex, didn't like a particular food, had anxiety, or some other issue. He would generally soil the front of his shirt. I would tell his parents, but all they said was that if he was sick they would take him home. I informed them that this wasn't a typical vomit situation; he spit his food back up. They did not seem concerned. I would need to change his shirt. It was rare for his parents to replace his spare clothes after I sent home his soiled shirt, so then he had nothing of his own to wear if he needed a change. I had to find a shirt from my collection of extra day care clothes. It got to the point where I would throw his dirty shirt into the wash so he would have something clean.

His parents didn't seem to care about this issue. I became frustrated, not with Cody, but with why this happened, and why his parents didn't seem concerned. When it occurred, I would quickly need to move Cody away from the table and the other kids, and clean up the mess. I had had standard/universal precaution guidelines ingrained into my mind through continuing education programs. Any bodily fluid may hold contagious germs, so whenever there was exposure to feces, urine, vomit, or other bodily discharges in the day care, I went into hyper-drive to get the kids out of the way and the offending substance cleaned and disinfected immediately.

At times, exasperated at the spitting up, I found myself sighing and saying, "Oh no, Cody, no spitting up." I realized this was inappropriate on my part, as some of the other kids said the same thing. I started to keep track of the times Cody did this and the foods I served. I could find no pattern. Days would go by with no incidents. I would get optimistic that the behavior had stopped, only to have it start up again.

On July 25, 2008, my sons had doctor appointments at 3:30 p.m., so I had asked all the parents to please pick up by three o'clock that day. I didn't often ask for an early close, but sometimes I needed to. I had put the request to the parents well in advance, and then reminded them all that morning.

Three o'clock arrived and all the children except Cody had been picked up. At 3:05, I gathered up Cody's things and took him up to the driveway to wait for his parent(s). At 3:10, I called Joe, who said he had no idea that there was to be an early pick-up. It was nearly 3:30 by the time he eventually arrived, making my boys late for their appointment. I was on vacation the next week, so I never got a chance to discuss the incident with the Marshalls. I also figured it was a fluke and I didn't want to dwell on it.

When Cody was picked up, it was common for Joe and often Maria to be on their cell phones. I thought that was rude. Greeting Cody seemed secondary to their conversations.

Two separate times during the summer of 2008, Maria told me that she and/or Joe had some behavior issues with Cody, and they used my name in reference to making him behave. One time they were eating out and Cody was naughty, so they asked him if he wanted me to come and make him be good. Another time, Cody did not stay in bed and they asked him if I should make him go to bed. I was appalled that they were using my name in reference to this. The phenomenon of kids behaving better at school or day care is unbelievably common. Parents find it surreal to see their child willingly take a nap or try peas at day care. Kids work hard to hold it together at day care; once home they may "let it all out." Cody's less than desirable behavior on these occasions was perfectly normal, yet his parents were threatening him with me making him behave, likely confusing poor Cody and painting me in a bad light.

15

On August 12, Cody was still at day care at five o'clock, my closing time. That was unusual, as he generally left by 4:30. I waited until about 5:10, at which time I called Maria. She was absolutely shocked that Cody was with me. She said that Joe was supposed to have taken Cody with him for the day. She assured me she would be right over to pick up Cody. I gave him a light snack while we waited; it was six p.m. when she finally arrived. She apologized.

The next morning when Joe dropped off Cody, he also apologized. Then he stunned me by saying that things were not going well at home. He did not elaborate, but asked me not to let Maria know that he told me. That request placed me in an uncomfortable position.

On August 15 and August 25, Joe asked if Steven, who was almost ten, could come to day care with Cody for a couple hours while Joe attended a counseling session. I wondered if this was related to his prior message of things not being well at home. I realized that Cody's behavior change and spitting-up issues could be connected to family conflict. It would make sense. I felt bad for Cody, and was determined to be extra loving and caring at this time. Maria still had not indicated to me that there was any trouble at home.

August 27, 2008 was Steven's tenth birthday. Maria dropped off Cody at my house and stated that they were going to Noah's Ark Waterpark in Wisconsin Dells. Steven had not come in with Maria and Cody; I had hoped to give him a birthday wish.

That afternoon, while we were outside playing, I encouraged Cody to stop riding the trike around in circles and join the other kids on the climbing structure. I started picking up some toys on the patio and all of a sudden noticed that Cody was on the ground; he must have slipped off the ladder. He was startled and cried a bit, but it didn't last long. I saw no injury, other than a red area on the left side of his face where he probably made contact with the side of the ladder. I observed him for a bit and he was fine. Joe arrived a short while later to pick him up, and I explained what happened. I recorded the incident in my day care medical log book. I was disappointed that Steven had not come along for the pick-up, as I wanted to give him his birthday greeting. Joe had no report on how the day at the waterpark had been.

When Cody arrived the next morning, I checked his face for any sign of a bruise or injury from the previous day's fall. There was nothing; had there been I would have noted that in the log book. Maria only asked me if he had cried when it happened. I reassured her that he only briefly cried and then seemed fine.

I heard no more from either Joe or Maria on any family issues.

On the afternoon of September 17, as we were heading outside to play, Cody tripped on the edge of the rug located in front of the open door, falling into the edge of that door. He hit his right forehead. I retrieved "Icy Bear," an orange, bear-shaped ice pack, from the freezer, with the intent to apply it to Cody's forehead. Before I could do so, Joe arrived. I explained what had happened. Joe was nonchalant about it and even laughed. The next morning, I noted that Cody had a goose-egg/bruise on his forehead.

Little did I know that in the very near future, these two recent incidents/injuries of Cody would be used to charge me with child abuse.

Reese Family

Tommy started with me in December 2007, at age two-and-a half. I got the feeling from his mom, Tina Reese, that his previous child care setting was not a good match for him. She had used many child care centers and providers over the course of his and his older brother Peter's young lives. It concerned me to hear that she so readily switched caregivers, but Tommy adjusted to my program easily and fit in perfectly with the group.

In early May 2008, Tina informed me that Tommy was leaving my care; she had a nanny for the summer for both boys, and then in the fall she wanted them both to attend the same preschool. I was disappointed because I wanted to keep Tommy for one more year, but I understood. She still wanted Tommy to come once a week for a half day in the summer; I agreed.

Tina asked if I could also care for Peter for a few days in the summer. He was four-and-a-half years old at this time, and had special needs, including sensory issues and autism. I wasn't sure that I could meet his needs without sacrificing the care I gave my other kids, but I said I would try. Mostly he was in his own little world when he was at my house. He was not aware of anything outside of his own reach. He would grab toys from others. He was oblivious to the other kids, even his brother. He was destructive with some of the equipment. He had a hard time following the routines the other kids automatically abided by, like nap, lunch, and circle times. I could handle him for those few days, but would not be able to care for him regularly without major changes to my program.

In early August, Tina asked if I would still have an opening for Tommy in the fall, as she changed her mind and wanted Tommy back with me. I did still have a spot and happily agreed to take him back.

Most of the kids in my care at that time would be with me for only one more year, and then I would send them onto a pre-kindergarten program. The parents were well aware of this, and I had encouraged them to start looking into programs early, as some fill up quickly. Tina suggested that I should keep all the kids another year and run my own pre-K program. I was pleased that she thought highly enough of me to make such a request.

<u>Other Families</u>

The other children in my care in 2008 were:

- David Christie, son of Bev and Mark.

- Eddie Ryan, son of Barb and Dean.

- Max Pickett, son of Brian and Elsie.

- Emma Byer, daughter of Jack and Jane.

Chapter 3

Annie Attends Day Care

*T*he life changing email arrived in the afternoon. It was early August 2008. The day care kids napped while I tackled the daily record keeping for the business. I noticed a new email from Holly Jeter, asking if I could take Annie for a couple days later in the month, August 27-28. I thought it would be fun to have Annie, now six years old, back again, and I was glad to help out the Jeter family. With no hesitation, I responded affirmatively to Holly's request, having no idea of the ultimate impact of that decision. No good deed goes unpunished, right? If I could have the hypothetical do-over or go-back-in-time moment, my email response to Holly would thus be, "Sorry, I won't be able to take her." That little girl unknowingly and unwittingly shattered my life by alleging that I harmed children in my care. Her accusations sent my life into a tailspin of emotional upheaval, legal battles, and financial ruin.

On August 27, I woke up with a headache. That was rare, and it had not gone away by the time I expected the kids' arrival. Looking back, I think this headache was nature's way of telling me to take

21

the day off and stay in bed. I knew I could make it through the day, however, and it was always an inconvenience to the families when I couldn't work. I was actually glad that Annie was coming that day; I thought she could be a good helper for me in case I didn't feel better.

She wasn't. Annie was bored. She brought a few of her own things in her backpack, but never took them out. I tried to have her participate in our activities—she did them, but I could tell she had no interest. She hung around Miles. She was rather sullen. She sat at the table when I served morning snack, but she picked at it. I told her she didn't have to stay at the table, and she went in the other room before any of the little kids were done eating. This was a day when Cody had a morning spitting-up episode. I told Annie that I needed to clean up Cody, and I asked if she could be my helper for a few minutes by keeping the other kids occupied. She sat down by Miles. Seeing that she would not be much help, I put the TV on while I cleaned up the mess in the kitchen and tended to Cody in the bathroom. Annie then wandered around the room, including up and down the wooden climber, while the kids watched TV.

She wouldn't eat much lunch, and, again, I told her she could leave the table to find something else to do. She wanted a cot to lie on during the little kids' naptime, even though I had told her she could play quietly anywhere in the room. Obviously, she was unhappy being at my house. I felt I had to make sure she was busy and appease her.

Annie came back for the second day, August 28. She didn't seem quite as unhappy, but still didn't participate in anything. I was preparing for pizza theme the following week, and I invited her to help me. She did a few things but didn't spend much time on them. Again, she spent most of her time hovering over Miles or wandering about the room.

Neither Miles nor Annie were scheduled to come the next day, Friday the 29th, although Holly showed up around five o'clock as I closed for the day. I was setting up for pizza week. She looked at everything in awe. She gave me a payment check, and then asked me about Cody, stating that Annie had concerns that Cody seemed sad. I couldn't share anything about Cody or his family (less than harmonious, from what Joe Marshall told me), but I told her I was working with him. She seemed satisfied.

Holly then called me on Sunday, August 31. She had received an email from Kids Express Preschool (on Friday evening, before Labor Day weekend?) that they had an opening, and she was going to take it and enroll Miles immediately. This was very strange. I felt bad for Miles—no transition to a new school or no chance to get closure at my house with his friends. With his physical/health issues and with him recently starting to walk on his own, was this the proper time to move him?

"I get the feeling that you're not telling me something," I said to Holly. "Are you upset or unhappy with me?"

She hesitated, but finally said that it was Cody—she didn't want Miles exposed to his sadness. Since she had an opportunity for another preschool, she took it. "I'll have to get a second job to pay for the additional cost of Kids Express," she joked. I wondered why, then, would she be sending Miles?

Earlier that week she gave me a pizza kit toy for the following week's pizza party, indicating that Miles looked forward to the fun week. Now, a few days later, she withdrew him. Warning bells should have been going off in my head, but I had no clue that anything could be wrong. I ended this unexpected conversation by stating that I would miss Miles and would welcome him back if the new preschool didn't work out.

Pizza Week was fun. I arranged the day care space as a pizzeria, complete with red-checked tablecloths, chef hats and aprons, pizza oven, pizza boxes, and plastic pizza food. We made and ate various types of pizza, and had pizza-related art projects, stories, and games. All the kids were excited, even Cody. I was pleased to see him participating on his own accord. Cody was back to full-time attendance and I hoped he would return to the happy, active, playful little boy he had been.

The next week, September 8, was baby theme. I set up the room like a large nursery, provided lots of dolls, baby furniture, and pictures of all of us as babies. We even tasted baby food and had a visit from a baby.

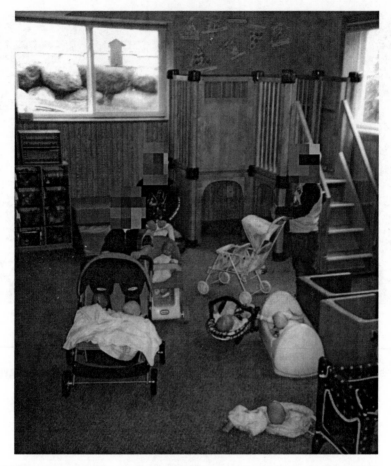

"Note the position of the climber in an L shape against the wall, in-between the two windows, in the corner of the room. This was its location on August 27-28, 2008, when Annie attended. This is an important detail."

At the end of this week, I moved the wooden climber from the corner of the room over to the wall by the door. Due to issues with Direct TV, I had to move the TV from its wall-mounted position over to the cable outlet in the corner, necessitating the climber move.

On September 17, Bev Christie (David's mom) told me that, although she didn't know if I had any openings, she had referred me to a friend needing child care. Up to this point, I hoped that Holly would change her mind and return Miles to my care, so I had not informed the other kids or families that he had left. Realizing now that he was not returning, I took this opportunity to inform Bev that I did have an opening due to Miles' departure. She looked surprised, but I got no hint of shock or alarm.

The following evening, Mark (David's dad) called. He prefaced his conversation by stating that there was no easy way to say this, so he was just going to say it: David would not be coming to my day care anymore. Mark was quite ill mannered; I had never heard him speak in such a way. I was speechless. Eventually I extracted from him that David had said something disturbing about Cody, so now David was going to attend Kids Express with Miles. Mark wouldn't expand on this, even though I pressed him for more information. I started to say that I was working with Cody.

"I'm not going to get into a he said/she said conversation with you," Mark rudely interrupted. "David is my son and I'm going to believe him." Believe him about what? Mark said they were paid up through the next week and I had their initial deposit, and then they were done with me. Since he wouldn't tell me anything else, I conveyed that he was free to withdraw David, of course, but he would have to cover what his prepayment/deposit didn't.

27

Without getting any other details, I attributed Mark's concern to that of Holly's—Cody's sadness affected David in a negative way. I was devastated. In the past two weeks, I had lost two long-term families. What was it about Cody that caused them to leave, and in such a rude and abrupt manner? I couldn't believe it was because he was sad and cried sometimes.

Ki had his bowling league that night, so I had no chance to talk to him about this issue. I stewed on my own all night, wondering what was happening.

Chapter 4

An Empty Day Care

The next day, I called Maria Marshall to tell her about the two families leaving due to Cody, but I had no explanation as to why. She was puzzled also, and asked if I wanted Cody to leave my care.

"Absolutely not," I replied. "I love Cody, but I want to get to the bottom of the concern." Maria divulged that she had actually received an email from Holly Jeter earlier that day, asking if she could talk to her. I said, "Well, you should call her and then maybe we can figure out what's going on." Maria said she would call me back after she talked to Holly. Joe came to pick up Cody at the usual time. He gave no indication of anything being wrong. I waited to hear back from Maria, but she never called.

I was finally able to tell Ki at suppertime what had transpired the past two days. He was as confused and shocked as I was.

I called the Marshalls the next day, Saturday, but no one ever answered. Since I hadn't heard anything further from Maria, I assumed I would see Cody as usual on Monday morning. I could not have been more wrong.

"I sent this email to Joe and Maria on September 19. It was "Talk Like a Pirate Day," and all the kids were AAAARRRRing. Note the position of the climber on this date—on the back wall between the window and door. I had moved it the prior weekend due to the TV placement issue."

Monday arrived. Our Internet was down, so I was unable to check email first thing in the morning. Ki attempted to fix the issue.

Cody had not arrived by 7:30 a.m., which was unusual since he normally arrived by seven. Emma arrived, as did Tommy and Peter (I had agreed to take him that day). I was then waiting for Eddie. He had not arrived by his usual time, and I had not heard from his parents.

Ki eventually got the Internet working and I could see my emails. There was one from Joe Marshall, succinctly saying that Cody would not be attending my day care anymore. That caused me worry, but the next email from Barb Ryan absolutely made my heart sink: "Eddie will not be coming to your day care anymore. We heard over the weekend that a child was being harmed in your care. While we do not believe it, we feel that you will be distracted by this and will not be able to give your best care to the children. We were going to send Eddie to preschool next fall; we will push that up now."

I called Ki over in panic to read these emails. What was going on, we both wondered. I called Barb to see if I could get more of an explanation. She said she wasn't comfortable talking about it.

"I need to know what's going on, Barb," I begged. "No one is telling me anything." Reluctantly, Barb revealed that she had received phone calls over the weekend stating that Cody was being hurt in my care. I could tell she didn't want to talk, so I assured her that no abuse had occurred, and that I understood her need to keep Eddie home. Why was she contacted? I had Emma and the Reese boys attending that day. Were those families contacted?

I called my friend Darlene and explained the weird things that were going on. She immediately changed her plans for the morning to come over. She was a recently retired child care provider, sometimes subbed for me, and was familiar with the kids. She graciously helped through lunchtime, as I was quite out of it.

After lunch, I contacted Tina Reese to see if she had heard anything strange about my day care. She denied knowing anything. I gave her a brief synopsis of what I knew, and asked her to let me know if she heard anything else.

I figured that I had better contact my day care licensor, Cathy Leaverton. She was a new licensor to me. I had only met her one time previously in May 2008, when she made an unannounced visit. She tried to unearth violations to the licensing rules, only finding that my blind cords were not tied up (they were inaccessible to the kids but not tied up to her satisfaction). She gave me a written evaluation with some token positive feedback, but it would have been nice to hear her say it, too. Her parting message was that she would return in the near future to check for violations, as she always found some. I found it odd that she focused on rule violations instead of positive things.

DEPARTMENT OF HEALTH AND FAMILY SERVICES
Division of Children and Family Services
CFS-809 (Rev. 12/2002)

STATE OF WISCONSIN

SITE VISIT
COMMENTS / RECOMMENDATIONS

Use of form: Completion of this form is optional and may be used by Licensing Specialists to confirm comments and recommendations. The information provided through its use should not be construed to be orders, mandates, or citations of violations which must be implemented.

Name - Facility
Lynn's Family Day Care

Address - Facility (Street, City, State, Zip Code)
1226 Velvet Leaf Dr. Madison WI 53119

Name - Licensing Specialist
Cathy Leaverton

Date - Site Visit (mm/dd/yyyy)
6-11-08

Great play space.
Good & patience with children.
Children have good verbal skills and social skills.
Children have great listening skills
Great theme ideas incorporating
crafts, books & play toys

**"This is the report from Leaverton in June 2008
after her first visit to my day care."**

Although I was not impressed with her, she was the licensor assigned to me. I left a message with her about the kids dropping out of my care. I did not hear back from her before the end of the workday.

Tina Reese and I talked again later in the day. In hindsight, this was not a good idea, but her family had not abandoned me and I was desperate to find out what was happening. I said I had no idea what was up with Cody and why families were leaving because of him. The only thing I could think of was his crying and spitting-up issues at meals. I explained what the spitting-up entailed and how I had to move him away from the table and the other kids when it happened. I speculated that the other kids were seeing me grab him quickly.

Tina said she would see if she could find out anything more. She also thought it best if Tommy did not come the next day, and I certainly understood.

My licensor, Cathy Leaverton called back that evening. I told her that things were bizarre with kids dropping out, and I wanted her to be aware. She took note, said she had not heard any complaints or concerns, and asked me to call her back if I learned anything more.

The next morning, Brian Pickett called to say that Max had a cold and would not be coming. Given the recent events, that sounded suspicious. I asked him if he had heard anything over the weekend about my day care. He said no. Much later I would learn that he had indeed heard something that prevented him from sending Max to my house.

A short email arrived from Tina Reese that afternoon, stating that Tommy would not be attending my day care anymore. There was no other explanation or clarification. Earlier that day, I had also received an email from Emma's mom, Jane, who said that Emma would not be returning to my day care. I was again stunned at these emails and had no clue what to think. What was going on? All my day care families were gone.

Later that afternoon, the licensor, Leaverton stopped by. She said there had been a complaint about me. We went down to the day care room to talk. She sat in the rocking chair next to my desk. I sat at the desk. Ki was present, also.

"This will be hard for you to hear," she began. "There has been a complaint lodged with our department saying that you were banging a child's head into the wall."

I almost laughed when she said this, until realizing she was dead serious. She said a six-year-old girl was watching TV and saw me bang Cody's head into the wall in the bathroom. Well, the only six-year-old girl in my care had been Annie those two days in August.

Leaverton asked me where the TV was. When Annie attended, it was mounted to the wall right above the rocking chair in which Leaverton sat. "The kids sit on the floor here to watch TV," I explained, indicating the position. "The bathroom is over in the corner; it's not possible to see in there while watching TV."

Ki asked her if she wanted to get up and look from different perspectives in the room; she refused, saying she didn't need to do that. Ki then went into the bathroom and opened and closed one of the cupboard doors. That made a banging sound, a common sound heard throughout the day. Did Annie hear that and her imagination went wild?

"Maybe the concern was with Cody and his spitting up issues," I pondered aloud.

"No, this complaint has nothing to do with anything in the kitchen," Leaverton responded.

I explained to Leaverton a bit about Cody, his behavior, and my work with him. For lack of a more appropriate term, I indicated I was "harder" on him with my requests to stop crying, make choices, etc. However, I had no explanation for why Annie would say what she did. Who bangs kids' heads against a wall? I was confused. I knew the bathroom head-banging allegation was ridiculous, but feared I was in for a challenge of getting this straightened out. I knew about false abuse allegations and how hard they are to fight. My mind immediately flew to the hysterical epidemics of the McMartin Preschool case and other day care scandals of the eighties and nineties, which began with accusations from disturbed parents or from the odd comments of a child.

Leaverton said her department would continue to investigate this. She departed, leaving me more confused than ever. At least I had some idea of what was going on, unbelievable as it was.

The mass exodus of children from my care finally made sense. Nevertheless, why hadn't the parents been honest with me about the reason? Holly Jeter especially should have shared the cause of Miles' departure. I had directly asked her if she was unhappy with me; she responded that Cody's sadness was the issue. She was a special education teacher. If someone had a problem with her, wouldn't she want to know the truth? Had she told me what Annie alleged, I would have been able to confront its ridiculousness immediately.

I called a couple more of my day care colleagues, Rima and Patti, to let them know what happened. They both responded incredulously with, "What?" Rima and Patti, as well as Darlene, were supportive, offering reassurance that this would be resolved, but I didn't share their confidence. I also alerted my good friends Jan, Kellylee, and Lynn S., who, again, were in disbelief, but offered their unconditional love and support. I didn't want to tell my sons what was going on until I knew more, although they could tell something was wrong.

I didn't hear anything back from Leaverton the rest of the week, prompting me to call her on Friday. She reported that nothing yet had been done. Was that good or bad news?

Chapter 5

Police Interrogation

*N*ot knowing what was happening was driving me crazy. I knew what Annie said was false, but, until I heard that things were straightened out, I was anxious and fearful. I couldn't eat. Sleep was erratic and filled with bizarre dreams. I had never had time off during the week, with the exception of rare vacation days, and the empty days, lack of eating and sleeping, and fear of the unknown were wreaking havoc on me. I had a constant knot in my stomach. I missed the day care kids; I had no idea if I would see any of them again, and I never got a proper goodbye.

After another poor night of sleep, I laid down on the couch in the early afternoon of Thursday, October 2, 2008. My cat, Purrsie, had been lying on my chest; suddenly she gave a low growl and leaped off me to run upstairs. I should have taken that as an omen and followed her.

There was a knock at the front door. Upon opening it, I saw two females. They identified themselves as Madison Police detectives, and asked if they could talk to me about the "Cody Marshall situation." I was surprised it was the police; I figured that if any-body came, it would be from day care licensing or child services. Anyway, I invited the detectives in. *Big mistake*. I always had respect for police and believed they could be trusted. That was the last time I ever had that thought.

We sat at the kitchen table. They identified themselves as Detectives Julie Johnson and Kris Acker. I was actually glad that someone was finally talking to me, and I simply thought we would get this issue resolved. It never entered my mind that I should not talk to the police. I unwisely assumed only guilty people had reason not to converse with police.

Detective Johnson asked how long I had been doing day care. "Sixteen years in family day care, and then since 1984 in other set-tings," I replied. Detective Acker said that was a long time. Johnson asked if I had ever had anything like this come up before. "Never," I answered.

Johnson asked what I thought was going on and what my con-cerns were. I told her what had occurred since Holly Jeter informed me that Miles would not be coming to my day care anymore. Johnson asked a few incidental questions during my explanation and made a few comments. I ended my account by saying I had no current day care kids.

Johnson said, "So what's going on?"

I replied that I didn't know, to which she rudely retorted, "Well, I think you do know." I didn't care for the manner in which she said that, but I guilelessly answered, "The only inkling I got that something was wrong was the email from Barb Ryan stating that she had heard about a child being harmed. Then there was Leaverton's licensing visit in which she mentioned the observations of Annie. I haven't heard anything back from state licensing."

Johnson continued. "So what can you tell me about the complaint? What do you think is going on? Why are these parents all pulling their kids out of your day care?"

"I don't know."

"Yeah, I think you do."

My heart dropped as Johnson's tone turned confrontational. That remark and her attitude should have set alarms off in my head to shut up, but I wanted to be cooperative. "According to Leaverton's complaint, I banged somebody's head into the wall."

"Is that true?"

"No."

"What happened?"

"I don't know. I've been racking my brain about why they would perceive something like that." I explained about the bathroom cabinets banging when they closed and how I suspected Annie heard that. I described some of Cody's issues, how I would need to guide and direct him both verbally and physically, and about his tendencies to not watch where he was going. I told them about my day care medical log book where I document injuries. Johnson asked if they could look at that.

39

"Is there anything else you can think of to explain why?" Johnson inquired.

"No. Can I get a drink of water?" I was feeling uncomfortable and intimidated in this interview and thought I had to ask for a drink in my own home.

The detectives then asked if they could see the day care area. I took them downstairs. Johnson didn't say much, but Acker literally "oohed and aahed" as she looked around. "This is very nice, very nice, very neat. I bet the kids have a good time here. This is really nice. Very, very nice down here. Very nice." She was fascinated by the child-sized equipment.

Johnson briefly looked in the bathroom, and I demonstrated how the cupboard doors bang shut. She was clearly not interested in exploring that possibility. She never attempted to look into the bathroom from the TV viewing area. As we were in the kitchen area, I explained about Cody's spitting-up issues.

We headed back upstairs. I had grabbed my log book. I felt confident that the detectives would be satisfied that nothing could have happened here that matched the claim made by Annie. Little did I know that the tide of accusations was about to turn horribly against me.

We sat back down at the kitchen table. Acker looked through the log book and noted some of my entries. She again complimented me on the day care space. Johnson then took over the interview, and asked me if I could think of anything that would cause the parents to be concerned. "No," I answered.

"Okay. Well, I've interviewed a whole bunch of kids and I have photos and kids on tape talking about you banging heads on walls, demonstrating you. I have pictures of unexplained bruises. What I'm wondering is, was there a time when maybe you were rough with one of the kids? Is that possible?"

"Oh my god," I said.

"Yeah. It's kind of interesting because we have Cody Marshall falling, having bruising, they take him to the doctor. You denied anything happening. We have August bumps on the head. The thing that concerns me is that I have all of the little kids pretty much telling me the same story, that you smack the heads against the wall, that you bang their heads against the wall and they cry and you're mean and you do mean things to them and they weren't coached by their parents. These kids are too young to be coached, to be so consistent with all of this stuff."

My mind went blank. I felt my soul leave my body. I couldn't fathom what Johnson was saying and I became flustered. At this point, my son Aaron arrived home from school. Johnson paused the interview. Why didn't I take that break to say that I wouldn't talk anymore? Things quickly turned against me and my mind reeled.

Aaron left for a neighborhood babysitting job, triggering another round of accusations by Johnson. I only half heard what she said, trying to process her comments about me hurting kids.

"When I ask the kids, they all tell me Lynn hurts Cody, Lynn hurts Emma, Lynn hurts Eddie, bangs heads on the table. Peter says that you bang Cody's head on the table, and he's only been there a few times. This isn't something that they're making up. If it was just one child, one incident, I wouldn't be here. We can understand how an adult can lose patience with a child, maybe be a little rough. One time, one incident, we're going to let that go and give the person the benefit of the doubt. The reason I'm here is because there's multiple times, multiple incidents, multiple children telling us of injury, bruising and crying, Lynn hurting Emma, Lynn hurting Cody, Lynn hurting Miles, Lynn hurting David, and I want to hear your side of it. I want to know if there's an explanation, if you're a little stressed out, if the kids are getting to you. You've been doing this a long time.

"Why do you think the kids would say this if it isn't true? It's not like these kids see each other every day and live in the same neighborhood and are twelve years old and can talk. It's not an isolated incident. I've got more than one child telling me pretty consistent things that concern me.

"I have to be honest with you, too, that the DA's office, you know, if you did something, you need to make it right. You need to talk about it. You need to bring it out, take responsibility, so that we can deal with this, and move on. No matter what you tell me today, I'm not arresting you. You're not going to jail. Right now, I'm just investigating. I'm trying to find out what happened. No matter what you tell me, we're going to walk out the door and you're going to stay home tonight, if that's a concern."

DA, jail, arrest? Johnson threw those words at me so fast and that's all I heard. I felt nauseous; if I hadn't been sitting, I likely would have fainted. She asked for an explanation. How do I explain all those accusations? Believing that police don't lie, I was astonished to hear that all the kids said these things.

I thought about Cody. I attempted to describe my dealings with him. All I could think of was that I maybe was verbally harsher with him, due to his spitting up and needing direction on playtime. I said I never hurt him intentionally, thinking aloud that maybe when I pulled him away from the spit-up at the table I did it too quickly or forcefully. However, he never would have gotten his head bumped from that. What were all these head-bumping allegations? Who does that to a child? I admitted that the spitting-up issue was frustrating since I didn't know its reason, but Cody was not a problem child or had temper tantrums.

Johnson then threw down a series of photos of Miles Jeter. The photos showed Miles standing in a bathtub, with some bruises on the left side of his head. The photos were date-stamped May 16, 2006.

"So when Miles was a year and a half and not really mobile, how do you explain these bruises on the side of his head?" Johnson demanded.

I stared at the photos.

Johnson went on. "Mom says he came home from day care that way, asked Lynn, no idea. What did you do to Miles?"

Her tone was nasty. I kept looking at the photos.

"Something happened, Lynn. They were concerned enough to take the photos and discussed it, but did not want to believe that you would do anything like that to a child."

"How do you get a bruise like this?" I asked.

"Well, I was hoping you could tell me because they think you did it. Again, they were concerned enough they took photos. Do you remember that?"

"No," I honestly replied.

"That looks like a thumb to me. And these look like hand prints. You can see better on that one; those look like fingertips, and that looks like a thumb. The common denominator is you with these injuries. Did you hurt Miles?"

"No."

"How did Miles get this? He didn't get them at home. Something had to happen here. How did this happen?"

"I don't know. He had special needs so I know that I was always very careful with him."

Where did these pictures come from? I had absolutely no recollection of Miles having any injury or bruises, and I don't recall Holly speaking to me about such. If anything had happened, or if Holly had spoken to me about suspicious bruises, I would have documented it in my log book. My log book had no such entries.

Johnson went on to drop more bombshells. "So, the parents take the kids to the doctor, get them checked out, the doctors are well, yeah, there's something up with her, these are not normal childhood injuries. These are injuries to the head. The parents did not do this, so I need to know, Lynn, what happened, and I need you to be honest with me and tell me. Are you frustrated with the kids, are you a big person and maybe you're too rough? You're not a small woman; is it possible that you're a little too much when you're dealing with the children?"

I was in shock hearing this. Frankly, I don't remember any more of this interview. The rest of this documentation comes from the transcript of the recording, as I went into a catatonic state of shock. I mumbled some responses, thinking that was what Johnson wanted to hear. Now I questioned myself. Was I some sort of Jekyll/Hyde personality who hurt the kids? As a police officer, Johnson wouldn't lie, would she? (*Yes!*)

"If I'm doing something that's inappropriate or causing harm, it's not intentional." I muttered.

Johnson persisted. "What do you think should happen from here on out? Where do you think we should go with this? I'm trying to figure out why this happened. Why these children are getting hurt, and you're the only one who can answer that. Do you ever find yourself losing your patience, getting frustrated?"

"No."

"That doesn't seem normal. I would think that anybody would get frustrated dealing with that many little kids."

"I don't know what to say."

Detective Acker jumped in. "I would love to hear some sort of explanation for these injuries. What I think is happening here is completely understandable. These children, especially Cody, are fraying at your last nerve. What I would respect you for is if you were to come forward and say you lost your patience. You would only be human, and you didn't intend to cause these injuries, but I would like to hear some sort of an explanation. You probably lost your patience, which is completely understandable. You wouldn't be human if you didn't get frustrated with children. Admitting that you were frustrated helps us understand how these injuries could have happened and we can understand that. It's either you didn't mean to do it or you did it intentionally. Do we want to leave here and think that you're beating the crap out of these kids because you're a bad person, or is this completely accidental and you're not meaning to hurt them?"

Acker continued. "Maybe you don't want to admit it, but does that make you a bad person? No. But otherwise we're going to come away thinking that beatings are going on here on a daily basis at this place, and I don't want to think that's true. So either you meant to do it or you didn't mean to do it, but somehow the injuries are here. I'd like to hear something, Lynn."

I either did it intentionally or didn't mean to do it. These were the choices I had? In my shocked and unnerved condition, I couldn't get out the words: "I did not do any of this!" I probably would have conceded to accusations of orchestrating Jimmy Hoffa's disappearance or any other unsolved crime.

The detectives wanted me to say something. I mumbled, more to myself than to them, "I'm not meaning to harm any child, of course, and if I am, then I'm doing it out of frustration, or that I'm not even aware of it, which is scary."

"That's completely understandable." Johnson said. "Your explanation is either you're beating these children intentionally or you're frustrated and perhaps things happen, and that people can understand because we are human. I haven't met a perfect human being. We get angry. We have good days and we have bad days. We're police officers. We carry guns. We also have good days and bad days.

"People do burn out in their job. I can't imagine anything more stressful than taking care of children, day after day, with no end in sight because they're coming back the next day and the next day and then the next day. That has to be stressful. We can leave our homes for eight hours. We can leave our stressful jobs, go home, and get a break. You can do neither. Day after day after day, this is your life, and it's a long time to have that kind of stress, with no break and no end in sight. I feel bad for you. So you didn't mean to do it?"

"No."

I wanted these women out of my house. What did they want me to say? I was intimidated by these officers, and unable to latch onto their devious interrogation techniques. My reasoning ability was compromised due to stress, anxiety, and exhaustion. They had me believing I did something. In my rattled state, I answered, "If I'm responsible for what's been happening, I'm terribly sorry, and it's not me—well, it is me, but. . ."

"It's not you." Johnson agreed. "I don't think it is either, or I think we would have been here a long time ago."

Johnson asked for a copy of my log book. Foolishly, I gave her one. "I'm meeting the DA tomorrow and we'll discuss everything you've told me. I'll tell them what you said, that your intent was not to harm a child, but that the injuries happened here. I have to tell you, the evidence is pretty overwhelming, but I do not make a final charging decision. The DA does. So that's why we're meeting tomorrow. I don't know what the DA will think. I know that you like kids. That's pretty obvious. But I have a lot of kids with a lot of injuries and I have a lot of kids that have been harmed, physically and emotionally. There probably will be consequences. It's not okay that this happened. Children were hurt. That's what it comes down to."

What had I said to them? It had been a mentally exhausting interview. How did suspects survive hours and hours of these interrogation tactics? After only an hour-and-a-half, I was stressed out and confused. I wanted them to leave and be finished with the psychological intensity and questioning.

Acker asked, "Are you going to be all right?"

"No," I responded.

"Well, don't hurt yourself." Acker continued. "This isn't worth hurting yourself over." I thought that was a bizarre thing for her to say.

They finally left. I collapsed. What just happened? What did I do? What had I said?

Chapter 6

Lawyering Up

I frantically called Ki at work and told him about the police interview. "I think I said something to them, but not sure what." He rushed home and tried to talk to me about it, but I was in shock and incoherent.

"We need an attorney," Ki said. He called Deb Johnson, a friend and former parent of day care kids. She came right over upon hearing what had happened. She was an attorney, although not in criminal practice, and gave us some attorney suggestions. I honestly can't remember her coming; later she would tell me that I was curled up on the couch and totally out of it. Ki had bowling league later that night, and, not wanting to leave me alone, called my friend Lynn to come over and stay with me. He also talked to my brother, PJ, who happened to call on another matter. PJ was absolutely floored, which would be the typical response whenever I told anyone.

I don't know how I got through that night. Deb called me Friday morning; she was in touch with Attorney Bob Burke, who agreed to call me. Lynn came over shortly before noon to take me for lunch. I didn't think I'd be able to eat anything, but it was good to get out of the house. As we pulled into the parking lot of Panera, Ki called me on my cell phone. He said that the detectives had come back to our house, wanting to talk to me again. Ki told them that I was not home, and Johnson demanded to know where I was. He laid into them about questioning me the day before without another person or lawyer present. He then said we had an attorney, and they left.

"What more do they want with me?" I fearfully asked. "Are they going to arrest me?"

Ki thought that was their intention. I had a few bites of tasteless soup for lunch before coming back home with Lynn. She graciously stayed with me for the afternoon.

Bob Burke called me a few hours later. I explained what had happened the past few weeks and about the meeting with the detectives. He agreed to come by and meet me at my house on Sunday.

I received another phone call later that afternoon from the state day care licensing department. It was not Leaverton, but the licensing chief, Diane Bloecker. She told me that due to the allegations of abuse, I could either voluntarily give up my day care license temporarily, or they would take it away from me. I was confused and asked for clarification. Bloecker was not very nice, and bluntly said, "Well, do you think we're going to let you keep a day care license after what you said to the police?"

What did I say? How did she hear about anything I allegedly said? It seemed that there was communication between agencies. Since I didn't have any day care kids, I agreed to close my day care business only on a temporary basis. Bloecker said she would stop by on Monday with paperwork for me to sign to this effect.

Ki called my dad on Saturday to tell him about the events of the past month. He was in disbelief, of course, but supportive. We thought it best not to share this news with my mom at this point, as she had MS with physical limitations, including not being able to speak well. We didn't want to overwhelm her with bad news, not knowing if she was capable of even understanding. We also had the hard conversation with our boys. They knew something was wrong the past few days, and wondered why I had had no kids coming to day care.

Bob came over on Sunday. He asked questions and looked around my day care space. I showed him the view to the bathroom. Bob agreed that it was impossible to see anything there. He said Annie's claims were absurd, but concurred that I needed legal representation. He assured me that he was a good attorney. I gave him a retainer check. Money worries began now; not only did I have no income, but I also needed to pay an attorney.

Bob said he would try to contact Detective Johnson. He assured me that the detectives couldn't talk to me anymore without my attorney present. I told him that they had me flustered. Why hadn't I asked for a lawyer when they threw abuse allegations at me?

Talking to Bob calmed me down a bit, but my contact with him now was like shutting the barn door after the cows escaped. I should have told the detectives to get the hell out of my house, but that was not in my nature. I was unsophisticated about my legal rights. A person with a stronger personality or one with more experience with the police likely would have asked for a lawyer. It never dawned on me to ask for one since I was innocent of these accusations. Believing as I did that police are not allowed to lie, I was astonished to hear the claims against me. As they were telling me I did all these terrible things, I thought I must be out of my mind or suffered from blackouts.

With my head starting to clear, and relieved that I had legal representation, I thought more about the interview with Johnson. I realized that I had been duped and taken advantage of due to my calm, easy-going manner and vulnerability. I had not wanted to displease or alienate the detectives, and in my anxiety about the false allegation, I had deferred to their authority. I have the inclination to subordinate my own wishes to a stronger person, resulting in the habit of being conciliatory and self-sacrificing, traits that do not bode well in a police interrogation. My attempts to deny allegations were brushed off by Johnson; she would quickly change the direction of her questioning any time I said "no" or gave an outright denial. Yet if I gave an unambiguous or no response, she was all over that. Johnson was biased against me from the start. I naively trusted her not to lie, and my natural reaction was confusion and hopelessness.

My mind flashed back to the interview and some of the things Johnson said that, now with the pressure off me, made absolutely no sense.

- "The parents take the kids to the doctor, get them checked out, the doctors are well, yeah, there's something up with her, and these are not normal childhood injuries." Really? A doctor gives that report, yet the parents keep the kids in my care?

- "Peter says that you bang Cody's head on the table, and he's only been there a few times." Peter and Cody overlapped on attendance only two days, July 1 and 2, 2008. Peter, with his self-absorbed nature and special needs, wouldn't know who Cody was if he was right in front of him.

- "It's not like these kids see each other every day." Well, yes, actually they do. Annie and Miles are siblings. If Annie said something, it is probable that Miles picked up on that.

- "We have bad days and we carry guns." What a terrible and unprofessional statement. I'm sure the Madison police chief, as well as citizens, would be shocked to hear that

Johnson not only had that attitude, but also was willing to verbalize it.

- Johnson kept referring to my size. "You're a big person and maybe too rough?" She insinuated that because I'm tall, I was a danger to the kids. That's an illogical statement, and, besides, I always crouched down or crawled with the kids to be on their level. I have the bad knees to show for it.

- "Your job is so stressful." Untrue. I loved what I did. At the end of the day I would go upstairs and be done with my workday. Talk about an easy commute. I could wear casual, comfortable clothes. I was home when repair or service people came. I was there when my kids came home from school. There was generally a two-hour quiet period in the afternoon during naptime. It wasn't stressful at all.

- Regarding the bruises on Miles' face: "The parents think you did it." Really? Then why would they return Miles to my care? And keep him coming during the summer when Holly was off work? What kind of parent keeps their child with a suspected abuser?

Hindsight being twenty-twenty, of course, I wish that I had been coherent enough to rebut those statements of Johnson, or, even more crucial, that I had never agreed to speak to her. I have chided myself about this repeatedly.

While I did not make any outright confessions to the child abuse allegations, I was drained by the persistent accusations and demands for explanations. I almost believed I had done something wrong. In my vulnerable state, I lost the ability for self-defense as I tried to make sense of the accusations thrown at me.

On Monday morning, Leaverton and Bloecker showed up with the paperwork about giving up my day care license. Leaverton said not a word. I called Bob to have him talk directly with Bloecker before I signed anything. After Bloecker and Bob hung up, I signed the paper, stating that I agreed only to a temporary, voluntary closure of my day care, and would re-open once these abuse accusations cleared up (which I believed would happen).

Chapter 7

Criminal Charges

or the next few weeks, I heard nothing. Bob called a few times to say that this was normal and he hadn't heard anything, either. I was a zombie, slinking around the house like an extra from *Invasion of the Body Snatchers*. I couldn't eat and lost a lot of weight in a short time, not a healthy thing to do. I had nightmares. I had a constant feeling of dread and a persistent knot in my stomach. Innocent people under a cloud of suspicion by the authorities live in a constant state of fear. Every time the doorbell rang, I thought it was the police coming to arrest me. Even to this day, the sound of someone knocking on our front door or ringing the bell causes my heart to skip a beat.

I don't know how I got through the days. I'd look out the window and see people passing by, going about their normal lives, seemingly without a care in the world, while I felt like my world was ending. A sense of hopelessness consumed me. Ki worried about me, and made sure that I had friends come over when possible to keep me company. He wanted me to talk about my feelings, but I couldn't get any words out. I attempted to keep up a good attitude for the sake of my boys, but when they weren't around, I fell apart. Why was this happening to me? What had I done to upset these parents, whom I had considered family, but who now turned on me?

Going down to the day care area was painful. I expected to hear delightful child voices and noises; the reality of the new normal jolted me as I faced an eerily quiet, cavernous space. Would this room ever be used for its intended purpose again? Would I ever be able to participate in my life's work and passion again?

On October 10, I received a letter from the Dane County Department of Human Services/Child Protective Services, stating that they had received a report on September 20, 2008 alleging that I abused Cody Marshall. This letter alerted me of their involvement in the investigation, and stated that I was named a "maltreater" in a report to the agency. I called the contact person and requested copies of any reports. She said it would take up to a month for me to get these. I forwarded this letter to Bob.

Early in the week of October 27, I called Bob. I was weighed down by the constant fear and lack of information. "I can't take this anymore," I said. "Can you please find out what is going on?" He asked me to come to his office so we could go over things. Ki and I met with him for a couple hours on the 29th. I once again explained everything I knew, recalled what I could of the police interview, and gave him a rundown on all the families and kids involved in my day care. Bob said he would try to get a meeting with the DA that afternoon. Ki and I left Bob's office and stopped at a restaurant for lunch, but I had absolutely no appetite. I couldn't shake the impending sense of doom.

We headed back home. Ki had a visit from a relative from Denmark that afternoon, so I left the two of them to visit. Bob called me a short time later. I took the call down in the basement so I wouldn't disturb Ki and his cousin. I had a bad feeling, and Bob wasted no time affirming that.

"I met with the assistant district attorney assigned to this case, Karie Cattanach. She is going to charge you with child abuse."

A wave of horror swept through me. I started trembling uncontrollably and mumbled something in the phone. Bob told me to take a deep breath and try to listen to what he was saying. I attempted to grab a pen and paper to make notes, but my hand shook.

Bob continued. "There is a child advocacy center called Safe Harbor, where children who are victims or witnesses to abuse can go to tell their story. The purpose of this place is for kids to tell their story one time instead of repeatedly in court proceedings. Annie was interviewed there and said she witnessed Cody being hurt in your care. She said she reported it because she was afraid it might happen to her little brother, Miles."

Bob described ADA Cattanach as a tough prosecutor. I would be charged with two counts of abuse, both at Level I Felony, the lowest level. I couldn't believe I heard the word "felony." Bob stated that Cattanach had no problem offering me a plea deal through the DA's Deferred Prosecution Unit, also known as the First Offender's Program. He explained that if I admitted responsibility for my actions, pled guilty, and followed the requirements of the program, I could avoid criminal conviction. All I heard was that I would have to admit responsibility for something I hadn't done. Bob told me to think about it; there was no immediate need for me to decide. He did tell me, however, that in the near future I would need to make an initial court appearance, at which time I would be booked (mug shot and fingerprinted). He assured me I would qualify for a signature bond and would not go to jail.

Upon ending my phone call with Bob, I remained in the basement. From this moment on, my life would never be the same. My friend Patti happened to call at that point, and tearfully I told her what I had learned. She was shocked and tried to comfort me, but there was nothing she could say to calm me. I told her I would call her back later. I went upstairs, wanting to tell Ki, but he was still talking to his cousin. He could tell I was upset and cut his visit short. I explained what Bob had told me. He hugged me and said we would get through this. I was too agitated to take consolation from him. I went upstairs and cried.

After a bit, I settled down enough to recall what Bob had told me. Ki looked up Safe Harbor on the Internet to find out more about that organization. Interestingly, he found that Safe Harbor was a client of Mark Christie's (David's dad) video production company.

Ki called Bob to see if that would be any type of conflict of interest, and Bob said he would look into it. He called later to say that Cattanach disagreed that there was any type of conflict.

Evan had his end of season football banquet that night. However, I was so far away in my mind that I did not enjoy any of the food or conversation, and actually had to leave early, as I thought I was going to get sick.

I slept fitfully that evening, and, upon waking up in the morning, had a full-blown panic attack. I had never experienced one before. I couldn't stop crying or trembling, my heart pounded, and I couldn't breathe. I felt like I completely lost control. My friend Jan called, and she and Ki discussed the idea that I needed to be seen by a doctor. Unfortunately, we had recently switched insurance carriers and I had not yet established care with a primary doctor. When Ki tried calling for an urgent care appointment, he was told that I should go to the emergency room for my panic attack. Darlene made an unexpected but welcome visit and she kindly accompanied me to the ER. By the time I arrived there, I had calmed down considerably, but still felt I should be seen. The ER doctor gave me some anxiety medication. Mostly it allowed me to sleep through the night. I felt better in the morning, but was still in anguish about my impending charges.

A few weeks later, I connected with a primary care physician who prescribed Celexa, an antidepressant. It took about a week to kick in, and I could finally decrease that awful feeling in the pit of my stomach (although it never fully went away) and start to think clearly again.

Meanwhile, I learned that Maria and Joe Marshall had filed for divorce in early October, 2008. Maria was the petitioner, meaning that she started the divorce proceedings. In her affidavit for temporary order, she stated, "It is in my best interest and the best interest of my minor children that my spouse be required to vacate the premises until I am able to locate other housing in that I fear my emotional and mental well-being will be jeopardized if the respondent is allowed to continue to reside in the same household with me." Here she admitted that she was fearful for herself and her children's well-being. Cody certainly could have been noticing the marital tension. Yet, I was the one who would be blamed for his sadness and change in personality.

The summons and criminal complaint arrived via a process server from the Dane County Sheriff's Department one evening in early November. It was intimidating to be served a criminal complaint, but at least I finally saw the charges and their substantiation. There were two charges—one for August 27, 2008, and one for September 17, 2008. What struck me first was the heading of the charges: Intentional Child Abuse—Bodily Harm (Class H felony). What happened to the Class I felony that Bob discussed with me?

The text of the criminal complaint explained Annie's claim of seeing Cody get his head banged by me. It went on to state that Cody had serious injuries on August 27, 2008. What? There was an incident that day with him slipping off the outdoor play structure ladder, but there were no injuries from that, other than a redness on the side of his head. Had there been more injuries than that, I would have noted them in the log book. Yet this complaint said there was a huge bump on both the front and back of his head.

The charge for September 17 was for a forehead bruise and laceration behind Cody's ear. Yes, he had a bump on his head from the episode of tripping on the rug and hitting his head on the door on the way outside. Laceration behind his ear? He had some crud behind his ear and maybe some type of skin infection. That was attributed to abuse? There were no witnesses to any abuse on the 17th, although the complaint states that Cody said, "Lynn wall." "Lynn table hurt."

Ki said that for either of these charges to go anywhere, everyone would have to lie. That was a prophetic statement.

My initial court appearance was scheduled for Monday, November 24, 2008. I had dreaded it all weekend. This all became real for me now. For the first time ever, I entered the Dane County Courthouse. Bob met me there. I appeared before the court commissioner, who, to my relief, confirmed that I only needed a signature bond for bail. The State requested that I have no contact with the "victim," meaning Cody Marshall. I did not like how he was referred to as the victim. I also was not to have any unsupervised contact with juveniles except my own children.

The worst part of this day was the humiliation of getting the mug shot and being fingerprinted. The female deputy who did this was quite rude and brusque. That certainly did not improve my ever-decreasing regard for police officers. I caught a glimpse of my mug shot, barely recognizing myself. My expression was a mixture of bewilderment and dread, and I was shocked to see how gaunt, pale, and drawn I appeared. I knew my emotional health had been affected, but now I realized the toll taken on my physical health, as well.

Thanksgiving arrived, and I tried to remain positive for the gathering with my extended family. My dad and my siblings were the only family members who knew about my situation. It was hard to answer the "How are you?" questions many times with a token response of "good," when inside I felt absolutely terrible and terrified. However, I didn't want to worry my relatives until I knew more.

My next court appearance was on December 8 for a status conference. Bob assured me it was nothing to worry about; the judge would want an idea of what was going on and some future court dates would likely be set. While waiting in the lobby, I observed other people coming and going. The courthouse is set up with four courtrooms on each floor, so there were proceedings scheduled in other courtrooms. I saw a uniformed police officer waiting outside the courtroom next to mine. A female ADA handed him a sheet of paper, stating, "These are the answers to the questions I'm going to ask you." Ki and I looked at each other in disbelief. This is how officers and DAs work? We were floored at the collusion and corruption this represented. Had I been more courageous, I would have walked right into that courtroom and told the judge what I had witnessed.

Chapter 8

Safe Harbor

J met with Bob the week before Christmas. He had obtained a copy of the Safe Harbor tape of Annie, recorded on October 3, 2008. According to Safe Harbor's website:

Safe Harbor provides a safe and friendly place for a child to talk about what has happened to them, so that hopefully the child will be interviewed only once. Safe Harbor brings professionals together from all the agencies involved with a case, and the child talks to a highly trained interviewer. The statement is recorded, and if charges are filed, the recorded statement may be used in court in place of the child's testimony.

Bob and I watched the recording. The interviewer was Erin Simpson. She told Annie that the most important rule during the interview was that everything talked about had to be the truth. "Do you know the difference between a truth and a lie?" Annie responded that she did. Simpson then asked what might happen if someone lied.

Pursuant to Wisconsin Stats. 908.08 (3) (c): Audiovisual recordings of statements of children may be admitted into evidence if the child's statement was made upon oath or affirmation or, if the child's developmental level is inappropriate for the administration of an oath or affirmation in the usual form, upon the child's understanding that false statements are punishable and of the importance of telling the truth.

Annie did not respond, so Simpson gave a hypothetical situation, and asked, "Do you think the big sister would get in trouble if the mom caught her telling a lie?" Annie responded, "Yeah."

That was a leading question. While I have no doubt that Annie, who was age seven at the time of this interview, knew that lies could be punishable, this showed the bias of Simpson in getting Annie to meet the statute requirements.

Simpson continued: "Have you ever seen anyone get hurt?"
Annie: At Lynn's, um Cody. It looked like in the bathroom, when Lynn was changing Cody's diaper, she would put his head, like slamming against the wall, Cody's head against the wall. I told my

mom and dad that it looked like when Lynn was changing Cody that she would bump Cody's head on the wall.

Simpson: Is that something that you saw with your eyes or something that you heard?

Annie: I heard and saw with my eyes. I just saw her, I saw her leg, and like Cody's head bumping against the wall. I heard Cody's head bumping against the wall.

Simpson: Did Cody say anything?

Annie: He was crying.

Simpson: Can you tell me where were Lynn's hands on Cody?

Annie: On his hair kind of pulling him, his hair.

Simpson got out a doll and asked Annie to show her what she saw. Annie held the doll by the upper shoulders and jiggled it a bit. "So you're showing me that his hair was being pulled?"

Annie: Yeah.

Simpson: Was that when he was sitting or standing?

Annie: He was laying.

Simpson: What happened before Cody got his diaper changed?

Annie: Well, she liked carried him into the bathroom.

Simpson: What happened before they went into the bathroom?

Annie: I don't know.

Simpson: When did Cody start to cry?

Annie: When Lynn was starting to bang his head on the wall.

Simpson: Do you know about how many times his head banged against the wall?

Annie: No.

Simpson: Did anybody else see Cody's head being banged against the wall?

Annie: No.

Simpson: You told me that you went to Lynn's day care a couple of times. Did you ever see anything else like that?

Annie: No.

Simpson: Did you ever see Lynn hurt anybody else?

Annie: Yeah, Emma.

Simpson: What did you see with Emma?

Annie: Well, Lynn picked her up and kind of banged her head on the wall, but not in the bathroom. I don't know where it happened.

Simpson: Tell me everything you remember about when Emma was banged.

Annie: I don't remember. Well, all of us were eating lunch, and then Lynn just came over and pulled Emma's chair back and carried her into the playroom.

Simpson: Did Lynn say anything?

Annie: No.

Simpson: What happened once they got in the playroom?

Annie: Emma's head banged against the wall.

Simpson: Did you see Emma's head get banged against the wall?

Annie: No.

Simpson: Did you hear something?

Annie: I heard her banging against the wall and I saw Lynn like carrying her over there.

Simpson: Did Emma say anything or make any noise?

Annie: No.

Simpson: When Lynn pulled Emma's chair out and carried her into the playroom, was Lynn happy or mad or something else?

Annie: She was happy.

Simpson: You told me that Emma banged her head on the wall, but it was not something you saw but something you heard. How do you know it was Emma's head that got banged against the wall?

Annie: Because she was the only one who was out there and everybody else was eating lunch.

Simpson: Okay. Right. What made you think it was Emma's head that got banged and not another part of her body?

Annie: I don't know.

Simpson: You don't know? Okay. Did you ever see any owies on Emma?

Annie: No.

Simpson: Okay, you said that when Lynn came to get Emma out of her chair she was happy. Did she stay happy the whole time?

Annie: Yeah.

Simpson: Did you ever hear Lynn say anything?

Annie: No.

Simpson: Have you ever seen any other kids get hurt at Lynn's day care?

Annie: No.

Simpson: Did you ever see Cody get hurt any other time besides when he was getting his diaper changed?

Annie: No.

My first impression of this interview was that Annie was speaking in a babyish voice. This girl was talking well before she was two years old. I wondered if she altered her normal voice to justify her stories.

I was not impressed with the interviewer; besides various leading questions, there was a huge component of her questioning missing. *Where* was Annie when she saw Cody's head banged in the bathroom? While it is impossible to see in the bathroom from anywhere in my day care space, other than standing right in the doorway, it would still be critical to know where Annie was when she "saw" this. What type of forensic interview doesn't seek the basic who, what, where, how, why? Obviously, the Safe Harbor interviewer didn't think that was necessary.

I had to laugh about Annie's claim that I banged Emma's head. She didn't see anything but jumped to that conclusion. And I was happy when I did this! There was so much wrong with her Emma story, I didn't know where to begin. Annie must have had something about head banging get into her mind to say that both Cody and Emma had it done to them.

Miles was also interviewed at Safe Harbor. At three-and-a-half years old, he had trouble verbalizing the difference between a truth and lie. Simpson asked him if he would promise to tell the truth. Again, this was bias by Safe Harbor. His interview should not have proceeded. Bob said it would not be admissible in court.

What struck me about the interview was Miles' response when asked if he liked going to day care. "It was bad," he said. This from a boy who was all smiles every day in my care. Who brainwashed Miles into thinking it was bad at my house?

Chapter 9

Preliminary Hearing

A preliminary hearing was set for January 7, 2009. I had heard the term before, but, having had no experience with the legal system, wasn't sure what that involved. Bob explained that it is a requirement in all felony cases, although you can waive your right to one. The purpose of the preliminary hearing is for the judge to find that probable cause exists, in which case the defendant would be bound over for trial. Bob warned me that the standard of proof was low for the prosecution to meet, merely requiring that the State show that a felony was committed and the defendant, meaning me, probably committed it. The benefit of this hearing, for our sake, was to assess the strengths and weaknesses of the State's case. It would be like a mini-trial in which we could cross-examine the State's witnesses.

Shortly before this hearing, Bob informed me that ADA Cattanach was on maternity leave, so I had a new prosecutor assigned, Lana Mades. I asked Bob what she was like. His response was, "Well, she's not likable." I didn't know how to take that.

I was nervous before the hearing, but also curious to see what would happen. I caught a glimpse of Joe Marshall outside the courtroom before I went in. This is the first I had seen him since Cody abruptly left my day care four months earlier.

This preliminary hearing was with Judge Moeser. As would occur with all court proceedings, the judge introduced the case by its caption: "State of Wisconsin versus Lynn Moller." I realize that is how criminal cases are labeled, but how daunting to hear those words. The whole State of Wisconsin against me? How would Wisconsin residents feel about the waste of their tax dollars in pursuit of this concocted case?

Bob's first attempt at this hearing was to get the charges reduced to the less serious felony, from Class H to Class I. ADA Mades argued that I repeatedly banged a two-year-old's head against a wall and table with sufficient force to sustain a large goose egg injury in the front and back of the child's head. She said it was reasonable to believe that that conduct and the young age of the child certainly was a high probability of causing great bodily harm, and I was fortunate to avoid that. Well, Bob's assessment of Mades was correct—I instantly disliked her and her accusations. Judge Moeser bought into her story and denied the reduction of charges.

Maria Marshall was first called as a witness. Mades asked her if she noticed any injuries on Cody after picking him up from my care. Maria replied affirmatively, stating that the most recent one was on September 17, 2008.

"He had a lump on the top of his head, a goose egg, um, and he had, um, some bruising and some scratching behind his ear. On August 27 he had a lump on his head again in the same spot; um, bruising behind the ear; and a lump on the back of his head where there was also some skin scuffed off."

Mades: Did you observe those injuries immediately upon picking him up?
Maria: Yes.

Bob took his turn on cross-examination. "On August 27th, did you pick up Cody from day care?"

Maria: Yes.
Bob: And you noticed the injuries to him right away?
Maria: Yes.
Bob: Did you ask Cody what happened?
Maria: I don't recall.
Bob: On September 17, did you ask Cody how he got his injuries?
Maria: I don't recall.

Detective Julie Johnson was the next witness. Mades inquired about her interview with Cody on September 22, 2008. "He started out very outgoing, playful, relaxed, but when I asked him about the lump on his forehead he got extremely distraught. He teared up and was anxious. His whole demeanor changed. He went from an outgoing friendly little guy to a scared, frightened little boy. He said 'Lynn's house table, Lynn hurt me.' I asked him what he was doing at the table. He said he was eating toast. I noticed some healing bruises behind one of his ears. I told him I noticed an owie behind his ear and again he got all tense and agitated. He started to tear up and he said 'Lynn's house wall.' I asked him to show me and he ran over and flung his head up against the wall. I asked him if Lynn hurt him. He said 'Yes.'"

On cross-exam, Bob asked, "Detective, at the time that you talked to Cody on September 22, was it just you and Cody?"

Johnson: Yes. I asked the parents to leave the room to give us some privacy. That was the first time I talked to Cody.
Bob: Do you know whether anyone, before you talked to Cody about his owies, anybody discussed the same issues with Cody?
Johnson: I don't know.
Bob: Was this interview with Cody on the 22nd recorded in any way?
Johnson: No.

Judge Moeser found sufficient probable cause to bind the charges over for trial. He assigned it to Branch Fifteen, Judge Stuart Schwartz.

A man wearing an unattractive sweater vest hovered around the Marshalls. He seemed to be in charge of them. Later I learned that this was Mark Kerman, a victim witness specialist/advocate from the DA's office. While I appreciate the protections in place to help victims navigate the court system, there were no victims in the invented case against me, and the liberal use of the term "victim" bothered me. How about an advocate for the falsely accused?

Although not pleased with having the charges bound over, I was glad to have seen Bob in action. He asked some key questions. Bob reminded me of Columbo, minus the trench coat. He was quiet, thinking, and then came out with a zinger.

Ki and I sat down with Bob after the hearing. I started commenting on Maria's statements, and Bob right away said, "Oh she's lying. At trial I'll be able to attack her statements; today was not the time to do that."

Upon returning home, I thought about some of the statements made by Maria and Detective Johnson at the hearing. It was interesting to hear that Johnson had done her interview with Cody with no parent present. The Marshalls let a two-year-old alone in a room with a stranger? I certainly would not have allowed that. With no recording of this interview, who knows how accurate Johnson's version was? Johnson portrayed Cody as a talkative child, yet he could barely speak at that time. Cody never had a Safe Harbor interview. Safe Harbor will not interview children under age three, for obvious reasons that these young children cannot give reliable statements. Yet Johnson was able to extract all sorts of information from two-and-a half-year-old Cody in her (unrecorded) interview with him, and report his statements as truthful and credible.

Johnson said Cody was eating toast when he got hurt at the table on September 17. I checked my menus; I had not served toast on that day.

Maria, when asked by Bob, claimed that she had picked up Cody on both August 27 and September 17. That was not true. August 27 had been Sam's birthday and I awaited their whole family to pick up Cody after their day at Noah's Ark. Yet, it had only been Joe who arrived. The only comment Maria made the next day, August 28, was to ask if Cody had been upset when he slipped on the ladder.

On September 17, Joe picked up also, as the episode with Cody bumping his head on the door had occurred minutes before his arrival. Maria picked up Cody the following afternoon, the 18th, and briefly commented on his bruised forehead. She also mentioned that he had a strange mark behind his left ear and didn't know what it was or where it came from. I saw a line of small crusted-over lesions. My first impression was that it was impetigo, dermatitis, or some other skin infection. I thought I might need to warn all the other parents of a potential contagious situation. Maria didn't think much of it and we decided to keep an eye on it, as it was limited to that one small area. Now she transformed it into an injury caused by my abuse. How would one even inflict that type of wound?

Moreover, what were all these injuries that Maria claimed happened on August 27? *"He had a lump on his head again in the same spot; um, bruising behind the ear; and a lump on the back of his head where there was also some skin scuffed off."* Was there any proof of this? Photos? Doctor report? You would think there would have been a doctor visit and documentation of such numerous and vivid injuries if the parents were concerned. There was no evidence presented in court. I checked my photo collection, and, while I didn't have any pictures of Cody that I could link with the dates of August 27-29, I did have many photos from the following week, pizza week. Maria's description of his injuries from the 27th sounded like he was beat up on both the front and back of his head. Yet, pictures from pizza week showed Cody's injury-free forehead. Major injuries to Cody on the 27th would still have been present and evident on photos taken the following week.

Chapter 10

Discovery

*B*ob had put in a demand for discovery, meaning that the prosecution needed to provide us the police reports, witness statements, medical reports, photos, and any other materials they intended to introduce at trial.

I also received the reports that I had requested from Dane County Human Services. I found the first report, dated September 19, 2008, enlightening. Holly Jeter had made contact by phone on this date, alleging that her daughter saw me hit Cody's head against a wall. No injuries to Cody were seen or reported. The agency's response to this report was to screen-out, meaning that all allegations in the referral were deemed as not rising to the level of maltreatment or threat of maltreatment, and no further assessment of the allegation was required.

So Holly called in a report on September 19, 2008, three weeks after Annie's accusations. Three weeks! There was absolutely no abuse occurring in my day care, but what if there was? What if a child actually had been hurt in those three weeks after Annie's allegations? Holly only had to call Human Services and make her report. It would then have been out of her hands. If Holly believed Annie, she potentially endangered other children in the day care by delaying this report. Holly is a teacher. By law, she is required to report suspected child abuse seen in the course of her work. She knew the procedure for doing so. Although the story told by Annie was not abuse seen in the course of Holly's job, any morally sound person would have tried to protect other children. Teachers are held to a higher standard in looking out for kids in general. The parents of the other children in my care should have been enraged at Holly for not reporting immediately, especially the Marshalls. Holly was selfish to remove only her children from a perceived dangerous situation. I wonder what her school district employer, or the parents of children in her classes, would think about her self-centered actions.

There were two other Human Services reports. One was dated September 20, 2008, and was a report from the Marshalls giving their version of the "abuse," after hearing from Holly Jeter the day before. At this point, the agency decided to screen-in the report for further follow up. The next report detailed contact between the Marshalls and staff from Human Services on October 28, 2008. Based on "reliable" and "credible" information obtained by Detective Julie Johnson, observation of the witness accounts, and the meeting with the Marshalls, this staff determined that physical abuse to Cody Marshall was substantiated. They closed the case, noting that Detective Johnson had forwarded two charges of abuse to the DA's office.

It was interesting, albeit painful, to read these county reports. What would be more fascinating, however, was reading the police reports that Bob had received. Included in these reports were the narratives of Detective Johnson's interviews with all the day care kids and their parents.

The first thing that came to mind was Johnson's interview with me:

*"When I ask the kids, they **all** tell me Lynn hurts Cody, Lynn hurts Emma, Lynn hurts Eddie, bangs heads on the table."*

"I have a lot of kids with a lot of injuries and I have a lot of kids that have been harmed."

*"This is what **all** the kids are saying."*

*"There's multiple times, multiple incidents, **multiple children telling us** of injury, bruising, and crying, Lynn hurting Emma, Lynn hurting Cody, Lynn hurting Miles, Lynn hurting David."*

According to the reports of Johnson's interviews with the kids, only Annie and Miles had said anything to her about me hurting Cody. Yet, repeatedly, she had told me that *every* child reported this. Johnson had lied to me.

Annie and Miles were siblings and lived together, contrary to Johnson telling me, *"It's not like these kids see each other every day and live in the same neighborhood."* Annie started the accusations. Miles likely heard Annie telling her stories, creating false memories for him. Holly Jeter admitted that Annie made her allegations in the car on the way to my house, with Miles in the car.

When Johnson asked about her time at my day care, Annie said that she observed me changing Cody's diaper. She said, "Lynn was making Cody's head go up and down and he started to cry." Annie said she was standing on the climber and she could see the diaper changing table. Johnson asked her if she ever saw me hurt any of the other children and she said she saw me bang Emma's head on the wall. Annie said I hurt Cody more than one time, but she does not remember how many times.

Johnson told Holly Jeter that she wanted the kids to have Safe Harbor interviews, so she didn't cover specifics with them. Holly then showed Johnson pictures that they had taken on May 16, 2006, of Miles with bruises on his lower jaw and on the left side of his head. Holly stated that at the time Miles would have been totally immobile because he had had brain surgery in November 2005. She said he wasn't even crawling, he could only lie there, and you had to pick him up and hold him. She stated that she remembers picking Miles up from day care, giving him a bath that night, and noticing these bruises. Holly knows for a fact those bruises were not there when she dropped off Miles at daycare on the morning of the 16th, and that's why she photographed them.

Holly told Johnson she always had concerns over the bruises on Miles from 2006. Again, I wonder, why did she keep him in my care?

Her claim that Miles was totally immobile at this time was false. The photos showed him standing up in the bathtub. Does an immobile child have the capability to stand up in a bathtub?

When meeting with the Reese family, Johnson got Peter to bang his stuffed duck on the table, insinuating that's how I harmed Cody. Why Peter was even interviewed is beyond comprehension— he had only been in my care on four days, and the overlap with Cody was two days (July 1-2). There is no way that Peter, in late September, would know Cody. Should anyone believe his duck-banging equated to something he saw with Cody two-and-a-half months earlier, well, I have the proverbial bridge in Brooklyn to sell.

At Tommy's interview, he blurted out "only Cody cried" before Johnson even asked anything. That sure sounds like there was an attempt to prep him before Johnson's interview. But there were no abuse allegations forthcoming from Tommy.

Emma was the most verbal child in my day care. She told Johnson that she never saw anyone hurt at my house, nor had she been hurt (in contrast to Annie's Safe Harbor claim). Emma's mom, Jane, relayed to Johnson that Emma told her that I pulled Cody's hair. This disclosure occurred only upon questioning Emma after Annie's allegations; funny how it never came up prior to that.

David denied anyone getting hurt at my house, although he acknowledged that Cody cried. David's actual words to Johnson about what happened at my house were, "Nothing, nothing, nothing," Johnson stated that was because David was "very traumatized."

David's parents, Bev and Mark, told Johnson that they had a videotape of David making allegations of abuse. I viewed that videotape and laughed. David obviously played for the camera—flopping around like a fish out of water. The questions were leading, and, if his parents didn't get the response they wanted, they would re-ask. "You told me that she puts his hands on her face, can you show me what she does? No, no, not that. Does she do something to his cheeks?" David was directed to look at his mom for cues, he was corrected when he did not make incriminating statements, and almost every question from his parents was leading. This certainly was not a credible interview.

Max's interview with Johnson did not reveal any abuse. He stated that Cody cried a lot. As with David, Johnson claimed that Max was upset and reluctant to talk about this. Brian Pickett, Max's dad, stated that one day when they were leaving my house, Max told him, "Lynn told Cody not to cry." Max never mentioned anything further, so Brian didn't think much of it.

Eddie Ryan, when interviewed by Johnson, just directed her to make a sad face on a drawing.

Johnson's attempts to elicit abuse accusations from kids other than the Jeters failed. They honestly responded that Cody was sad, but couldn't say that I was harming him. Johnson's remedy to that was to proclaim that they were all upset or traumatized by the topic and refused to discuss it. She had never met these kids, yet declared that they were distressed about questions regarding Cody. Was she an expert on child behavior? What qualified her, after just meeting these children and spending only a few minutes with them, to give this psychological diagnosis? She didn't get the responses she wanted, so conveyed the impression that they were all too scared or distressed to talk about it. She went into these interviews already biased against me. She wouldn't accept the children's statements that nothing happened. To her, "nothing happened" meant the children were denying, repressing, or traumatized.

Johnson met with Joe and Maria Marshall on September 22, 2008. There was no mention at this interview about any August 27 injuries to Cody. Johnson's interrogation with me on October 2 allowed her to see my log book, referencing the August 27 ladder incident. Then, in a follow-up call from Johnson, Maria suddenly recalls dramatic injuries to Cody that had no substantiated medical report or photos.

The term *"dramatic"* seemed to come up a lot. Johnson used the term in her interview with me. *"What's happening to these kids with the bruising? You know, it's pretty dramatic."* Was this a favorite term of Johnson's that she projected onto Maria's report?

The report from the county dated September 19, 2008 indicated that no injuries were present. This was the initial report from Holly Jeter. Cody, Miles, and Annie were all at day care by 7:15 a.m. on Thursday, August 28, after Annie informed Holly about harm to Cody the previous day. Holly did not see any injuries on Cody on the 28th or she would have noted their existence in her county report.

Johnson's report specified that Annie was on the climber when she "saw" Cody harmed. The Safe Harbor interviewer never asked her where she was. Cathy Leaverton, my licensor, had only told me that she was watching TV and did not give a specific location.

There was never any abuse occurring in the bathroom, or any-where else, but I was curious to check out the alleged "scene of the crime." I examined the view from the climber to the bathroom from every angle. I twisted and contorted from every possible posi-tion; I even tried getting up in the windowsill to see how far into the bathroom I could see. I asked others to attempt a view, also. There was absolutely no view to the diaper changing area unless you were right in the bathroom doorway. I dubbed Annie "The Girl with X-ray Vision," due to her seeming ability to see nonexistent abuse through walls.

**"This is the view to the bathroom from the climber.
You can't see the changing table."**

Chapter 11

More Charges

*M*y next court proceeding was an arraignment on February 6, 2009, with Judge Schwartz at the helm. ADA Lana Mades was not available for this meeting; Deputy DA Judy Schwaemle appeared instead. She was much nicer and treated both Bob and me respectfully; she actually regarded me as a human being instead of a guilty defendant. I wished that she could be the DA on the case. Bob entered not-guilty pleas on my behalf for both counts. Judge Schwartz set the trial date for April 27. Proceeding to this step scared me, but I naively held out hope that the system would not fail an innocent person.

With a trial date looming in the near future, I decided to tell the rest of my family and friends about the situation. I also informed previous day care families, as I didn't want them to learn about it from any potential news reports or gossip. Reactions varied among disbelief, shock, anger, sadness, and reassurance. Generous friends and relatives offered money to help with legal fees and household expenses (I still was unemployed), and many wrote letters in support of me or as testament to my character. I took comfort in these kind acts. Comments to me had the same prevailing theme: "There's no way you would have ever harmed a child."

I was amazed by how many people told me that they knew of others in the education or human services fields who had faced similar allegations. I always knew that my profession carried a risk of abuse allegations, but never thought I would be falsely accused. I had just begun my early childhood education career in 1984 when the McMartin case in California became widely publicized. I remember thinking, "Great. I begin my career working with children amidst the hysteria."

I tried to keep busy through March. I engaged in some household projects and spent time helping my grandma, but my mind whirred with thoughts of the upcoming trial. I volunteered at the local Humane Society; those few hours a week caring for the cats at least provided me some distraction.

Bob had hired a private investigator, Gwen Dunham. She attempted to interview the day care families, but met resistance and obtained nothing helpful to my case. I found that telling; the parents had no trouble talking to the police, but if there was anything in my favor, they were unwilling to take that leap.

I anticipated the April trial with mixed feelings. I knew the worst could happen, but I didn't see how, once we got the chance to present our case. For the charge of injury to Cody on August 27, 2008, it would be easy to prove that there was no way Annie could see into the bathroom to have witnessed anything like she claimed. There was also no proof of any injuries to Cody on this date — no photos, no doctor visit, even though Maria contended there were "dramatic injuries." Holly Jeter even admitted in her report to the county that she did not notice any injuries to Cody.

For the charge of injury to Cody on September 17, 2008, I admit that he did have an incident of bumping his head on the door, resulting in a bruise. This was documented in my log book and told to Joe upon pick-up. Cody was seen at the ER on Monday, September 22, for concerns of abuse, after the Marshalls first heard from Holly Jeter. This ER trip resulted in a diagnosis by Dr. Mark Bellazzini of "bruising." I could have given that diagnosis and I am not a doctor. There was no confirmed diagnosis of child abuse, no significant head injury. Cody had a skeletal survey done at this visit, which was normal. Something surely would have shown up on that imaging if this poor child was getting the "crap beat out of him on a daily basis."

According to the American College of Radiology, a skeletal survey is a series of radiographic images that encompasses the entire skeleton. The goal of the skeletal survey is to accurately identify focal and diffuse abnormalities of the skeleton, including healing fractures of varying ages, and to differentiate them from developmental changes and other anatomic variants that may occur in infants and children. The skeletal survey is frequently critical to diagnosis of child abuse and is often presented as critical evidence in care and protection cases and criminal proceedings.

There were no witnesses to any alleged abuse on September 17, 2008; Annie, with her X-ray vision, was not in attendance that day. Therefore, I was confident that I would be acquitted of both charges. After all, the standard of proof in a criminal matter is "beyond a reasonable doubt," and there was nothing but doubt here.

On April 10, Bob called me, stating that ADA Mades had added another child abuse charge to the existing two—a charge for injuries received on September 17, 2008, making that the second count for that day. That was the day he bumped into the door on his way outside, and received the forehead bump. Now she added another injury—what, the crud behind his ear? How could I be responsible for that? I was upset, but pissed off more than anything. I certainly lost any small modicum of respect I had for ADA Mades. I also began to dread any time Bob called.

I arranged to meet with Bob on Monday, April 13· to discuss this new development and trial strategy. As I approached his office, he waved me in; he happened to be on the phone with Mades. He put the phone on speaker. My heart immediately dropped to the floor. She stated she was adding yet another charge, this one being the facial bruises I allegedly inflicted upon Miles Jeter in May 2006 when he was a year old. This charge was based on those photos I first saw at Johnson's interview with me. I was never made aware of those bruises to his face. They were never reported to me at the time and I had nothing in my log book about them. Had they shown up when he was at my house, or if he had arrived with them, I most certainly would have noted that.

In addition to the new charge of abuse toward Miles, Mades indicated that she intended to introduce "other acts evidence," consisting of injuries I allegedly afflicted on other children in my care. What injuries? What other children?

"Can she do this?" I asked Bob.

"Yes, unfortunately," he responded. "ADAs can basically do anything."

I had no idea what the principle of "other acts evidence" even meant, but, as with other terms I encountered in this unpleasant journey, my legal vernacular was rapidly expanding.

Bob explained that "other acts evidence" establishes the conditions under which factual evidence of past misconduct of the accused can be admitted at trial for the purpose of inferring that the accused committed the misconduct at issue. What past misconduct did I ever have? None of the parents had ever lodged a complaint, or even voiced suspicion about any injuries their children sustained in my care.

The log book in which I recorded any instances of injury was now being used against me — injuries listed in there now became questionable for abuse. It's not like there were even that many injuries or incidents that occurred in my day care. There were the occasional minor bumps and bruises. No child ever had to seek medical care for any injury occurring on my watch. Parents had never had any reason to suspect these isolated prior injuries of being anything other than normal and reasonable in the course of daily day care events, because that's what they were. Once Annie's allegation emerged, however, the snowball of suspicion started rolling.

I had always followed the state licensing requirements for the medical log book. Injuries received at my home or injuries the children arrived with needed to be included. The book itself had to have numbered pages and a stitched binding.

A provider shall note in a medical log book any injury or evidence of unusual bruises, contusions, lacerations or burns received by a child in or out of the center and any incidents requiring the services of medical personnel. The licensee shall maintain a medical log book with pages that are lined and numbered and a stitched binding. A provider shall record in ink any injuries received by a child, evidence of unusual bruises, contusions, lacerations or burns received by a child in or out of center care or medication dispensed to a child in the medical log and sign or initial each entry.

We were told that this protected us because the log book could be used in court proceedings. I never envisioned a day when mine would be used against me. Among my many regrets in this whole debacle was giving a copy of my log book to the detectives, absent any type of court order. Yet I had nothing to hide and simply thought it would be helpful.

Mades tried to buttress her case by introduction of other bad acts in order to increase the likelihood of convicting me. There was a great danger a jury could convict even when the evidence on the actual charges was insufficient, solely because of the other acts evidence. The addition of the charges and other acts evidence was also a way to overwhelm me and pressure me into taking a plea deal. This trick of the trade of prosecutors to overcharge with everything but the kitchen sink is enough of a threat to induce an innocent person to accept a plea bargain. Prosecutors have no reason not to overcharge; there are no adverse consequences for improper charging decisions and they enjoy immunity from lawsuits over misconduct in their prosecutorial capacity. Although feeling overpowered and bullied, I would not budge from my decision to reject a plea deal. I was innocent and wanted my day in court to prove it; I hung on to the belief that the truth would prevail. Had I been guilty, I would have had the integrity to admit it and jumped at the chance for the best deal.

Bob said that Mades would have to submit motions for these charges/other acts; he would counter her motions with compelling arguments. I had entered Bob's office that day thinking we had a good defense against the original charges, but I left feeling scared and hopeless. I wanted to sink into a hole in the floor and never get up. Why was this happening to me? This was completely spiraling out of control.

These recent changes by Mades also reduced the charges to "Reckless Child Abuse Causing Bodily Harm," a Class I felony, compared to the original charges by Cattanach of "Intentionally Causing Bodily Harm" Class H felony. It was of little consolation; these four charges were still felonies, inherent with the risk of three-and-a-half years in prison for each count. The State would not have to prove intent now. I did not assert myself well at that terrible interrogation back in October, but I did stress that I never intentionally harmed a child. Mades probably realized she could never make an intentional charge stick.

Bob submitted memoranda opposing Mades' intent to introduce other acts evidence and the new charge of the bruises to Miles' face. His main argument against the other acts was that the power of suggestion applied equally to the parents and children in this case. Earlier injuries to the kids, which were normal accidents young kids experience, had now been converted into allegations of abuse, which the State was trying to introduce as other acts evidence.

Admission into evidence of any earlier injuries to any of the children in my care would unfairly prejudice me. Bob urged the court to review my log book, venturing to say that the few injuries sustained by the kids were typical of similar home daycares. Parents viewed those injuries at the time as normal childhood incidents and their opinion changed only after they heard what Annie allegedly saw on August 27, 2008. The State attempted to show a pattern of injuries, but the evidence concerning the earlier injuries was far too tenuous to support its admission as other acts evidence. Clearly, the State could not prove by a preponderance of the evidence that these injuries were caused by me. Bob urged the court to not allow the other acts evidence, citing the high risk of an injustice.

As to the new charge of bruises on Miles' face, if there was a question of possible abuse it should have been raised at the time (May 2006) when the injuries were seen on the child. Three years later, it was impossible to defend. Moreover, as this was a completely new unrelated charge, I had not even had a preliminary hearing on it.

Bob also submitted a motion to suppress statements I had made in my interview with the detectives. Considering the totality of the circumstances surrounding my interrogation, Bob asserted that my statements were made involuntarily, contrary to the fifth and fourteenth amendments to the U.S. Constitution. He asked the court for an evidentiary Goodchild hearing on this motion. A Miranda/ Goodchild hearing decides if a defendant was advised of his/her Miranda rights when there was a need and that his/her statements were given freely and voluntarily.

Obviously, the April trial date was removed from the court docket. No trial dates were available until September. I was devastated when I heard this—four more months of this hanging over my head. The court system is nothing like you see on TV, where someone is charged with a crime and the trial is the next day. It is, in reality, slow as molasses. I realize that is necessary for attorneys and judges who need time to draft motions and make rulings, not to mention fitting a trial time into the overloaded court calendar, but when it is your life hanging in limbo, the long wait times are agonizing. At least I was fortunate that I was not in custody; in fact, Judge Schwartz stated that was why he was comfortable pushing the trial out to September. I can't imagine how hard it is for defendants in custody to wait amid inevitable delays for their day in court. Bob explained that we had to have time for rulings on these new charges and other acts evidence, and, depending on those outcomes, he would need more preparation time for trial. All I could do was hope that the judge would be fair when reaching his decision on these new motions, which would be discussed at a hearing on July 3. I anxiously awaited this date to hear the arguments and the judge's rulings.

Chapter 12

Protect, Serve…and Lie

riday, July 3rd was a gorgeous summer day. Ki and I were expecting friends the next day for a Fourth of July gathering. I hoped I would have good news to share with them after the motion hearing.

The courthouse was eerily quiet when we arrived—there was not a lot scheduled, as it was the day before a holiday. Bob met me outside Judge Schwartz's courtroom. Mades and Detective Julie Johnson arrived shortly after us. Why was Johnson attending? I was bothered by seeing her again, knowing what she put me through. The last time I saw her was at the January preliminary hearing, where she made it sound like she and Cody were the best friends in the world and he allegedly said damning things about me. Seeing her now sent me into a mini panic attack. I tried to be polite by acknowledging her as she walked past me, but inwardly my mind called her nasty names.

We settled into our respective seats in the courtroom and waited for Judge Schwartz's arrival. Each time I sat in that courtroom

I asked myself why I was there—it was still all surreal to me. Judge Schwartz arrived and asked Mades and Bob to start with the motions for adding charges and other acts evidence. Bob began, arguing that the DA abused her discretion by attempting to add the totally unrelated charge of Miles from 2006.

"It's beyond her power to do it. It adds to the unfairness of it. We were close to trial and all of a sudden this was charged." Bob cited case law that supported his view; Mades, in rebuttal, attempted to twist that case law to fit her point of view. The legalese went above my head, but I was glad to see Bob fighting for me.

He argued the gross unfairness of the new charge. "This charge is based almost exclusively on a photograph taken in May 2006. That's it. You're handed a photo and told, here's the charge, May of 2006. Think back two-and-a-half-years. This wasn't brought to anybody's attention. How am I supposed to defend this now? If it's going to be charged, it should be charged the right way under the system. It should be charged as a criminal complaint and we'll have a preliminary hearing on it."

Schwartz said that he would need time to look at the cases cited and how they fit with the motions in front of him, including the other acts evidence. He indicated he would make every attempt to get his decision made as quickly as possible. I was disappointed that I would leave without any firm ruling on this issue today, but realized that he was being fair in taking the time to study this.

Other motions were discussed by the parties. Most were referred to by number only, so I had no idea what the discourse involved. Most of these motions were granted; I trusted that Bob agreed to things that were in my best interest. One of them garnered a bit of discussion: Mades had moved to disallow any testimony that my day care had never received any prior complaints and had had only positive reports. Mades believed that this was an impermissible attempt to get character type evidence in front of the jury. Judge Schwartz stated that he was concerned about how Bob was wording that.

"I'm going to deny the State's request because I will let you ask some questions, but they need to be limited. I don't want to get into character evidence." That astonished me. It seemed that it was easy for the State to get any prior "bad acts" admitted, but anything good in my past or character couldn't be admitted. I was glad there was somewhat of a positive ruling on my behalf for this issue, but I got the uneasy feeling that the State had a clear advantage in getting their motions approved. This view would become solidified in the upcoming months.

After a short break, we resumed the hearing to address the Goodchild motion. Judge Schwartz stated that my recording of the October interview with the detectives needed to be played in its entirety in court so it would be on the record. We had received a copy of that recording on CD and I had listened to it a few times, each time berating myself for talking to the detectives. I hated the idea of having to listen to this tape again, here in court. Detective Johnson was called to the stand by Mades to give some pretext for the interview; the recording was then played.

After the recording finished, Mades asked Johnson a few more questions. The best question was, "In your presentation of your investigation of the defendant, were you dishonest to her in any way?" Johnson responded that she was not.

Bob took over. "During the interview, would it be correct to say that you had indicated to Lynn that all of the kids were consistent and all of the kids were saying there was abuse?

Johnson: I don't remember the exact words, but their statements were consistent on the ones that I had interviewed.

Bob: Do you recall using the words "all of the kids?"

Johnson: I may have. I don't remember exactly. If it's on the tape, then I said it.

Bob: Did you talk or try to talk to all of the kids in the day care during the time in question?

Johnson: Yes, I tried to talk to all of them.

Bob: Would I be correct that a number of the kids that you talked to, when asked if they saw any abuse at the day care, said no?

Mades: Objection—relevance.

Bob: Well, I'm trying to determine whether at any point in the inter-rogation the detective was dishonest with the defendant.

Judge Schwartz: I'll give you some latitude. Go ahead.

Bob: Do you recall talking to Eddie and his mother?

Johnson: Yes.

Bob: Would I be correct when questioned, Eddie told you that he saw nothing; he saw no abuse at the day care?

Johnson: I don't remember his exact words. I would have to review my report.

Bob: Well, I don't want to belabor the point. Could we have her look at her report?

Judge Schwartz: If your point, Mr. Burke, is that Detective Johnson, in the course of her questions, may have misled by saying *all* of the children. If that's where you're headed, the point is made. Otherwise, we are going to presumably go through each one of these children. If you want to do that, that's fine.

Bob: Just so the record is clear, the police report will eventually come in evidence and I believe it will indicate one, two, three, four, five of the kids, when questioned about whether there was any abuse, indicated they didn't see any abuse. Detective, would you agree with that or would you have to review your notes?

Johnson: I would have to review my notes.

Bob: But isn't it correct that you led Lynn Moller to believe, in the process of questioning, that all of the kids you talked to were consistently pointing the finger at her and saying abuse; isn't that essentially the thrust of what you were saying to her?

Johnson: Essentially, yes, that's what I did say to her.

Bob: Judge, I could introduce the police report at this point to complete the record.

Judge Schwartz: Well, however you want to do it, Mr. Burke. The point is that she's now testified that not all of the children were able to say there was abuse, but she did not share that with Ms. Moller. So that's part of the record. Detective Johnson has already said although some of the children indicated to her that they were not able to attribute any abuse, but she did not share that and in her questioning she said something to the effect of all of the children are consistent. I think that's the point you want to make. If you want to supplement that by going through the records, I will give you the opportunity to do that. I'm saying you've made the point as far as I'm concerned.

Bob: That's fine.

I was impressed with Bob's tenacity in getting Johnson's deceit on the record. Mades then tried to argue that this interview was not coercive. "The most you could say is somehow if this was coercive, it was just by the sheer niceness of it. You heard the total of the interview which was very pleasant conversation, and nothing coercive about it."

That interview was pleasant conversation? On what planet would accusations thrown at you constantly be considered pleasant conversation?

Bob stated to the judge that he was diametrically opposed to what Mades said. "Police conduct does not have to be egregious or

outrageous to be coercive. This is one of the most coercive interviews I've ever heard. I counted like twenty times where Lynn said
no, I didn't. I didn't do this. I didn't cause these injuries, didn't
do anything intentional. So after an hour and thirty-five minutes,
I'm not saying they whipped, I'm sure Detective Johnson is a nice
person, but after being told over and over that all of the kids are
saying consistently the same thing, after being told that all of the
injuries occurred there, what you're saying doesn't make sense.
Finally, Lynn saying, well, if the injuries occurred in my house, I
didn't know it, didn't realize it. If I'm responsible, I'm sorry. But
every time she was given an opportunity to explain what she did
with Cody, none of it is consistent with any kind of intentional act
or any physical abuse.

"But faced with all the insurmountable evidence, dramatic evidence, all of the kids being consistent, all of the kids saying the
same thing—the logical conclusion of this interview was the pressures of the questioning, the disbelieving of the detectives. They
believed the kids. The pressure caused Lynn Moller to make a
concession, not because she admitted something, but just making
a concession because it seemed, based on what the detectives are
saying, there was no other conclusion. It was the product of the
pressures, questioning, the coercion of the questioning, the failure
of the questioning, and the misrepresentation of the State's case.
I think it's very, very important, during the process of this questioning, that Lynn was made aware that every one of these kids is

saying the same thing. Would it have made a difference if the detectives had said we talked to five of the kids who didn't say anything, but three of these kids said they saw something? It's the State's burden, and I don't think they have met it—based on the reasonable interpretation of that interview, any admission they try to get from this statement is not voluntary and the product of coercion."

Bingo, Bob. He nailed it. Mades had no retort. The judge would now have to rule on the admissibility of my statements during that interview. His job would be to assess the totality of the circumstances surrounding my statements, including the interrogation tactics used and their effects on me.

The final motion to be reviewed at this hearing was Bob's request for a jury view. He wanted the jury to look at my day care space. Judge Schwartz indicated his issue with a jury view was the coordination it would require. Bob responded that generally the defense arranges for transportation. Schwartz stated he did not have any problem with that, should he grant the motion. Bob said that a jury view was necessary to have the jury see the child care.

"It's very important for the jury to understand the testimony, the size of the child care center; you don't get it from photographs. I think the jury needs to see this to understand the testimony of the witnesses."

Mades objected to this, saying that, because it was in my sole custody, she didn't know how it had been changed. Of course she objected; the jury would have the opportunity to go up on the climber and try to see the diaper changing area, and no way would they be able to do so.

Judge Schwartz replied that it's one thing to move a sofa, but far more difficult to shift a basement window, etc. He asked Bob to submit a more detailed jury view motion to address exactly how it would help the jury.

The hearing was finally over; it took most of the morning, and I left feeling drained. However, it was a better feeling than I had had any other time leaving the courthouse. I didn't understand everything that went on, but was pleased with how hard Bob was fighting for me. Although I was initially bothered by seeing Johnson at this hearing, it turned out to be a good thing, as she was caught in her lies. I wondered how much I could trust her other statements, specifically her interview with Cody. How do I know that was properly communicated? It wasn't recorded and she was alone with Cody.

After this hearing, I did some research on police tactics during interviews, specifically about lying or fabricating evidence. Had Johnson been truthful with me in the interview that only Annie and Miles were saying things, along with some supposed comments from David, I would have been in a much better position to analyze her allegations.

I familiarized myself with the Reid Technique of Interrogation, and realized I had fallen in its trap. Developed by Joe Reid and Fred Inbau, the Reid Technique has a powerful capacity to elicit confessions from innocent persons as it strips them of the ability to provide credible denials and to advance an innocent account of their conduct while subjecting them to relentless pressure. This technique is less about finding truth as it is about using psychological manipulation to get a confession. Police officers are trained to get a confession, even if it means lying to the suspect and using trickery or deceit. Most people are surprised to learn this is entirely legal. Police use the Reid Technique because they know how vulnerable you are and will take full advantage of this. Even if you don't give a confession, you could be manipulated into saying enough to give a prosecutor evidence to convict you.

The Reid technique's nine steps of interrogation are:

Step 1 - Direct Confrontation. Lead the suspect to understand that the evidence has led the police to the individual as a suspect. Offer the person an early opportunity to explain why the offense took place.

Step 2 - Try to shift the blame away from the suspect to some other person or set of circumstances that prompted the suspect to commit the crime. That is, develop themes containing reasons that will justify or excuse the crime. Themes may be developed or changed to find one to which the accused is most responsive.

Step 3 - Try to discourage the suspect from denying his guilt. Reid training video: "If you've let him talk and say the words 'I didn't do it,' the more difficult it is to get a confession."

Step 4 - At this point, the accused will often give a reason why he or she did not or could not commit the crime. Try to use this to move towards the confession.

Step 5 - Reinforce sincerity to ensure that the suspect is receptive.

Step 6 - The suspect will become quieter and listen. Move the theme discussion toward offering alternatives. If the suspect cries at this point, infer guilt.

Step 7 - Pose the "alternative question," giving two choices for what happened; one more socially acceptable than the other. The suspect is expected to choose the easier option but whichever alternative the suspect chooses, guilt is admitted. There is always a third option which is to maintain that they did not commit the crime.

Step 8 - Lead the suspect to repeat the admission of guilt in front of witnesses and develop corroborating information to establish the validity of the confession.

Step 9 - Document the suspect's admission or confession and have him or her prepare a recorded statement (audio, video, or written). *Zulawski, David E.; Wicklander, Douglas E. (2001). Practical Aspects of Interview and Interrogation. Ann Arbor: CRC Press.*

I trusted the police and wanted to be helpful. Yet the detectives were telling me that I committed these terrible acts against Miles and Cody. I trusted the investigator not to lie to me and was astonished to hear that there was evidence against me that I couldn't explain. Had I been stronger or had more experience with the police, I may have said the magic words: "I want a lawyer." I didn't believe I needed a lawyer if I was innocent, thinking that would only make me look guilty. On the contrary; that would have made me look smart. Lesson learned, albeit too late.

Chapter 13

The Judge's Logic

On July 14, 2009, our investigator, Gwen, met with my day care licensor, Cathy Leaverton. Gwen's report of their encounter contained the following information:

- Leaverton said that she has no comment regarding whether a person would be able to see the bathroom changing table from the loft. She said that she didn't check it out; she only sat in the blue rocking chair. She confirmed that there had been no prior complaints against Lynn's Day Care.

- Leaverton said Lynn didn't say she did it (the abuse).

- Leaverton said that Lynn's log descriptions are briefer than some other day care providers who write more. But, she said, there are no violations in her log. Leaverton said Lynn's log notations match the Wisconsin administrative code ("a daily record of injuries including the child's name, date, and time of injury and a brief description of the facts surrounding the injury").

Ki and I went to Green Bay on July 25 for my thirtieth class reunion. While at my parents' house before the reunion, Ki received an email from Bob. Judge Schwartz's ruling had been submitted. I heard Ki whoop with joy as he read the email: neither the other acts evidence nor the charge regarding the injuries to Miles would be allowed. I was beyond thrilled to hear this. Schwartz acknowledged that parents of the other children with the alleged injuries never considered them serious or suspicious at the time. "Nor did these parents feel the necessity to contact any investigative authorities. In fact, none of those allegations were voiced by any parent until other parents or authorities contacted them in the course of this current investigation. Furthermore, none of the parents opted to remove their children from Moller's care. I find that the proposed other acts evidence goes only to other conduct that the State wishes to use to bolster its charge that Moller abused Cody Marshall. Allowing the other acts evidence would certainly arouse the jury's sympa- thies, provoke its instinct to punish Moller, or otherwise cause the jury to base its decision on something other than the established propositions in the case. Therefore, I must prohibit the State from introducing other acts evidence involving children other than Cody in its case-in-chief."

As to the charge of injury to Miles, Schwartz wrote, "Because count four is a completely new felony charge that was not tested at the preliminary hearing, I must apply the sufficiency of the evidence test to that count. To do otherwise would lead to the absurd result of allowing the State to file new charges, even though the evidence at the hearing failed to demonstrate the requisite probable cause. Motion to dismiss count four is granted, without prejudice."

I felt a tremendous weight off my shoulders with those two rulings. The other acts would have been extremely hard to overcome; the judge even said there was a high risk that a jury could convict based on an inherent distaste for child abusers if they heard testimony that I may have engaged in such behaviors previously with other children. In addition, Schwartz was correct that count four regarding Miles was not related to any charges related to Cody, and did not have sufficient evidence to support probable cause for a charge related to Miles.

I was, however, disappointed that some of Bob's other motions were denied. The jury view was disallowed; apparently, Bob did not provide enough information to provide a basis for which a jury view would be necessary to a fair adjudication.

Schwartz wrote, "If the view is being sought to show the jury the position of furniture, play equipment, etc., I have no information demonstrating that the current placement of such items is identical to their placement back in August and September of 2008. Nothing prohibits the defendant from presenting a detailed description of the facility as it was at the time, or from arguing that witnesses could not have seen what they may claim to have seen based on the facility's internal configuration."

Bob and I had thought it would be extremely helpful to have the jury view to impart the significance of not being able to see into the bathroom diaper changing area from *anywhere* in the day care room. Unless one stood right in the doorway to the bathroom, the view was restricted. Annie's claims of seeing into the bathroom from the climber across the way started the abuse allegations; discrediting her initial accusation would be the first step in knocking over the house of cards built upon it.

I was bothered by Schwartz's decision that my statements in the police interview would not be suppressed. He ruled that the circumstances surrounding the interview supported the conclusion that my statements were voluntarily made. Because I did not testify at the evidentiary hearing on July 3, the testimony of the detective remained unchallenged. I did not even know that I had the opportunity to testify.

It was also frustrating to read that count three would be added. This was evidently the second "injury" to Cody on September 17, 2008, the crud behind his ear. I was to blame for him having some kind of skin infection? The picture showed a line of crusted dots; how would I have inflicted that type of symptom on the space behind his ear? Johnson claimed this was from me hitting his head against the wall. Can someone show me how one would get this type of mark behind the ear? I hoped the jury would have enough sense to figure out that this charge was bogus.

I wished that Schwartz had ruled favorably to me on all motions, but at least the motions most damaging to me were ruled to my advantage. I also learned from Bob that Judge Schwartz had put in his notice for retirement, and he would be done in October. I was glad the trial was scheduled for September so Schwartz would be the judge; while I disagreed with some of his rulings, I still felt he was fair. I wouldn't want a new judge to step in at this stage.

We filled my dad in on these latest developments. My mom still knew nothing. Her health was declining rapidly, and we had no desire to burden her with bad news. I enjoyed the weekend with my parents and the class reunion. The black cloud that had been hanging above my head dissipated a bit, and I felt a sense of relief I had not known for many months.

Unbeknownst to me, however, was the reemergence of a key player in this game, causing that black cloud to reappear, darker and angrier than ever. Cue ominous music.

Chapter 14

Return of ADA Cattanach

About a week after I returned from Green Bay, Bob called with devastating news. He said that the original ADA, Karie Cattanach, had returned from her maternity leave and taken this case over again. She was going to reissue count four, the Miles charge. In addition, she wanted to ask the judge for reconsideration of the other acts evidence. My heart sank (again). Here I had had, for the first time, a judge's ruling in my favor, and now the ADA was trying to wipe that out. I was livid. I never did anything to Miles other than love and care for him.

I remembered what Bob initially told me about Cattanach being a tough prosecutor. That worried me. The only thing I knew about her was that she was a former University of Wisconsin women's basketball player. Therefore, she probably had a competitive nature, and I wondered how much that came into play in her role as a prosecutor.

So, on August 12, I made another trek to the courthouse. The Dane County Courthouse is a cream-colored, triangular-shaped, architecturally bland building located a block from the Wisconsin Capitol in downtown Madison. Unlike other historical Wisconsin courthouses, this building is devoid of charm and character. Near its entrance is a sign with a picture of Lady Justice, her symbolic image complete with a blindfold, balance scales, and a sword. I would come to dread any time I came near this building, and was often tempted to add a sign of my own below Lady Justice: Abandon all hope, ye who enter here (from Dante's *Inferno*—the inscription at the entrance to Hell).

While waiting for Bob, I engaged in people watching. I wondered why others had court appearances and couldn't help but feel bad for anyone caught up in the criminal justice system. I had not yet met Cattanach and did not know what she looked like. A tall, dark- haired woman in her mid-thirties carrying an armload of documents approached Schwartz's courtroom and checked the schedule. I wondered if that was Cattanach; this was confirmed when I heard her greet a colleague, who welcomed her back and congratulated her on her new baby. Cattanach's reply was, "Thanks. I love my daughter but there's no way I could be home with her all day."

That statement bothered me. Over the years of my child care career, the majority of my parents had to work and wanted to be able to stay home with their kids. A big reason I started my family child care business was to care for my own children as well. Yes, people have their own goals regarding careers and family, but

115

knowing that Cattanach wanted to leave a new baby in order to pursue invented child abuse charges against me tainted my perception of her.

Bob arrived and we entered the courtroom. Judge Schwartz started the proceedings by asking the attorneys for an update. Cattanach jumped in. "Upon my return about three weeks ago, I inherited the case."

Inherited the case? She initiated the charging decision last fall — two counts of child abuse intentionally causing harm. She had to have known it would not be resolved by the time she returned from her maternity leave.

She continued; it was obvious by her tone that she was not pleased that Schwartz had issued his decision to dismiss count four. "You issued your decision in the motion hearing that I was not part of."

Unfortunately, Schwartz had dismissed it *without prejudice*, another legal term to add to my ever-expanding repertoire, meaning that a new case or order may be brought on the same basis as the dismissed one. Dismissed *with prejudice* is the term you want when trying to get rid of a case for good.

Cattanach rattled on. "Based upon that ruling, I intend to reissue count four based upon an opinion by Dr. Knox that the pictures did depict child abuse. I will immediately be issuing that complaint. The State then intends to file a motion to join the new complaint with the current charges, and then we will be filing a motion for reconsidering the other acts based upon the joinder of those. We currently have a trial date in September. The proposal of the things the State intends to do is not going to be anywhere near complete in that short a period. The State requests a setover."

My head was spinning. I thought she would never stop talking about what the State wanted. Postpone the trial again. Adding charges and other acts. Requesting a joinder. What was this woman trying to do?

Bob immediately objected to the setover. He chastised Cattanach for adding the Miles charge at this late date. "We want to proceed on the trial date. I object to having it set over. My client has been living with this longer than she can bear and wants the trial to proceed."

Judge Schwartz somewhat rebuked Bob. "At the July 3 motion hearing, you argued that if the State thought they had enough to pursue count four, they could have filed a separate motion giving you an opportunity for a preliminary hearing. I forced them to do that. So you're getting what you asked for, which kind of puts me in the position of saying to you maybe you should be careful what you wish for; you got what you asked for now because the State wants to pursue that."

Bob asked to wait and see what would happen at the preliminary hearing. "I will be fighting bindover vigorously. If the State is successful, that's one issue. If they're not successful, then we're back on track." Cattanach and Judge Schwartz were satisfied by Bob's proposal. I can't say I understood all that went on, but I knew

117

I would face another preliminary hearing for the charge of those bruises to Miles' face that I never saw. I knew Bob would do all in his power to prevent the charge from going any further, but I remembered that a preliminary hearing was only a probable cause determination, and the burden was low for the State to say a felony had occurred and I probably had done it.

After this hearing, Ki and I googled ADA Cattanach. What types of cases did she handle? What were her results? This woman determined my fate. She wielded all the power and resources of the State, and could deprive me of my liberty. I had a right to investigate her prosecutorial career.

"Wait till you see this article I found!" Ki exclaimed, calling me over to the computer. "Looks like Cattanach engaged in some inappropriate behavior in the course of her job."

I read the article with interest. It was written by Bill Lueders in October 2001 and published in the *Isthmus,* an alternative weekly newspaper based in Madison. Cattanach, while working for the DA's office in 2000, posed as a prostitute in a sting operation set up by the Dane County Narcotics and Gang Task Force. Cattanach was chastised by the DA for her role; she had created a conflict by participating in a law-enforcement action. This forced the DA to dismiss solicitation charges against the man nabbed in the sting.

This *Isthmus* article focused on the friendly and personal relationship between Cattanach and the Madison Police Department. In 2007, Cattanach married an assistant police chief, twenty years

her senior. While I reserve judgment about May-December couples, this relationship seemed to validate the article's "cozy with
the cops" viewpoint.

Further research on Cattanach turned up noteworthy cases,
encompassing questionable tactics. One involved a defendant who
refused to plead guilty to misdemeanor possession of marijuana
after passing a joint to a friend during a parade. Cattanach dismissed that charge only to re-file it as a felony distribution charge.
For passing a joint at a pot rally? What a frivolous charge, not to
mention a waste of time and resources for the DA's office and Dane
County courts. Another case had her continuing with a battery and
disorderly conduct trial even after knowing her main witness lied.
My impression of Cattanach was sinking. What was her motivation—to win at all costs? That was scary to me. How would she
manipulate the evidence, or lack of evidence in my case, to get her
conviction?

I also searched for information on Dr. Barbara Knox, who,
according to Cattanach, had authored a report that Miles' bruises
were abuse. I couldn't find much information, other than that she
worked at American Family Children's Hospital Child Protection
Program. Her profile on the web page stated:

Dr. Knox's mission for the UW Children's Hospital Child Protection
Program is to ensure the safety and well-being of infants, children,
and adolescents from throughout Wisconsin, Northern Illinois, and

Eastern Iowa. She cares for children who have been or are suspected of being victims of physical abuse, sexual abuse, neglect,
and factitious illness by proxy. She also provides medical review
of child abuse cases for social services agencies, law enforcement,
and prosecutors.

I found inherent bias in the fact that she advertised working for
law enforcement and prosecution. I was curious to hear her rendi-
tion of these mysterious bruises.

Chapter 15

Another Preliminary Hearing

*O*n August 19, 2009, I made my initial appearance for this new charge of abuse to Miles. I knew what to expect now, but that did not make it any easier to hear the court commissioner read the charge against me. Since we did not waive time limits for the preliminary hearing (these hearings must be held within twenty days for a defendant who is not in custody), it had to occur soon. The court commissioner gave me a date for the following week. He said it would be with Judge Sumi. Judge Sumi! I smiled. I had had her two children in my care at University Avenue Day Care. I adored her children and greatly respected her and her husband, Carl. She would know that these charges against me were bogus. However, as much as I wanted her to be the judge for this preliminary hearing, she would have to recuse herself. Bob informed the court of the conflict and a different judge was assigned.

I couldn't believe it when the court commissioner said I would have to go through the booking process again. They already had my fingerprints and mug shot on file. Now I had to do this again?

I trudged next door to the jail building and once again subjected myself to the humiliation of the booking procedure. At least this time the officer was friendly and did not make me feel worse than I already did. I even attempted a small smirk for the new mug shot. Take that, I thought.

I tried to prepare myself mentally for this second preliminary hearing. I knew I would see Marty and Holly Jeter. Remembering that Maria Marshall had lied in the first preliminary hearing, it would be no surprise to hear falsehoods spew from the Jeters. They would have to lie to make this work in their favor.

August 25th was the date of this preliminary hearing, with Judge Flanagan. I had about ten friends and relatives accompany me and sit in the courtroom; they all wanted to see for themselves how these court proceedings work. My favorite detective, Johnson (*insert sarcastic tone here*), attended. I saw the Jeters arrive with the victim witness advocate, Mark Kerman, and once again was struck by how much protection the "victims" receive.

Holly Jeter was the first witness called. Cattanach asked her to look at the photos of Miles.

Cattanach: What day were these photos taken?
Holly: May 16, 2006.
Cattanach: On the morning that those photos were taken, did he have any sort of injuries to his face?

Holly: No. Upon picking him up from day care at Lynn Moller's, I observed the bruise on his cheek.

Cattanach: And when you brought him to day care that morning, the bruise was not there?

Holly: No. Then during his bath that night when I washed his hair, I noticed the bruises on his head.

Cattanach: And those were not there that morning?

Holly: No.

Bob started his cross-examination. "When did you see the bruise on Miles' cheek?"

Holly: I believe I saw it immediately when I saw him at the day care

Bob: Did you ask Lynn about the injury to the side of his face?

Holly: Yes, probably. I most likely said. . . I would have asked her, yeah.

Bob: Do you specifically recall asking her?

Holly: I specifically remember talking to her about them.

How was that for inconsistency—from "probably" and "most likely" and "I would have asked" to a definite recall of asking. Yet, she never did. If I had seen the bruises, whether he received them in my care or not, I would have recorded them in my log book. Even if I hadn't seen any, I would have noted Holly's concern had she actually spoken to me about them.

Bob tried to ask if she had ever seen any similar injuries prior to May 16, and why she had taken the photos, but these questions were met with objections by Cattanach. He did get Holly to admit that Miles could sit and stand at this point in time, contrasting Johnson's claim of him being totally immobile.

Bob attempted to ask Holly if Miles had any type of medical condition, if he was on medications, and if she had taken him to the doctor after seeing these injuries; again, these questions were met with objections. I wanted to shout out, "Let her answer these!" Holly admitted that she continued to take Miles to my day care right up until August 2008. Bob tried to ask her if she served as a reference for me (she did), but that was objected to as going towards credibility, which the judge said was not an issue here.

Holly was dismissed from the stand, and I couldn't help but think how unfair a preliminary hearing is to a defendant; any good information Bob tried to get from Jeter was not allowed.

Next on the stand was Dr. Barbara Knox. She exuded a quality of arrogance as she took her place. She rambled on about her occupation and background; Bob finally stepped in and said we would stipulate to her expertise in the area of child abuse. My supporters in the courtroom were rolling their eyes at her conceited introduction of herself.

Cattanach asked her if she viewed the seven photos of Miles, and if she made any findings regarding them. Knox responded, "Yes, I did. I diagnosed this case as gravely concerning for adult inflicted fingertip contusion injury to this child. The pattern appearance of this bruising appears consistent with an adult inflicted grab mark fingertip contusion injury to the left side of this child's face."

I had glanced back at my supporters; they were trying to simulate the action she described of a grab to the face. I had to smile at everyone with their hands on their faces trying to get this face grab scenario down. It wasn't an easy or likely motion, and I certainly never would have done that to Miles' or anyone's face.

Knox admitted that some of the photos were clearer, and, in some of them, she couldn't see bruises, just some discoloration. She indicated that she always likes to check for bleeding disorders in children with bruises to see if that explains the bruises. Miles was actually hospitalized during summer 2009 for spine surgery and she checked his blood then; results were normal.

Her reply to Cattanach's last line of questioning was to state that there was no plausible mechanism of injury presented to her, therefore she found that this injury was consistent with abuse.

Bob took his turn at cross-exam. "Doctor, in this case would I be correct in saying that your opinion concerning child abuse is based almost entirely on looking at the photographs?"

"Looking at the photos and getting some select historical information such as any history of trauma that was reported, yes."

Bob attempted to get her to admit that seeing photos only and not seeing the actual child or even a doctor report was not the best basis on which to make a diagnosis, but she stubbornly stuck to her opinion that five of the seven photos showed a pattern that was consistent with adult inflicted fingertip contusion injury.

"I feel that this is a definite contusion injury, despite the fact that I did not see the child and there was no medical care sought for the child at the time. No independent medical provider had confirmed that this was bruising, but that by photo documentation it does appear consistent with bruising."

Bob asked her if she could give a time frame for the bruising, such as the earliest or latest it could have happened. Knox replied, "I don't date bruising. The literature clearly documents we cannot effectively date bruising. I can just tell you that, by history, there was no bruising on the child at the time of day care drop off, and this was noted at the time of pick-up, which I would say this would be consistent with that statement. But beyond that, I cannot date them by looking at these photos."

Within the half-hour or so that Knox testified, I could tell that she had favorite catch phrases. Everything was either "gravely concerning for" or "consistent with" abuse.

Bob asked Knox if she was aware that prior to May 16, 2006, there had been no suspicious injuries at my day care. She admitted that there were no concerning facets in the day care and that no reports had been called in to state licensing. Bob finished by asking her if she was aware that this child remained in the same day care until August 2008; she replied, "Yes," before Cattanach objected.

Knox left the stand, and there were no more witnesses. Cattanach, of course, asked the judge for bind-over. Bob moved for dismissal of the case. "I know that the State at this stage just has probable cause, but I don't feel that the State has met its burden. Dr. Knox hadn't examined the child, her opinion is based on photos and nothing else. I think there's a serious limitation on her opinion. If the court accepts her opinion that there were signs of abuse, then the leap is to state that Lynn Moller was responsible for the abuse, and I feel the evidence is insufficient. I think the State has presented a case that's speculative and doesn't rise to the level of probable cause, and I would ask that the court dismiss the charge."

Cattanach rebutted. "I think it's clear from Ms. Jeter that Miles had no injuries going to day care. She picks him up around 4:30, she notices the bruising, and later that night observes he has more injuries to the head. Dr. Knox testifies that these injuries are intentional inflictions, and I think that's crucial in finding the abuse here that she diagnosed. And based upon that, the defendant is the one who probably did it, and that's the standard."

I was filled with trepidation as Judge Flanagan gave his decision. "I think it has been demonstrated to the level of probable cause that probably a felony was committed and that the defendant probably is the person who committed it. Exhibit number seven with the testimony of Dr. Knox is pretty strong evidence that this injury was caused by an adult-sized hand. I don't have any difficulty finding probable cause in this matter."

Bob entered a plea of not guilty on my behalf. The judge set this case over, again with Judge Schwartz. Bob, my friends, and I all moved into the side room to discuss what transpired. Everyone was abuzz with disbelief and disgust.

"Every reasonable inference went to the state," I exclaimed in misery. "How unfair is that?" Bob reiterated that the probable cause standard was absurdly low, but he had optimistically thought he could overcome it in this case.

He glumly stated that the big problem ahead of us was Cattanach's threat of moving my cases for joinder, meaning that the three Cody charges and the Miles charge would be joined together for trial. He would oppose the joinder, of course.

"If the Miles charge stands alone, the jury would not even need to leave the box to render their verdict. Holly Jeter kept Miles attending your day care, the injuries were over two years ago and nothing was done at that time, no other injuries happened to Miles in his entire time with you, there was no medical report, and Knox is only diagnosing based on photos. We couldn't bring these things up in this hearing, but at trial, they will provide a strong defense. There is nothing but reasonable doubt here. However, if the joinder occurs, the State has another charge to strengthen their case. Prejudice to you will be extremely high. I will fight it vigorously, of course, but we need to be aware of the possibility that joinder will be allowed."

Chapter 16

Joinder

*C*urious about the joinder issue, I researched the pertinent statute.

WI §971.12-JOINDER OF CRIMES. Two or more crimes may be charged in the same complaint, information or indictment in a separate count for each crime if the crimes charged, whether felonies or misdemeanors, or both, are of the same or similar character or are based on the same act or transaction or on two or more acts or transactions connected together or constituting parts of a common scheme or plan.

A common scheme or plan? Hardly. But I could predict how Cattanach would play that wording in her quest for the joinder.

I thought about Knox's testimony. She admitted that she couldn't see all the bruises on some of the photos. I looked at the CD of photos we were given in discovery. There were seven photos, but, in examining the properties of the photos, the numbers from the camera were 1733, 1734, 1737, 1738, 1743, 1744, and 1750. That meant that photo numbers 1735-1736, 1739-1742, and 1745-1749 were not included in our discovery. Why not? Did they not show anything? Were they not included by Holly when she first emailed them to the police, or were they not included by the police in evidence to us? All photos in that sequence should have been included, showing bruises or not. If there were photos of Miles that did not show anything, that would have been exculpatory evidence. It seems highly unlikely that Holly would have taken any other subject matter photos in those missing numbers. Miles was in the bathtub so I don't think she would have been leaving him there to go snap a picture of the family cat, for instance. Moreover, how do we know the accuracy of the time stamp? Was there any forensic study done to authenticate these photos? Were there any photos from the day after this—were those bruises still present? I hoped Bob would explore these issues before trial.

Knox was adamant in her testimony that the bruises were caused by adult fingertips. I did not inflict them, so what other adults in his life could have done this? The only injury Miles received while in my care was on December 4, 2006 when he slipped down the steps of the climber and bumped his head. Miles arrived to my house three times in 2007 with injuries he had received at home. These were properly documented in my log book, as was required when a child arrived to my care with injuries.

Then there were the inappropriate acts of Marty letting his kids sit on his lap while driving, and Holly making her kids go back to my day care even after she suspected abuse. Which entity engaged in imprudent conduct regarding the children's welfare? The only reason I was accused, over two years after the fact, was due to Annie's allegations about abuse toward Cody. The little girl with the superhuman ability to see nonexistent abuse through walls was again the bane of my existence.

In reading the criminal complaint regarding Miles, I discovered that the information listed the date of the alleged abuse as April 5, 2005, not May 16, 2006. April 5, 2005, was actually Miles' date of birth. I joked about that with Ki; not only was I the cause of these mysterious bruises, but I inflicted them on the day he was born. I knew this error would be corrected, but it was irritating that the information was wrong in the first place. This wasn't the only error I had found in the State's documents—they were rampant with misspellings and grammatical errors. If prosecutors were going to ruin someone's life with their allegations, couldn't they at least be professional in their document preparation?

On Bob's suggestion, I contacted my telephone provider to see if I could get a copy of my phone records for May 2006, to see if Holly Jeter had called me regarding these bruises. Unfortunately, the records from that far in the past were no longer available. I was, however, able to get the records from 2008, so I found the calls I had made to the Marshalls on the occasions where they had forgotten to pick up Cody. I hoped to use them to show their lack of communication.

I didn't have to wait long for my next court proceeding; a status conference was scheduled for three days after this preliminary hearing. I started to feel like I should rent a room at the courthouse. Once again, Detective Johnson showed up. She and Cattanach proceeded to the side room before the start of the hearing. I overheard Cattanach ask Johnson if the Jeters took Miles to the doctor regarding these bruises. The door shut before I could hear Johnson's answer. Why would Cattanach have to ask that question? She should have known if there was such a visit. At the preliminary hearing, Bob attempted to ask Jeter if she took Miles to the doctor; his question was not allowed. Dr. Knox said that there was no medical care sought. If there was, that medical report should have been provided to us as discovery. I remember what Johnson had told me in my interrogation with her strange statement of, *"The parents take the kids to the doctor, the doctors are well, yeah, there's something up with her, these are not normal childhood injuries."* I don't think that was actually in reference to Miles but rather a blanket statement Johnson threw at me. It was a ridiculous thing to say; if true, why would parents send their kids back to my care?

The status conference itself was rather quick. The judge gave some dates for Cattanach and Bob to file their briefs in support/ opposition of the joinder motion. He made it clear that his replacement would be ruling on this issue. Well, there went Schwartz being

132

the judge for the trial. The trial date was completely taken off the court calendar. No date could be scheduled until the joinder issue was decided. Yet another delay. The trial would have been over if the prosecution had stuck to their original two charges. The prosecutors were dragging this out by adding charges, making amendments, and asking for other acts evidence and joinder. Yet Mades, after adding charges, had the nerve to complain about her young child witnesses losing memories if the trial was postponed. "With every passing day the memories of children get worse. A setover can have a significant impact on the case."

The gist of Cattanach's memo in support of joinder was that the offenses charged were of similar character, meaning that the "crimes" were the same type of offense, occurred over a relatively short period of time, and the evidence as to each overlapped. She urged the court to promote efficiency by trying the charges together. It was interesting to read in the "Facts" section of her brief: "Upon his arrival home, MJ's mother noticed the bruises, took pictures, and contacted both medical personnel and Lynn Moller to ask about injuries and potential causes." Contacted medical personnel? Where was this report? And Holly Jeter had never asked me about those bruises.

Bob's memo for opposition of joinder addressed the lack of medical care sought for Miles. He also argued that Judge Schwartz's ruling on the other acts and the Miles charge was a done deal; Schwartz had made a ruling that prior acts would not come in, including Miles. Based on case law, the ruling by Schwartz meant that these charges should not be joined. He also fought against Cattanach's claims of the acts occurring over a "relatively short period of time" as there was a two-and-a-half-year time period between the alleged bruises of Miles in May 2006 and the alleged abuse to Cody in August and September 2008. No other case in the state had that long of a period between crimes allowed for joinder.

With the briefs submitted, there was nothing to do but wait for the judge's ruling. I learned in early October that a new judge had been assigned, Stephen Ehlke. It sounded like most of his experience was in prosecution, although he had been in private practice for a time. I could only hope that he would be fair.

Fall 2009 was a hard time for me. In addition to waiting on the joinder decision, my mom's health was quickly declining. She had had several scares in the past few years, but managed to bounce back. Now, sadly, it was clear that her condition was terminal, and her needs were beyond my dad's capabilities of caring for her at home. We made the hard decision to admit her to hospice care. I made several trips to Green Bay to visit her and give my dad some respite time.

During this period I also lost some special relatives; in late October, my uncle Doug died, and in early November, my great aunt Violet died. Her graveside service was the morning of November 11, which happened to be the day that I would hear the judge's ruling on the joinder motion. My brother PJ and I attended her service, and then headed to the courthouse. My fate was in the hands of a brand new judge, on the job less than a month.

Ki and my friend Jan met me shortly before the hearing. I had a knot in my stomach, and feared the worst. Bob and I took our places at the defense table, while Cattanach and Detective Johnson (again) sat across from us. Judge Ehlke made his appearance; he was accompanied by retired judge Robert DeChambeau serving as his mentor. Ehlke made some cursory introductory statements, and then cut straight to the chase. "I am going to grant the motion to join the two cases together."

I dropped my head into my hands and tried to keep tears from forming. I essentially stopped listening while the judge justified his reasoning. My mind went back to what Bob had said about joinder and the risk of the jury seeing so many charges that they would be likely to convict on at least one. Bob tried his best to sway the judge into changing his decision. "To say I'm disappointed with the joinder decision would be an understatement. I'm raising my concerns at this time." Ehlke let Bob make his arguments, but he would not change his mind. I could imagine Cattanach and Johnson smirking at the next table over their victory.

Cattanach then jumped in with her request to submit a motion to reconsider the other acts based on this joinder. Fortunately, Ehlke stated he was not likely to overturn Schwartz's decision on that. That took some of the wind out of Cattanach's sails, but it was not much consolation to me. The damage had been done by the ruling to allow joinder.

The hearing ended with trial dates being scheduled for the first week of March 2010.

Bob and I discussed things after the hearing. It was obvious he thought we had a much harder battle ahead of us with the joinder decision. He stated repeatedly how this ruling was a mistake and that this was definitely an appealable issue, should I lose my case. I didn't like thinking about that aspect—it felt like conceding defeat already.

For a brief moment, I reconsidered taking a plea. The deck seemed to be stacked against me. Did I want to risk taking this to trial? Nevertheless, the thought was fleeting. I would not admit to hurting these children for the sake of a plea bargain. I was innocent. I wanted to vindicate myself. My own family and all the day care families I had cared for over the years needed to know I was ready and willing to fight these charges.

I barely had time to absorb the impact of the joinder ruling when my family had to make critical end-of-life decisions regarding my mom. Her condition was quickly deteriorating and there was no chance that she would rebound. We knew death was inevitable within days. We had an extended family gathering at the hospice center on November 21, at which people were able to say goodbye to her. On Wednesday, November 25, 2009, the day before

Thanksgiving, she passed away with my dad, PJ, and me at her side. We had a wonderful memorial service on the weekend.

Over the next few weeks, I spent a lot of time with my dad, helping him with thank you notes and other tasks necessary after a family member's death. These tasks kept me busy, but thoughts of the upcoming trial consumed me. I did not have a chance to fully grieve for my mom with the dark cloud looming over me.

Chapter 17

A New Attorney

*B*ob called me in early December and dropped a bomb-shell. He explained that he had some health issues and his doctor had recommended surgery in February. That meant that he would not be able to see my case through to trial. I almost dropped the phone. What else could go wrong for me? I had had a change of prosecutors, a change of judges, and now I would need a change in defense attorney. How was I going to get a fair trial?

I told Bob I was sorry to hear of his health issue, but I was worried. I didn't see how the trial could go on as planned in March, two-and-a-half months away. A new attorney would never be able to get up to speed on this complex case. Would the judge even allow me to postpone the trial (again) due to this new complication? Bob said he would do whatever he could to ease the transition. I had no doubt about that, but it was unlikely that I would have an attorney as prepared as Bob. Bob recommended a colleague of his; he said that he had already spoken to him about the case. Not knowing where else to turn and pressured by the trial in the very near future, I agreed to meet with this attorney.

Aside from my worry about the closeness of the trial date, I was concerned about how I would pay for a new attorney. Bob had agreed to take my case through trial for a flat fee, and I had already paid him. Now I had to come up with funds for another attorney. The average person does not have a contingency fund for legal expenses, and I was no different. I had not been working in over a year, and our savings was quickly dwindling. Our household expenses were based on both Ki and me having good paying jobs, and my job had been ripped away from me. Twenty-five years building a career were wiped out with one false allegation. There were no other jobs that I felt qualified for or desired. With my future uncertain, I had not wanted to pursue employment until after the trial.

I met with Attorney Eric Schulenburg, Bob's recommendation, a few days later. He was an extremely nice man, and I felt an immediate connection with him. I told him about my mom's recent death and we shared some stories about interests that they had in common. We talked about my case, and he indeed was familiar with it, as Bob had shared the background. I expressed concern about the trial being close. While Eric stated that he would like more time, he said that he would be ready in time. We discussed payment of his fees; he was willing to work with me on a payment schedule.

I liked Eric, as his personality and style was similar to mine. In hindsight, however, I needed an attorney who had the exact opposite style from me—someone who was aggressive and not afraid to confront the antagonists in my case. It turned out that Eric would do me no favors with his nice guy and low-key manner.

I met with him several times over the next few weeks to go over the case. Bob's theory of defense had been that my case was a house of cards with Annie's allegation as the base; discredit that and the whole thing would tumble down. Eric's take on the case was similar; he likened it to a spark (Annie's accusations) that set off a wildfire. I thought that both of these analogies would make good opening statements to a jury.

The first court appearance I had with my new lawyer in tow was on January 29, 2010. It was for a Ludwig hearing/status conference. In Wisconsin, a Ludwig hearing is held for the defendant to formally accept or reject any prosecution plea offers. Judge Ehlke asked Cattanach what the State had offered. "The State has offered a possible First Offender's disposition contingent on full acceptance of responsibility in regard to the facts and that has been rejected."

Ehlke asked if I understood that this was on the record and that the State may withdraw that offer at some point. "Yes, I understand," I replied. In my mind, I was telling Cattanach what she could do with her offer. I wondered how many innocent people succumbed to plea deal offers rather than risking a guilty trial verdict and harsher punishment.

The remainder of this hearing involved discussion among the parties regarding jury instructions, dates, and witness lists. At the end, Cattanach brought up the wrong date of offense for the charge against Miles. "The date of offense is listed as the date of the victim's birth. I move to amend that." There was that term "victim" again. The least she could do was add the term "alleged." After all, at this stage wasn't I supposed to be considered innocent? Judge Ehlke asked me if I understood the amendment of the date; I acknowledged that I was aware of the error. I had to bite my tongue from shouting out that I had not only not abused this little boy, but I certainly did not do it on the day he was born. I appreciated Ehlke addressing me personally to confirm that I knew what was going on. Unfortunately, I would not have that same courtesy in the next and last hearing before the trial.

I am generally an organized person, and I had kept all the legal documents for the case in well labeled-binders or accordion folders. I spent the next few weeks making sure I had everything ready for easy access during the trial. I also wrote down many ideas and thoughts for Eric to pursue when he questioned the witnesses. I wanted to actively participate in my defense. After all, it was my life on the line.

I thought about the claims that I picked up Cody to knock his head into the wall. How could we let the jury know how ridiculous that was? Cody weighed about forty pounds. There is no way I could pick up a child that size and bang his head into the wall. A bag of salt for the water softener is forty pounds. Yes, it is a different weight distribution than a two-year-old child, but forty pounds is forty pounds. A jury could relate to the pain of picking up one of those bags and emptying it into the water softener tank — now try to pick that up and bang it into the wall. Eric agreed that that was a good analogy, and said he would be sure to bring it up as a point of reference.

I wondered why Annie's statements were taken as gospel. Annie "seeing" the abuse was speculative. Why was it allowed? Holly automatically assumed that she told the truth? My whole case was based on tunnel vision. Everyone was obsessed by Annie's initial statement. If Holly had done any investigation right away, this would have all been over. It wouldn't have taken much on Holly's part — asking Annie to show her where she was when she saw this.

If my child had said something like that, I would have made him accountable. It's one thing when kids tell stories or make things up, which they do and should do to strengthen creativity and imagination, but there is a big difference between childhood fanciful tales and allegations that could ruin someone's life. We need to be open to children's statements when they tell us that something is wrong. However, believing everything a child says without investigation does no one any favors and gives too much power to the child.

In 1985, the *Sesame Street* story line about Snuffleupagus, the wooly mammoth seen only by Big Bird, ended due to researchers worrying about the message this sent to children. At that time, increasing numbers of stories about child molestation and abuse were being told in the media. The *Sesame Street* educators worried that if children saw that the grown-ups didn't believe what Big Bird said (even if true), they would be afraid to talk to adults about dramatic or disturbing things that happened to them. Therefore, the *Sesame Street* writers and producers decided that it was time to have Snuffy become real and seen by the adult cast. While I feel that the "invisible" Snuffy story line may have eventually run its course, it is sad that it took these day care hysteria stories (most of which were unfounded) to end it. Even the character of Bob, in response to Snuffy's "outing," said to Big Bird, "From now on we'll believe everything you say."

Tunnel vision led everyone to think that I had abused children, when in fact there was no abuse. Conclusions were drawn without proper investigation. Had I been banging Cody's head into the wall on a daily basis, there surely would have been some evidence on my walls—hair, blood, DNA. No forensic investigation was ever done. How, if I banged the back of Cody's head, did he obtain forehead bruises? Was he like one of those classic cartoon characters where head injuries immediately resulted in a huge swelling, and attempts to shove the lumps back into the head were answered with a lump of equal size appearing somewhere else? Plus, everyone knows that it hurts like a son-of-a-gun when we accidentally bump our head on something. Had I been constantly banging Cody's head, he would have screamed bloody murder any time he came near me. I was the sole focus of this non-abuse, and they built a case for conviction based on a child's mistaken perception and subsequent panic that every innocent bump or bruise was abuse.

Eric said he had received a box of discovery from Cattanach. It held over a thousand pages of Miles' medical records. I said I would look through those and let him know if I found anything interesting or helpful to my defense. I hoped to find something exculpatory to clear me. Had the prosecution even looked through all these records?

In my examination of the documents, I specifically looked for any report regarding those puzzling bruises of May 16, 2006. The records were mostly from specialists covering the period through summer 2009, and dealt mainly with Miles' Chiari condition. These records made for interesting reading, notably for what was lacking—any mention by the parents that Miles had been "abused." Many of these records were dated after fall of 2008, when the Jeters had started their claim that I inflicted those bruises, and criminal charges were pending against me. Not one doctor report mentioned this concern by the parents. Had they believed there was abuse, they should have been making it part of Miles' medical history.

I even found a hospital record dated July 7, 2009, during Miles' spine surgery, where the parents were asked: *"Violence/abuse is an increasing problem in our society. Have you or anyone in your home been hurt, threatened, frightened, or neglected?"* The Jeters' answer? "No." That would have been the perfect opportunity to present the abuse allegations, but their response was negative. I found this very revealing.

The medical records also revealed that Miles had had over the years, including near the time of May 2006, some low hemoglobin lab results. I didn't know if that could cause easy or unexplained bruising, but thought it should have been something Knox looked into before making her abuse diagnosis. Knox didn't see fit to reveal that; in fact, she said his bloodwork was normal.

Lacking in this big box were any records from Miles' primary care doctor or routine well baby/child visits.

February, already a short month, flew by. My siblings, dad, many friends, and other extended family members had made plans to attend at least some of the trial. I gave permission for Evan and Aaron to miss that week of school so they could attend. They were seventeen and fifteen at the time. I kept thinking how terrible it was to see their mom go through this.

The last pre-trial hearing was set for Wednesday, February 24, five days before the trial. Eric had called me the day before, revealing that Cattanach had asked him one more time if I would take the plea deal. She said that Cody was a "basket case." What a terrible thing for her to say about one of her witnesses.

Cody hadn't seen me for well over a year. He probably wouldn't know me from Adam; what made him react in the basket-case manner? Did his parents keep reminding him of what a terrible person I was? That wasn't fair to him or me. Given their prior conduct of threatening him with me when he misbehaved, I harbored the thought that they were keeping the "Evil Lynn" scenario alive in his consciousness.

I pondered the enigma of the First Offenders/Deferred Prosecution Program deal. If I accepted "meaningful" responsibility for the abusive acts, I would, in effect, receive a slap on the wrist. Successful completion of this program, including minimal requirements such as counseling, aggression treatment, community service, or restitution, would result in dismissal of the case with no formal adjudication or conviction. Therefore, someone who actually harmed a child could get off easy, but the falsely accused person standing by her innocence risks a guilty verdict and sentence. Where is the fairness and justice in that? I stuck by my decision to reject any plea deal.

I made my appearance at the courthouse for this final hearing. I took my place and waited for the usual suspects. Cattanach arrived, and I noticed that she was pregnant again. I worried that it may be prejudicial to me, facing a child abuse trial, to have a pregnant prosecutor. Would the jury, on a subliminal level, let that sway their verdict? Eric didn't share my concern.

Detective Johnson handed Eric a folder. "Here is some discovery we just received. It is Miles' medical records from his primary care doctor."

Here were the primary care doctor reports that I had found lacking in the big box. I noted on the cover sheet that they hadn't even been requested until February 12, 2010. I told Eric I would read them that afternoon.

Judge Ehlke's first order of business was to do some "house-keeping." He said we needed to have a formal arraignment of the Amended Information for the Miles charge, which we discussed at the last hearing (to correct the wrong date). I understood this, meaning that I would formally have to plead "not guilty" to the charge. Unknown to me, however, and I would not find this out until the start of the trial, was that the date of one of the Cody charges was also changed. Unlike the last hearing, where Ehlke asked me specifically if I understood the changes, I did not receive that consideration. Eric did not inform me of any changes, so I thought we were again addressing the date of the Miles charge.

I was not pleased with Ehlke's announcement that he over-turned Schwartz's ruling allowing testimony that my day care had never received any prior complaints. He explained, "I have reviewed that and I disagree with that ruling. I do not believe that it's proper to introduce testimony that there are no prior reports of abuse related to Lynn Moller's day care. Absence of report is not relevant to whether anything happened." Well, there we go, I thought, chipping away at something in my favor. A major sense of unfairness engulfed me, as it seemed that the prosecution was allowed to put its thumb on the scale of justice.

More discussion was held regarding the details of the trial. I didn't understand much of it, and could only hope Eric had my best interests at heart. Cattanach and Eric both stipulated that Dr. Landry's report of March 3, 2008 would be allowed to come in without a doctor's authentication. This was the report from a day I noticed Cody tugging on his ear, and suspected an earache. Dr. Landry's report found no ear infection but did note some small superficial ecchymotic areas in the auricle. Now this report would be admitted in trial? It had been briefly discussed in the preliminary hearing a year ago, with Maria Marshall greatly embellishing the symptoms as injuries; her version did not match the doctor's. The report also stated that Dr. Landry was not concerned about these small bruises; Cody had other bumps and bruises that were not suspicious, and Cody played roughly with his brother. How would this report be used? I could only imagine Cattanach would spin it against me.

The last part of the hearing addressed how the child witnesses would give an oath to truthfulness. Judge Ehlke proposed asking, "Do you promise that you will tell the truth today for all questions that are asked of you and only tell the truth?" Cattanach responded, "I can tell you that two of the children will have no idea what the truth will mean and will have no response to that whatsoever. I can cite a Wisconsin Supreme Court case, State v. Hanson, 439 NW 2d 133, which states a child is not rendered incompetent if unable to distinguish between the truth and a falsehood. I think we definitely have that situation with children who are not at a level where they can comprehend that." I'm sure she referred to Peter and Cody.

Why would Peter even be a witness? He was hardly ever in my care and would have no clue who Cody was.

Eric stated he was generally okay with Ehlke's oath, but did want to reserve the opportunity to ask if the child could verbalize the difference between the truth and a lie. I thought the oath and truth/lie issue was moot. I suspected that these children had been fed the stories of my alleged abuse so often over the past year-and-a-half that what they actually believed or knew at the time would not matter. Children under age five often can't tell the difference between something they were told and something that actually happened to them. If these preschoolers had overheard adults exchanging rumors about me, they could come to believe they actually experienced the event themselves. An oath would do no good if these children were exposed to their parent's fears and prejudices about me.

As I left the courthouse, I thought, "The next time I'm here will be for the trial." I still couldn't believe I was in this situation. Would I ever wake up from this nightmare?

Chapter 18

New Discovery

I was anxious to get home and look through those new medical reports. I still hoped to find something to clear me of the Miles charge. Right after lunch, I delved into the reports. They were all authored by Miles' pediatrician, Dr. Conrad Andringa. The records dealt with his well-child checkups, visits for minor things like a cold or ear infection, and the appointments leading up to his Chiari diagnosis. Then I found it! I saw the words "This 13 month-old-comes in with Mom because she is worried about some bruising and sores around the ears and the cheeks." A medical report existed, after all. As I looked closer, I noticed that the date of the report was May 15, 2006, a day before Holly Jeter said the bruises appeared.

Pediatrics Conrad L. Andringa, M.D.

05/15/2006

SUBJECTIVE: This 13-month-old comes in with Mom because she is worried about some bruising and sores around the ears and the cheeks. She has noticed this for the last 3 or 4 days. Dad thinks it may be just a discoloration of the ear. Little fussy and irritable, not quite himself, but no cold or cough or sore throat. No bruising anyplace else on the body, just in, around and above the ear on the scalp.
At first, I thought they were worried about abuse, but believe the mother is worried that something is wrong inside the head again causing the bruises on the skin because of injury to the head. This child had a Chiari malformation that was corrected surgically. That is why the mother is so concerned. She is more worried about coming from inside through the scalp onto the skin.
PHYSICAL EXAMINATION: He looks great, vigorous and active, normal and healthy. Cranial nerves are intact. I do not see anything that I would call a bruise at the ear itself, on the scalp, anyplace else. There is a little bit of discoloration at the cheek that might be a bruise, but nothing on the head or the ear. He looked absolutely fine with no bruises or petechiae anyplace else on the body. Otherwise was vigorous and active. Ears, nose and throat are just fine. Lungs are clear. Heart: No murmurs.
ASSESSMENT/PLAN: He looks just fine except for mother's concerns. We are going to watch, observe and see back if needed if things do not go well. Mother was reassured.

Conrad L. Andringa, M.D.   Pediatrics DWPED
CLA/ust15   8377679   DD: 05/15/2006

I literally screamed out to my friend Jan, who had been with me. "Look at this report! Check out the date, and what it says about the bruises being there for three or four days!"

Jan grabbed the report from me and a big smile emerged on her face. "This is in complete contrast to her claims that the bruises appeared on May 16. Call Eric immediately." He was not available, so I left a message for him to call me right away. I read and re-read this report.

Dr. Andringa even said he thought the parent might be worried about abuse, opening the door for Holly to express any such concern, but that was not the issue at all. She was worried about his underlying Chiari condition. The doctor did not see any bruising on the head or by the ear, maybe just a bit of discoloration on the cheek that might be a bruise.

I knew I had never seen those bruises. If Dr. Andringa couldn't see them, how was I supposed to? And what was with Holly's testimony at the preliminary hearing?

Cattanach: What day were these photos taken?
Holly: May 16, 2006.
Cattanach: On the morning that those photos were taken, did he have any sort of injuries to his face?
Holly: No. Upon picking him up from day care at Lynn Moller's, I observed the bruise on his cheek.
Cattanach: And when you brought him to day care that morning, the bruise was not there?
Holly: No. Then during his bath that night when I washed his hair, I noticed the bruises on his head.
Cattanach: And those were not there that morning?
Holly: No.

So she took him to the doctor the evening of May 15, 2006, with concerns about the bruises, yet, according to her testimony, those bruises were not present when she dropped him off at my day care the next morning. This did not make any sense. I called Ki and told him what I had found, and I could hear his elation. The case against me regarding bruises to Miles began unraveling. I was not able to confer with Eric until later that evening. I filled him in on what I found and said I would bring the report to his office first thing in the morning. I actually slept well that night for a change, hoping that the tide had turned in my favor.

The next morning, however, Eric's reaction to this report was puzzling. "How does this help us?"

"What do you mean?" I asked, baffled by his lack of enthusiasm for what I thought was an exculpatory piece of evidence.

"Well, this doctor is saying he doesn't see any bruises on this date," he replied.

"I know." I shot back. "But he says Holly noticed them for three to four days. That contradicts her statements that they appeared after she picked him up on the 16th. Why would she bring him to an appointment on the 15th if she claims the bruises didn't occur until the 16th?"

Eric said he would have to think about this report and its use. I left his office with an uneasy feeling. I didn't expect him to jump for joy, but I certainly felt that he should be happy we found some evidence to contradict Holly's claim. At the minimum, this report provided reasonable doubt. I was troubled by Eric's response, and got the foreboding feeling that maybe he was not up to speed on this case. After all, he had not been on the case to hear Holly's pre-liminary hearing testimony in which she was adamant that those bruises were not there on the morning of May 16. I hoped that over the next few days he would get on top of things.

We had given our witness list to the judge at this final hearing. There weren't many—since there was no abuse, how could I have any witnesses to that effect? Gwen Dunham, our investigator, would testify as to taking the photos of the day care space and her interview with Leaverton. Darlene would testify, as she was my substitute care provider, but her testimony would likely be short since the judge would not allow character witnesses. M.D., a former parent, was on my list. She and her husband had gone through a divorce when their child was in my care, and they were open and honest with me so I could help their child with this tran-sition. I wanted M's testimony in this regard to show how con-cerned parents handled this situation, in contrast to the Marshalls.

I had requested that Eric get someone from the food program to testify that my records showed I did not serve toast on September 17, 2008, contrary to Detective Johnson's claim that Cody got his head banged on that day while eating toast. I knew the prosecution would argue that that didn't necessarily mean I didn't serve toast that day. However, I watched what Cody was eating due to his spitting-up issues, and I would have made note of that as a way to narrow down causes for this behavior. I was displeased that Eric had not followed up with this witness suggestion; eventually he would claim that he never remembered this request.

I was as ready as I could be. Nervous, of course, but still optimistic that I could beat these false abuse charges. My big concern was how to prove a negative—that abuse never happened—especially when it became clear from the preliminary hearings and interviews that the parents and the detective were willing to lie.

The charges, as I knew, and their defenses, were:

1. August 27, 2008—Annie's claim that I banged Cody's head while changing his diaper. This charge could be easily fought by discrediting Annie and her X-ray vision. The Marshalls, despite their claim of "dramatic" injuries to Cody on this date, had no photos or medical report to substantiate any injuries, and Holly Jeter said there were no injuries on Cody in her social services report. Refute this allegation by Annie and the house of cards should tumble.

2. September 17, 2008—The bump on Cody's forehead. This was caused by his fall into the door edge on the way outside. It is documented in my log book, and was reported to Joe Marshall right away. It was a typical toddler fall that happens to all children in spite of the best care. The parents would have thought nothing of it if not for Annie's claim.

Medical advice was sought only *after* Annie's allegations, and the diagnosis was "bruising," not child abuse. The skeletal survey was normal.

3. September 17, 2008 — Strange marks behind Cody's ear. Possible impetigo or skin infection? How could I have caused that? There was no medical finding of abuse.

4. May 16, 2006 — Bruises to Miles' face. Miles had an extensive medical history with the Chiari diagnosis and possible immunization reactions, he kept attending my day care for two-and-a-half years after these mysterious bruises, Knox's diagnosis was based only on photos, he had no other injuries in all the time at my day care, and there was past unsafe behavior toward Miles by his father. Add all that to this newly discovered Andringa report, and there could be nothing but reasonable doubt for this charge.

Bring on the trial. Whatever happened, at least it would be over, and I could move on with my life. It was, however, terrifying to think that a conviction could come with a three-and-a-half-year prison sentence, on each charge. That could potentially be fourteen years. What would happen to my family? Once again, the plea offer of the First Offenders program returned to my mind. Should I rethink my decision to reject that? Nope. I couldn't, in

good conscience, admit false guilt. I was caught in the innocent person's Catch 22—maintain integrity by not admitting to something
I didn't do, or concede guilt to achieve a better outcome.

Chapter 19

The Trial Begins

$\mathscr{S}$omehow, I made it through the next few days. Monday arrived, which was jury selection day. Ki, my dad, PJ, and a few friends attended to observe the voir dire. There was some time before the judge appeared. Eric presented Dr. Andringa's report to Cattanach and Detective Johnson. Cattanach read it. "How are you presenting this?" she demanded. "It's hearsay." Hearsay? It was a medical report prepared in the normal course of business, for an "injury" in which child abuse was suspected. How could it not be used? Eric said he would introduce it during Holly Jeter's testimony.

Cattanach left the courtroom. I wondered if she called Holly to ask about this doctor visit. Johnson remained at the prosecution table, staring at that report like there were tentacles growing from it. Obviously, neither she nor Cattanach had ever seen it. They never looked at the medical reports they requested? Johnson had told me that kids were taken to doctors. Cattanach referenced a medical consult in her motion for joinder. Now a medical report shows up, containing conflicting information provided by their key witness, and they are in disbelief?

Cattanach finally returned. How would Holly explain the bruises on the 15th when she swore in court that they weren't there until the 16th?

Jury selection began. One potential juror had to be dismissed, as she knew the Jeter family. Our side struck a potential juror who stated that a child of his had been abused; their side struck a juror who said a family member had been falsely accused of abuse (although I surely wanted to keep that one). The rest of the voir dire was uneventful. We ended up with twelve jurors and three alternates. That process took most of the morning; we were dismissed after that with the trial set to begin right away Tuesday morning. I spent the rest of the day making sure I was ready with all my documents. I tried to relax, but that was impossible.

Upon arrival at the courthouse on Tuesday morning, I was immediately struck by the number of family members and friends who were there for me. My sister Nikki and brother Andy had made the trek from Minneapolis, my Aunt Sherry and Uncle Wayne came from Portage, Wisconsin, and many friends and fellow child care providers showed up. Many who couldn't attend had contacted me over the weekend with good wishes. I had warned everyone that terrible things would be said about me. They all said that they knew the real me and weren't going to be swayed by exaggerations or lies by Cattanach. Those who were at other court proceedings were already aware of her tactics. Eric was impressed by the show of support. Throughout the three days of the trial, the defense side of the courtroom gallery would be full, while the prosecution side was empty. I was extremely grateful for all the support.

Judge Ehlke arrived. He asked Eric and Cattanach if anything needed to be done before starting. There was not, so the jury entered. My heart was beating so fast I thought it would leap out of my chest. These people held the rest of my life in their hands.

Judge Ehlke gave some welcoming remarks to the jury, as well as some preliminary instructions. He stated that I had entered "not guilty" pleas to all the charges, meaning that the State had to prove every element of the offenses charged beyond a reasonable doubt, and that I did not have to prove my innocence. I sure hoped the jury would take his instructions about reasonable doubt to heart.

Ehlke went on to read the charges:

- One count alleges that Lynn Moller, on or about, August 27th, 2008, in the city of Madison, Dane County, Wisconsin, did recklessly cause bodily harm to a child, CM, in violation of Wisconsin law.

- A second count alleges that Lynn Moller, on or about, August 27th, 2008, in the city of Madison, Dane County, Wisconsin, did recklessly cause bodily harm to a child, CM, in violation of Wisconsin law.

- A third count alleges that Lynn Moller, on or about, September 17, 2008, in the city of Madison, Dane County, Wisconsin, did recklessly cause bodily harm to a child, CM, in violation of Wisconsin law.

- A fourth count alleges that Lynn Moller, on or about, May 16, 2006, in the city of Madison, Dane County, Wisconsin, did recklessly cause bodily harm to a child, MJ, in violation of Wisconsin law.

Wait a minute. What was the second charge? That should have been on September 17, not August 27. Why were there now two charges on the 27th? I glanced back at Ki; he shrugged his shoulders and had a puzzled look on his face. I jotted a note to Eric about that second charge being on the wrong date; he looked at it and shook his head. Obviously, he wasn't going to contest that. Confused, I knew I'd have to wait for a break before I could address it with Eric.

Cattanach began the opening statements. The judge had cautioned the jury that opening statements were not evidence. Cattanach started out by saying that I had run a day care for a long time, but I only took children up to age four. "She did not go beyond age four. At around four that's when children start to develop and articulate more, their vocabulary increases, they can report what happens to them. They can tell what occurred during the day."

Well, I could see where this was going. Her theory is that I only kept kids until age four so I could beat them and none of them would be able to tell anyone. Her knowledge of child development was sorely lacking. Had she never heard a two-year-old girl talk? I thought, wait until her daughter chatters non-stop. Plus, if she claimed that kids under age four can't verbalize, how does that give credence to the child witnesses she intended to use in this trial—they were all under four when initially interviewed. She can't have it both ways.

Moreover, I certainly had had kids over age four in my care— obviously, since Annie was six when she was there for those two days. If I beat kids on a daily basis, why would I have let a six-year-old attend?

Cattanach continued with a brief synopsis of Annie coming to day care, observing the harm to Cody, telling her mom, and the subsequent investigation that determined abuse occurred at my day care, with many child witnesses. She said I had a bad day and a headache, so when Cody threw up again, I got ruffled. She warned the jury that the child witnesses might not say the same things in court that they said initially. "I truly hope that the children are able to recall what happened a year-and-a-half ago. But when you hear the different versions of everything they saw and they heard and what they witnessed this defendant do to Cody Marshall, the conclusion you'll find is guilty of abuse of Cody Marshall on August

27th and September 17th. And I hope you'll find her guilty of the adult-inflicted fingertip injuries to poor Miles Jeter."

It was hard to sit there and listen to these falsities and assumptions. She started to sound like Johnson with her "all the kids are saying this" statements. And I had a headache that made me go off? I'm sorry, but anyone with a bad headache knows that the last thing you'd be doing is yelling or grabbing kids to bang their heads.

I didn't like how she tried to arouse sympathy by saying "poor" Miles. I was glad when she finished; I sure hoped Eric had prepared an opening that would show the real me.

Eric began his opening statement by sharing my background and my passion for children. He spoke about different themes and equipment that I had in my day care. He mentioned how I took tons of photos to document the daily happenings. I thought he did a good job with this part, and I looked forward to hear him introduce the problem with Annie—how her accusations were the spark that started a wildfire. All of sudden, though, he was done with his opening. That was terrible, I thought. He didn't even mention how Annie's statements would be discredited. The jury needed to have that front and center in their minds as they heard testimony. I was getting nervous about Eric's competency.

Cattanach called Miles Jeter as her first witness. He came through the courtroom, accompanied by Mark Kerman. He got up on the stand, looked over at me, and gave a huge smile and wave. That brightened my day. Cattanach asked him if everything he said today would be the truth, and he answered affirmatively. She asked him a few things about his time with me, such as who the other kids were and the types of things he did. He answered "yes" when asked if he had fun.

Cattanach: When you were there, was anybody ever sad?

Miles: Cody. Hmmm. I don't know.

Cattanach: Do you remember why Cody was sad?

Miles: Cuz Lynn was banging his head on the wall and that's about all I know.

Cattanach: Did you see Lynn bang Cody's head on the wall?

Miles: Yes.

Cattanach: What was Cody doing when Lynn banged his head against the wall?

Miles: I don't know.

Cattanach: Was he making any noises?

Miles: No.

Cattanach: Did he cry?

Miles: No.

Cattanach: Do you remember why Lynn banged his head against the wall?

Miles: No.

Cattanach: Do you remember Cody ever having any problems eating or throwing up at all?

Miles: No.

Cattanach asked Miles to take a doll and indicate what I was doing with Cody. He picked up the doll, face out, and hit the back of its head against the wall. She asked him how many times he saw this happen. "I don't know." She asked him how many different days he saw me bang Cody's head against the wall. "Probably like every day. It was in Lynn's play room."

Eric took over the questioning. He asked Miles to clarify if Cody's feet were lifted off the ground when his head was banged; Miles affirmed and demonstrated it again with the doll. "So it happened every day that she would hit his head against the wall?"

Miles: Yes.

Eric: When she did that, was Cody crying?

Miles: Yes.

Eric: Do you think Cody had fun at day care?

Miles: Yes.

Eric: Did you have fun when you were there?

Miles: Yes.

Eric proceeded to ask Miles if he remembered specific things that happened at my house, such as dinosaur week or circus week. Miles responded negatively, but upon being asked what he liked doing he said, "Playing with dinosaurs." Eric asked him to name some dinosaurs, but Miles said he didn't have any names. He was then dismissed as a witness.

What five-year-old boy does not know a few dinosaur names? I suspected Miles had worked hard to remember what his answers to the Cody questions should be and he was thrown for a loop when asked a general question any child could answer. How much had he been coached? I had wanted Eric to ask him if he had practiced for his testimony. I'm sure that line of questioning would have met with an objection, but it would be important for the jury to think about how much prep these child witnesses had.

Chapter 20

Annie Testifies

*N*ext up was Annie Jeter, the State's "star witness." I was anxious for Eric to challenge her X-ray vision abilities.

Cattanach asked her if she remembered going to Safe Harbor and answering questions about Lynn's Day Care. Annie responded that she did. That video was then played in its entirety, including Annie's absurd allegation that I banged Emma's head on the wall. That was wrong; as ridiculous as that accusation was, it went toward other acts and another alleged "victim." Judge Schwartz had denied the admission of other acts, and Judge Ehlke had preserved his judgment. Why was this part of the Safe Harbor tape played, and where was Eric's objection to it?

After the video finished playing, Cattanach told Annie that she would ask her a few more questions. Didn't that defeat the purpose of going to Safe Harbor? (*The statement is recorded, and if charges are filed, the recorded statement may be used in court in place of the child's testimony*).

167

Cattanach: I want you tell us only things that you saw, not things that you heard.

Annie: Okay.

Cattanach: You talked about seeing Cody get hurt. What room was Cody in when he was being hurt?

Annie: The bathroom.

Cattanach showed Annie several photos of the bathroom and diaper changing area. "When you saw Cody get hurt in that area, where were you?"

Annie: I was out on the play climber. It has stairs that go up and you can play on it. It was over on the wall on this side. If you're looking that way from the diaper changing station, it was on this wall.

Cattanach: For the record, you're gesturing that it was on that wall outside the door of the diaper changing area?

Annie: Yes.

Cattanach showed Annie more photos of the climber and the area. It was difficult to discern via these photos exactly where Annie claimed the climber was, but Cattanach sure tried to get Annie to say it was right outside the bathroom. That would be impossible.

Cattanach continued. "When you were there, did you ever see Cody get hurt another time?"

Annie: Yes.

Cattanach: Can you tell us about that?

Annie: Umm, on the wall where she was banging his head on the wall, but not in the diaper station in the bathroom.

Cattanach: What wall was that where you saw her bang Cody's head?

Annie: I can't remember.

What was this? On the Safe Harbor recording, played minutes before, Annie was directly asked if she had seen Cody get hurt any other time besides when his diaper was changed, and her answer was "no."

Simpson: Did you ever see Cody get hurt any other time besides when he was getting his diaper changed?

Annie: No.

Now, a year-and-a-half later, she changed her story, with some vague reference to seeing him hurt somewhere she can't remember. "But not in the diaper station in the bathroom" sure sounded like a coached statement—was she told to report another incident that didn't occur in the bathroom? If it made such an impression on her, why wouldn't she remember where it was? Moreover, if she saw through walls to observe non-existent abuse in the bathroom, what are the odds that this second incident was imagined, also? This second story of Annie's must have accounted for the change of offense date for charge number two, of which I was not made aware until this morning. That also would explain why the prosecution would want Annie to testify at trial rather than relying on the recording—she needed to now account for another incident. I had been prepared to defend one "sighting" by Annie; how unfair to me now that, at the eleventh hour, this was changed. How did Annie's memory of this second incident appear after such a long period?

Cattanach asked Annie to demonstrate with the doll how I held Cody. "Well, I saw Cody standing up. She was sort of banging his head on the wall like this (indicating), but holding on to him. His feet were touching the ground. I think she was holding him, maybe, underneath his arms."

Cattanach asked Annie a few more questions about why I banged his head, what else Cody did before I clobbered him, and if he cried; Annie claimed she didn't remember any of these details. Cattanach finished by asking Annie why she told her parents about this. "So my brother gets out of there so he doesn't get hurt."

Eric took over the questioning. I wanted to hear him confront Annie about her inconsistent statements. He again showed Annie some photos of the climber. "Can you point with your finger where you were standing on the climber?" Annie responded that she was on the stairs. When Annie attended, the climber's configuration had the stairs against the window on the far wall. She put herself farther and farther away from any bathroom view.

Eric: When you were standing on the stairs, were you turned around and looking toward the bathroom?

Annie: Well, the other kids were all playing around so I wanted to see if I wanted to go play with them, but then I saw that when I was looking around.

Eric: Those kids were littler than you. Was it much fun to be there with all those little kids?

Annie: Well, sometimes.

Eric: I'd like to ask you about some words you used. One time you said that Lynn had slammed Cody's head against the wall, and another time you said that she bumped Cody's head against the wall. Do you know which word you like better?

Annie: Bumped.

Eric: Is bumped closer to what you think it was?

Annie: Yes.

Eric: Did the word slam come from somewhere else? Did someone say that to you?

Annie: No, I just thought of it sometime else.

Eric: All right. Where you were standing on the stairs of the climber, you said you could see Lynn's hands on Cody's head?

Annie: Yes.

Eric: Could you see his head bump against the wall?

Annie: No.

Eric: But you heard something thinking that it was?

Annie: Yes.

171

Eric: Do you know how many times his head bumped the wall?

Annie: No.

Eric: You heard once?

Annie: Yes.

Eric: Was he crying then?

Annie: Yes.

Eric: Could you hear him crying in the bathroom?

Annie: Yes.

Eric: Were the other smaller children there playing and making noise?

Annie: Yes.

Eric thanked Annie for answering his questions. What—he was done with her? What kind of cross-exam was that? While he got her to admit that she couldn't see but only heard Cody's head bump against the wall, he failed to confront her about that second incident and her inconsistent story between Safe Harbor and Cattanach's question about it. I hoped that he had another chance with her.

Cattanach followed up with a few questions. "Eric asked what word you liked better, bumped, or slammed. Is bumped a nicer word?"

Annie responded, "Yes."

What a leading question, and no objection from Eric. Cattanach tried to put words and thoughts into Annie.

Cattanach attempted to elicit more information about the head banging. "When you saw Lynn's hands on Cody's head, how would you describe what you saw her doing with his head, in your own words?"

Annie: She was bumping his head on the wall.

Cattanach: Was it on accident or purpose?

Annie: I don't know.

Cattanach: When you talked about how Lynn banged Cody's head against the wall in the other room, is banged the word you used?

Annie: Yes.

Cattanach: And is that how you would describe what you saw Lynn doing?

Annie: Yes.

Cattanach: And how many times did you see Lynn bang Cody's head against the wall at that time?

Annie: I don't know.

Cattanach: More than once?

Annie: Yes.

Annie was excused from the stand. I was furious. Eric did not get another chance with her, and his cross-exam was sorely lacking in fundamentals. Cattanach had taken Annie's vague reference to another incident and run with it, now getting her to say it was in the other room and more than once, when earlier in her testimony it was "I can't remember what wall."

Eric had not even attempted to challenge Annie about her second incident story in an unknown place. I couldn't believe it. It would have been easy. He should have reminded her that we just watched the video where she made it clear that she had not seen Cody get hurt any time other than when his diaper was changed, yet now she was referring to another time. Why did she change her story? In addition, there was no clarity to all the references to the head banging on the wall. Was it the wall from the diaper changing area of the bathroom, or was in it this mysterious "other room?"

Moreover, this second incident sounded suspiciously, if not exactly, like Annie's claim in the Safe Harbor recording of Emma getting hurt. Had Annie somehow morphed Emma into Cody?

Simpson (interviewer): Did you ever see Lynn hurt anybody else?
Annie: Yeah, Emma.
Simpson: What did you see with Emma?
Annie: Well, Lynn picked her up and kind of banged her head on the wall, but not in the bathroom. I don't know where it happened.

Was Annie's young memory playing tricks on her? Or was there something else at work? Did Cattanach manipulate Annie's Safe Harbor statement to strengthen her case?

Eric treated Annie with the proverbial kid gloves, and, while you don't want to be unkind to kids in court, he needed to confront her about her inconsistent stories. Why was her memory better now, a year-and-a-half later, than it was at Safe Harbor a few weeks after the alleged incident? What was the benefit of Safe Harbor if testimony taken there was changed for trial?

We took a break after Annie's testimony. I immediately asked Eric about the change in the date of the charges. It was clear to me now why that was done, after hearing Annie's testimony about the "second incident." I figured Cattanach knew we could easily contest the bathroom diaper-changing event, so she had to make sure there was another incident reported by Annie.

Eric said that we knew about that change. No way did I know about that, and, if Eric had, why didn't he even attempt to deal with it? We started to walk out of the courtroom, and Ki met us. "What's with that second charge on the 27th?" he asked Eric. Eric brushed by him and said he didn't have time to talk. I worried about my lawyer and his defense strategy. It seemed like he didn't have one. Holly Jeter would be the next witness; I sure hoped Eric was ready to rake her over the coals.

Chapter 21

Holly's Story Changes

After the break, Cattanach called Holly Jeter to the stand. She started with some introductory questions about her family. Holly said that Miles attended my day care starting in the fall of 2005.

Cattanach: Was there a period in the fall of 2005 when he was removed from that day care?

Holly: Yes, he had gotten sick.

Cattanach: And were there any medical surgeries that were performed on Miles?

Holly: Yes.

Cattanach: Did it take some rehabilitation before he was able to go back to day care?

Holly: Yes. He went back to Lynn's in January 2006, five days a week.

Cattanach: Was there a time that something caught your attention in regards to Miles when you picked him up from day care?

Holly: Yes.

Cattanach: Do you recall the specific date of that incident?

Holly: No.

Well, that answer sure was a lot different from her answer at the preliminary hearing, when she was adamant that it was May 16, 2006.

Cattanach: I'm going to show you some photos. Before I show them, when you picked him up from day care, what do you recall seeing?

Holly: That he had a bruise on his cheek, right about here (indicating).

Cattanach: Did he have the bruise that day when you dropped him off at day care?

Holly: (hesitantly) I don't know.

Again, this answer was different from her prior testimony; it was "no" at that hearing. Would the charges have even been bound over at the preliminary hearing if she had given such indeterminate answers then?

Cattanach continued by asking her about the photos. "Who took these photos?"

Holly: I did.

Cattanach: Do you know exactly the day that those photos were taken?

Holly: May 16.

Cattanach: And how do you know that day?

Holly: Because they're on the photo.

Cattanach: Do you have any specific recollection of taking that photo on May 16, 2006, or is it the date on the photo why you know it's that day?

Holly: It's the day on the photo is why I know it was that date.

Cattanach: What point of the day were they taken?

Holly: In the early evening.

Cattanach: Do you remember at all discussing these injuries with Lynn?

Holly: I recall asking her about them. She said she did not know how they happened. She gave me no reason for what occurred.

Cattanach: Were you at that time hypersensitive to any injuries or bruises to Miles?

Holly: Yes, he had had brain surgery six months earlier.

Cattanach: Do you recall if those photos were taken the same day you first noticed the injuries or not?

Holly: No.

Cattanach: Do you recall specifically going to the doctor in reference to those bruises?

Holly: No.

Cattanach: If there is a doctor's report that says you did, would you dispute that?

Holly: No. I know I went to the doctor, but I took him often. I have no specific recollection of going to the doctor for these injuries. I knew I did something but I don't recall specifically. That was out of concern for the bruises, and Lynn had no reason for them.

Cattanach: Do you recall the weekend before the injuries occurred?

Holly: Yes, we were up north at my parent's cabin.

Cattanach: Had Miles been injured up there at all?

Holly: No.

Cattanach: Did he have any marks while you were up there?

Holly: Not that I'm aware.

Cattanach: So the first time you can recall seeing the bruises are either the day these photos are taken or the day before these photos are taken.

Holly: Correct.

Cattanach: Did these bruises occur in your care at all?

Holly: No.

Cattanach: And Miles would have been in day care all of Monday and Tuesday, May 15 and 16?

Holly: Yes.

Cattanach: If the medical record indicates you went to the doctor on the evening of Monday, May 15th, 2006, do you know why the pictures are taken Tuesday, May 16th, 2006?

Holly: I remember taking them just because when I was washing his hair, I felt I noticed it more and it looked worse.

Cattanach: Did Miles continue to go to Lynn's day care?

Holly: Yes.

Cattanach: In August of 2008, was Miles attending Lynn's day care?

Cattanach's focus segued to Cody. She asked Holly about Annie attending day care for a couple days. Holly explained that the school where she taught started earlier than Annie's school, and she needed care for those days, August 27-28. Cattanach asked if anything unusual happened when she picked up Miles and Annie on August 27. Holly replied "no."

Cattanach: Do you recall any conversation with her [Annie] that night?

Holly: Yes. When she was going to bed, she just told me that she didn't think she wanted to go to Lynn's tomorrow and she didn't think Miles should go. I asked her why and she said she saw Lynn bang Cody's head on the wall. So I had her get one of her dolls and show me, so she showed me. And then we talked about telling the truth, and that was basically it.

Cattanach: Did you explore that any further?

Holly: Not at that time.

Wow. This was the first that I heard about Annie saying something on the 27th. According to Detective Johnson's interview with Holly, it was the morning of August 28, 2008, as they were pulling into my driveway, that Annie told Holly she did not want to go to my house because she saw me hit Cody's head. Annie had said something the night before? And Holly didn't do anything about it? There would have been plenty of time that evening to call me and express her concerns about what Annie had told her. She hears this disturbing report and doesn't do anything about it? How unfair was that to both Annie and me?

Regardless of whether it was reported at bedtime on August 27 or the next morning, why did Annie wait so long to tell her mom about the alleged troublesome behavior she "witnessed?"

If she was bothered by it, wouldn't she tell her mom immediately? I'm sure Holly asked Annie how her day was when she picked her up. Wouldn't Annie say something like, "Mommy, it was bad. Lynn was hurting Cody." Holly admitted that nothing unusual happened when she picked up Miles and Annie on August 27. Right away at pick-up time would seem to be the opportune time for Annie to tell Holly that something bad happened.

I don't profess to psychoanalyze Annie, but I wondered if she devised a story to avoid another day at my house, where she would be bored and stuck with the little kids. Many children invent stories in attempts to get out of something. I know I did; fortunately, my parents had the backbone to call me on it.

Cattanach continued. "What happened the next morning?"

Holly: We were driving to Lynn's; we were just coming up the road almost to Lynn's when she said, "Mom, I don't think I can start school next week." I asked why, and she said she's going to have to go to Lynn's house to make sure Miles is safe. And I stopped and I just said "Do you think you'll be safe today?" She said yes, and I said I would make some phone calls and see if today will just be your last day and Miles' last day.

Again, wow—her child tells her this bombshell and she makes her attend day care? They came into my day care as if nothing was wrong. She should have made Annie tell me about her concern; it could have been investigated and cleared up immediately. Annie could have shown her where she was on the climber, and it would be obvious that she couldn't have seen the diaper change area. Cody was already at day care, allowing Holly to see that he had no injuries consistent with getting his head banged. Instead, Holly drops her kids off with a potential abuser. I wasn't, of course, but what if Annie's claim had merit? Pardon me if I don't nominate Holly for mother of the year.

Cattanach pressed Holly for more details about what Annie told her. "She just said it was in the bathroom when she was changing, and then after they were done eating and watching movies she saw Lynn do it, but she didn't specifically tell me where then. I gave her a doll to demonstrate, and she just held it like she was looking at it, and then she turned to the wall and bumped it."

Was this Holly's attempt to corroborate Annie's "second sighting?" Again, was this the impetus for the change in date of the charges? Moreover, how vague were these statements, by both Holly (*"she didn't specifically tell me where"*) and Annie (*"not in the diaper station in the bathroom. I can't remember."*) How can one possibly defend such inexplicit allegations? If Annie was bothered by seeing abuse, you'd think she would be cognizant of where it occurred.

Cattanach continued. "Were you familiar with the play area that she was describing where the head was somewhere in there banged against the wall?"

Holly: Yes.

Cattanach: Were you familiar with the bathroom area where she was describing that injury, and the play climber?

Holly: Yes.

Cattanach: To your knowledge and in your experience in those areas, did you believe that Annie would have had a vantage point to see what she was describing she saw?

Holly: Yes.

Holly was shown a picture of the day care room.

Cattanach: Can you show us where the play climber was located on that day?

Holly: Well, it was in the corner in an L-shape. This area was where the kids could stand up. She was on the stairs, so she was standing about there, I would imagine (indicating). The bathroom is right in here behind the TV; you can't see it on this picture.

Cattanach: So if someone were on the play climber as Annie had described, where would they be able to view?

Holly: They could view straight into the bathroom.

Well, at least Holly was honest in saying that the climber was in the far corner, not outside of the bathroom, like Annie said and like Cattanach tried so hard to place. Holly was correct that someone on the climber could look straight into the bathroom; I don't dispute that. However, all you could see would be the shower and part of the toilet. The counter with the changing pad on it would not be visible. Furthermore, if Annie was actually on the stairs of the climber, that straight view to the bathroom would not even be possible. Cattanach was desperate to get the climber right outside the bathroom. She had never been in my day care, but took the liberty to arrange things to make her case. There is no way that large climber could be next to the bathroom; there would be no way to access the bathroom. Also, since my day care was in the basement, the ceiling was lower in that half of the room due to the duct work;

there would be no head room on the upper level of the climber if it was in that position.

Regardless of any view into the bathroom, I did not bang Cody's head against the wall, there or anywhere else. However, discrediting Annie's bathroom view was the easiest way to show the absurdity of her statements.

Cattanach's questioning focused next on what Holly did after hearing Annie's allegations. Holly stated that she enrolled Miles at Kids Express. "Basically I believed my daughter, that she felt her brother was unsafe, and I didn't want to her think I didn't believe her. I just felt it was the best thing to do."

Cattanach: Did you have occasion to view Cody Marshall during pick-up and drop-off times?

Holly: Yes.

Cattanach: Can you describe those?

Holly: I guess what I recall most is possibly in the morning, if he was there first he might be crying, not adjusting to being there, and Lynn would redirect him and tell him to go find something to do instead of just standing there crying.

Cattanach: Did you notice a difference between her treatment of Cody versus treatment of other children in day care?

Holly: Well, I don't know. Most of the other kids appeared to know what to do; he just didn't and so the interaction I saw was her giving him choices. She would basically say, "Cody, you need to go find a book," or sometimes she would redirect him and show him how to get there or go there.

Cattanach: In what manner or demeanor would she relay those offers or choices to Cody?

Holly: Just direct and stern.

Cattanach: And did she speak in those direct and stern manners to other children in her interactions with them?

Holly: Sometimes.

Cattanach: After August 28, you removed Miles from Lynn's care?

Holly: Yes.

Cattanach: Did you have a conversation with her about this?

Holly: Yes. Well, first on that Friday, the 29th, I went to her house toward the end of the day to take payment. Nobody else was there, so I kind of tried to talk to her a little bit about what Annie saw, but not directly. I just said that Annie saw some things with Cody that were uncomfortable; is there anything you can share? And basically it was just that, no, Cody has a hard time adjusting, sometimes cries during the day and that was it. And I didn't push for more information.

Cattanach: After that point did you inform Lynn that you were going to be completely terminating Miles' care?

Holly: Yes, I called her. I just told her Miles was going to be starting Kids Express. From what I recall it just basically turned into more of a business discussion on breaking our contract, how much we'd have to pay her, and then getting kind of upset about that. Then I started to try and bring in some of the concerns without specifically saying them all.

Cattanach: How did you bring in those concerns?

Holly: I guess she kept pushing the money part of it, and then I'm like, "Yeah, but in"—and then it was my—you know, I think it happened through a couple conversations, so then my husband said we'll just pay her what we've got to pay her just to have them be done.

Cattanach: But what information did you share with her about why you were terminating Miles' care?

Holly: I basically recall saying that Annie saw some things, but I didn't specifically say what they were.

Cattanach: Did you contact Cody's parents that day or that weekend?

Holly: No. I contacted his mother at a later point a week or two later. I don't have a specific recollection of the date. The only person I told that weekend was Jane, Emma's mom, since Emma came over for a playdate with Miles.

Cattanach: After that initial disclosure, did you contact any of the other parents right away?

Holly: No.

Cattanach continued with her questioning about why she didn't contact the Marshalls. "I guess I just didn't want everybody to think I was calling just to tell people. Basically, it was wanting to get Miles out of there. Then I told Jane, who chose not to do anything about it. Once Bev Christie called me, where she's like, 'Oh my goodness'—then people started to pull their kids out on their own, not based on what I had told them. Then everybody is like, 'Well, we have to get ahold of Cody's mom,' and it was like, 'Well, I guess I should be the one.'"

Cattanach: Had you ever wanted to contact Cody's mom?

Holly: Every day.

Cattanach: What made you wait?

Holly: What made me wait was basically getting my family adjusted to Miles' new day care, just time.

Cattanach: Were you concerned?

Holly: Very.

Cattanach: After the initial report by Annie, did you report anything to the police?

Holly: No.

Cattanach: How did the photos of Miles come forward to the police?

Holly: When Detective Johnson came to our house to interview us, she asked us if there had ever been any concerns of bruising on Miles, and it was kind of a moment when I'm like, "Well, there is one time," and then I showed her those photos.

Cattanach finished her questioning. Holly claimed that parents started pulling their kids out on their own; not based on anything she said. No; if not for her telling others, no parents would have left.

Again, I couldn't stop thinking about Holly getting her own kids out of a seemingly dangerous day care, but leaving all the others there. How selfish. Holly stated she was concerned about Cody, but did nothing. Cody's parents should have been furious with her.

Chapter 22

A Frustrating Cross-Examination

ric started his cross-exam of Holly. He said he would divide his questions into first Miles and then Annie. "I think on direct exam you said you might have seen a physician just before you took those photos of Miles; is that accurate?"

Holly: It is. I knew I had done something, but maybe I said I might have.

Eric: Do you remember if you did see a physician just before you took the photos, specifically Dr. Andringa?

Holly: Well, no.

Eric: So you don't remember seeing him at all?

Holly: Well, I knew that I'd either called the neurosurgeon—I knew I had done something, but I made several phone calls, but I don't recall because at that time it wasn't unlikely for me to have Miles in the doctor's office every week or every other week. So that's why I probably don't recall that specific time.

She doesn't recall that specific time, but now claims those bruises were abuse? I'm sorry, but if you suspected abuse, you would recall making a doctor appointment about it.

Eric: What were Miles' medical issues then?

Holly: After his six-month immunizations, he was paralyzed from the waist down. To this date, it's a spinal cord injury of which they don't know the cause. So he had brain swelling, had the decompression surgery, so I was always overly careful with him.

Eric: So you link that to the vaccination?

Holly: Yes. That's still a question. Yes.

Eric: Have you taken some action about that to try to recover for it?

Holly: Not so much to recover but to get answers.

Eric: What was that action you took?

Cattanach: Objection. May we approach?

At this time, a sidebar conference between the judge and counsel took place, outside the hearing of the jury and me. It was a major discussion, but I wouldn't learn anything about it until obtaining the trial transcripts many months later.

The sidebar ended and Eric told Holly he would withdraw the question about action she took regarding the immunizations. What? The jury needed to know that she had submitted a claim to the National Vaccine Injury Compensation Program (NVICP), alleging that Miles suffered neurological injuries because of the receipt of his vaccinations on October 10, 2005. Why wasn't this allowed? What objection did Cattanach have that barred this testimony? It was critical to know if Holly submitted those photos of bruises to NVICP as evidence of adverse vaccine effects. That would be fraud to the NVICP if she did, since she now claimed that they were from abuse. Conversely, if the bruises were from a vaccine injury, she engaged in deceit to strengthen the case against me. Either way, the jury deserved to know. Why would the judge forbid the jury from hearing all information about Miles' condition?

Eric continued his questioning about the doctor visit. "I asked whether you had seen a physician just before you took the photos and you weren't sure. May I show you a document to see if it refreshes your memory?" Eric handed Holly the May 15, 2006 Dr. Andringa report.

Eric: Does that help you remember that physician and what happened during that visit?

Holly: Yes.

Eric: Is it accurate to say that the date you made the visit was May 15, 2006?

Holly: Yes.

Eric: Is that the day before the photographs were taken?

Holly: Yes.

Eric: I'm not going to ask what he said to you, but I am going to ask what you might have said to him. Do you remember saying to him that you were worried about some bruising and sores around the ears and cheeks?

Holly: Yes.

Eric: And that you noticed those for the last three or four days?

Holly: That part I can't recall.

Eric: Is that shown here as one of the things that you said to him.

Holly: Yes.

Cattanach objected for foundation. Why? A "lack of foundation" objection normally refers to a piece of evidence presented without an explanation of where it came from, or that it lacked authenticity. What could be more authentic than a doctor's report? It was requested by Holly for use in these criminal proceedings.

Eric continued. "But you don't remember saying it, is that right?"

Holly: Right.

Eric: The date on this is May 15th. Is that the day you made the visit to Dr. Andringa?

Holly: Yes.

Eric: Does this show that the report was prepared by him on the same day? At the bottom it was signed 6:33 pm on that date?

Holly: Yes.

Eric asked the judge if they could approach. There was another sidebar conference to which I was not privy. After that sidebar,

Eric changed the direction of his questioning. "Now after taking those photos and looking at Miles, how much longer did he stay in Lynn's day care?"

Holly: Until August of 2008.
Eric: So a little over two years?
Holly: Yes.

Eric spent a bit of time asking if Miles required any special care at my house after his operation. Holly replied that he didn't, other than having the Neurontin medicine given.

He then changed the topic of questioning to Annie. "Did your daughter tell you where she was standing when she saw what she described?"

Holly: She said she was on top of the climber. I knew where that was, in the corner.
Eric: Did you view the bathroom from that spot to satisfy yourself that it could be seen?
Holly: No.

Eric showed Holly a photo. "Do you recognize what that is?"

Holly: Yes. It's the bathroom counter with a changing table on it.
Eric: Have you been in that bathroom before?

Holly: Yes.

Eric: To your memory, is the play area at the far end of that room?

Holly: No. It's just straight out the door.

Eric: All right. And the climber is at the other end of that room in the corner?

Holly: Just out the door is a book shelf with little trinket toys in it and then the climber was in the corner in an L-shape.

Eric: Were you able to tell from where that climber was that a person standing there could see the changing table where a baby is lying?

Holly: You wouldn't be able to see this part (indicating), but you could probably see from a certain point on.

Eric: So if you got close enough to the bathroom you might be able to see inside?

Holly: Yes.

Well, good for Eric. He got Holly to admit that you wouldn't be able to see anyone on the diaper changing area from the climber.

Eric: I'd like to ask a couple of questions about your direct testimony. You said part of the reason you removed Miles from the day care is because Annie told this to you and to do anything else would be giving a message that you didn't believe what she was saying. Is that accurate?

Holly: That's a part, yeah. That was a piece. I didn't disbelieve her at all.

Eric: Right. But certainly you wanted to reinforce what she said by doing something that was responsive to what she had noticed.

Holly: Yes.

Eric: Did Annie tell you this on the first day she went or on the second day?

Holly: It was on the night of the first day.

Eric: So she told you about something she had seen the first day and then returned one more day?

Holly: Yes.

Eric: When either you or your husband would take the children to day care, do you remember if there were times when your husband may not have put them in the child seat? Do you remember being talked to about that by Lynn?

Cattanach: Objection — relevance.

Eric: The purpose is to show a concern for the safety of children.

Judge: I'll sustain the objection.

Why was this question not allowed? Not only was Eric trying to show my concern for the children's safety, but also we needed to let the jury know that Marty had deliberately put his kids at risk. This was unfair to me that the jury couldn't hear about the parents' questionable behavior.

Eric asked Holly about her observations of Cody. She said that it was not uncommon for him to be sad or crying when she saw him at drop-off or pick-up times. She admitted that those were the only times she would see him.

Eric: On the morning of the 28th when you arrived with Miles, the second day of Annie's visits there, did you notice any injuries on Cody?

Holly: No.

Eric was done with his questions. Cattanach had a few brief follow-ups. She asked if bruising would be a manifestation of Miles' underlying medical condition. Holly replied no.

Cattanach: Attorney Schulenburg alluded to the fact that you removed your son basically to please your daughter. Is that what happened?

Holly: No. After what she said, things I've observed, I just thought I needed to do it. And so I just thought he would be better out of there.

Holly was excused from the stand. I asked Eric why the Andringa report wasn't allowed. He said that it was considered hearsay since the doctor or his staff was not there to authenticate it. Hearsay? This was a child abuse trial that wouldn't allow a medical report from the alleged date of injury into evidence. The issue seemed to be that Holly had said the bruises were there three to four days prior. Because Holly didn't recall saying that, the report was not allowed? The doctor wouldn't write that if she hadn't said it—the doctor had no agenda to invent details for his report. That statement would throw a wrench in the prosecution's case, so they got around the report by claiming it was hearsay. Plus, we weren't even given that report until five days before trial. It would have been much more useful if we would have had it earlier. We could have subpoenaed Dr. Andringa as a witness, or stipulated that the report would be allowed without doctor authentication.

The closer to trial a piece of evidence is found, the less opportunity there is for its effective use. Cattanach referenced a medical visit in her motion for joinder, so where was it, and why didn't we get it at that time? Eric should have worked harder to get that report admitted. I was upset at him for dropping the ball on it. If there was information in that report beneficial to the prosecution, it sure would have been admitted.

I was also upset that he let Holly off easy with his cross-exam. Again, as with Annie, this was one of the prosecution's key witnesses, and Eric was a doormat with his questions. Yes, he got her to admit a few things about the climber and sight lines about not being able to see the changing area, but he should have grilled her about her changed statements from those of the preliminary hearing. He probably didn't know about her testimony at that hearing since that occurred with Bob. However, it was Eric's duty to have studied that and to be prepared for any inconsistency at trial. Why did her answers change? If trial testimony deviates, it creates reasonable doubt about all testimony.

When Eric asked Holly if Miles continued to attend my day care for two-plus years after these bruises, why didn't he follow up with the obvious question of "Why?" Had she really suspected abuse then? Obviously not, since Miles remained in my care; she even kept him enrolled during the summer of 2006, when she had a chance to withdraw him without payment because her neighbor wanted the spot. Eric did not ask about Miles ever receiving any other injuries in my care. He made no attempt to question her about the date stamp accuracy on those photos, or if those photos had been authenticated in any manner. He also should have asked her why, if she believed Annie, she didn't call social services to report abuse, instead of leaving other children in potential danger. He should have asked if, as a teacher, she knew the process for doing so. In addition, why didn't he question her about failing to tell me her real reason for withdrawing Miles?

Holly dodged a bullet with Eric's questioning, or more precisely, lack of questioning. He could have nailed her not only on all these topics, but impeached her as a witness for inconsistent testimony.

I again thought about the joinder of the Cody and Miles charges. If that hadn't been ordered by the judge, and the Miles charge was allowed to be tried on its own, Holly would have had to say why, two years after these suspicious Miles bruises, she thought they were abuse (she should have had to explain that, anyway, but unfortunately my attorney didn't pursue that line of questioning). Can you imagine the jury response? How would Holly have explained keeping her son in my day care for over two years? I know it was a moot point since the joinder was in place, but there is no way the Miles charge would have survived on its own. It's quite telling when a case can't stand on its own and has to be joined with others to bolster the State's position.

The last witness of the morning was Marty Jeter. He didn't say much. He didn't know when the May 2006 injuries to Miles occurred. He didn't know when he first observed them. He said that Miles had not received any injuries while in his care on May 15 or 16. He said he never had a conversation with me about them. I wanted Eric to ask him about the car seat issues, but knew it would be useless given the objection after the attempt with Holly. Again, that denied me the opportunity of showing the parents' poor behavior and judgment.

We took about an hour break for lunch. Most of us went downstairs to the courthouse cafeteria. While we were eager to discuss events of the morning, we knew it was not the time or place. It was an exhausting morning for me to hear all that testimony. I hoped my attorney was going to step it up. My brother-in-law, Dave, said, "When is your attorney going to start fighting?" I guess I wasn't the only one who thought the defense strategy was deficient. I had had all my notes with potential questions ready, right in front of Eric, and he never looked at them.

Wasn't a defense attorney's major strategy to discredit the witness? Holly and Annie were the State's main witnesses, and Eric didn't bother to discredit them. It would have been simple, given their inconsistent stories. They could have both been impeached as witnesses and their credibility questioned. I admit I was naïve about criminal defense strategies, but it sure seemed that my attorney lacked that tactic. I hoped that he was better prepared for the remainder of the trial.

Chapter 23

Liar, Liar

*M*ax Pickett was the first witness after we resumed from lunch break. Cattanach asked him about kids he remembered at Lynn's house. "Tommy, Emma, Miles," he recalled.

Cattanach: Do you know a Cody?
Max: I forgot him.

Cattanach showed him a photo of Cody; he responded that he forgot who that was.

Cattanach: Do you remember anyone being sad at Lynn's day care?
Max: Well, yeah.
Cattanach: Who was that?
Max: I forgot.
Cattanach: Do you remember telling somebody that Cody was sad?
Max: I don't think so.

Cattanach: Do you remember talking with Detective Johnson? Do you remember telling her that Cody is sad at day care and he cries because Lynn gets mad at him?

Max: I don't think I ever done that.

Cattanach: Do you remember telling your dad that Cody was sad and would cry there?

Max: No.

Cattanach: Do you remember ever telling your dad that Lynn would tell Cody not to cry?

Max: No, I don't think she ever does that.

Cattanach, even with her leading questions, couldn't get Max to say anything. Eric followed up with some general questions about what Max remembered from my house; Max responded with some accurate descriptions about the outside play area.

Max's dad, Brian Pickett was next up. After some introductory questions, Cattanach asked what led to Max no longer going to Lynn's day care.

Pickett: One night we received an email from one of the other parents, Tina Reese, who said she had had an alarming phone conversation with another parent. We called her and she described some allegations involving Lynn hitting Cody or doing something with Cody. She gave us the phone number of Holly Jeter, so we called her, and she described some events that her daughter had reported seeing to her. That was Monday, September 22, 2008.

Well, that conflicts with what he told me on Tuesday, September 23, when he called to say Max would not be coming that day due to having a cold. When I specifically asked him if he had heard anything about my day care, he said no. Why had all these parents lied to me? If this had happened to them, wouldn't they want to know the truth? Why were they all so quick to accept Annie's story?

Cattanach: Did you ever have a conversation with Max about any of the information that was provided to you by any of the other parents?
Brian: Yes, we asked him some very brief general questions, along the line of "Did anything ever happen while you were at Lynn's house that upset you?" He said no, and we dropped it at that point.
Cattanach: Can you tell us your observations of Cody?
Brian: I noticed that when I would pick up Max in the afternoon, the other kids would be playing together and Cody usually would be sitting apart and often looked kind of unhappy. His facial expression was kind of glum.
Cattanach: Do you recall any statements ever being made by your son to you about the treatment or anything of Cody?
Brian: There was one afternoon in August or September of 2008 when Max got in the car and said that Lynn told Cody to stop

crying. My impression was that Cody had gotten on Lynn's nerves perhaps a bit and she snapped at him verbally. That's all he said, and I didn't think much about it beyond that.

Cattanach: Were you present during an interview that Detective Johnson conducted with Max?

Brian: Yes. Johnson asked him about Cody, and I know he said something about Cody crying.

Cattanach: Do you remember if Detective Johnson asked him why Cody cried?

Brian: Yes, and Max said that Lynn gets mad at him.

Eric had no substantive cross-exam questions for Brian. He just confirmed that they had no desire to pull Max out of my care until talking to Holly Jeter on September 22.

It was 1:30 at this time, and Cattanach announced that her next witnesses, the Reese family, had not yet arrived. She apologized, and she was clearly disconcerted. "They were supposed to be here at 1:30, so hopefully they'll be here some time shortly. My staff is trying to track them down." The judge said we would take a break until they arrived, and the jury was excused. I thought that was unprofessional of Cattanach for failing to ensure that her witnesses arrived on time, and disrespectful behavior on the Reeses' part. If they felt so strongly about participating in this court proceeding, they should have arrived on time. If one of my witnesses had been late, would I have been given the same consideration?

Peter was the first witness after the Reese family finally arrived. Why was he was forced to participate in this matter? He attended my day care for only a few days, and he was oblivious to any of the other kids or activities.

Cattanach began her questions. "Is your name Peter? Yeah, I think he nodded there. Do you remember Lynn? Did you ever go to day care at Lynn's? For the record, for the last few questions he shook his head no. Can you answer out loud with your voice? Head shakes, no. Do you remember saying anything about what happened at Lynn's? Do you remember who Cody is? Do you remember Cody crying at day care? Do you remember showing how you saw Lynn hit Cody's head on the table with the stuffed animal? No. No further questions."

Peter, to Cattanach's disappointment, made a terrible witness. He wouldn't succumb to her leading questions.

Tommy was next up. Cattanach asked if he remembered me. He said yes, but when asked if he saw me in the courtroom he said no, even when directed to look my way. Cattanach asked him if he remembered his friends who went to Lynn's house with him. He said he didn't know, until she specifically asked if he remembered Emma, Cody, David, and Miles; then he replied "yes."

Cattanach: Do you remember any of the kids being sad?
Tommy: Yeah.
Cattanach: Who was sad?

Tommy: I don't know.

Cattanach showed him a photo of Cody. "Do you know who this person is?"

Tommy: He's one of my friends.

Cattanach: Do you know his name?

Tommy: No.

Cattanach: Do you remember if this person was sad at Lynn's day care?

Tommy: No.

Cattanach: Do you remember anybody yelling at Lynn's day care?

Tommy: No.

Cattanach: Do you remember telling your mom that Lynn would yell at Cody?

Tommy: Yeah.

Cattanach: Did Lynn yell at Cody?

Tommy: Yeah.

Cattanach: Did Lynn hit Cody?

Tommy: Yeah. I think.

Cattanach: You think. Did you see Lynn hit Cody?

Tommy: I don't know.

Cattanach: Do you remember telling your mom that Lynn would hurt Cody because he would cry?

Tommy: Yeah.

Cattanach: Did Lynn hurt Cody?

Tommy: Yeah.

Cattanach: Do you remember how Lynn hurt Cody?

Tommy: No.

Cattanach: Do you remember telling your mom that you had to be brave when you were at Lynn's?

Tommy: Yeah.

Cattanach: What does brave mean?

Tommy: It means you should not be scared.

Cattanach: Why did you tell your mom you had to be brave when you were at Lynn's?

Tommy: So then I wouldn't get in trouble.

Cattanach: And if you weren't brave, how would you get in trouble?

Tommy: When I go home

Cattanach: Do you remember telling your mom that you and Emma both had to be brave so that Lynn wouldn't yell at you?

Tommy: No.

Cattanach: That you and Emma had to be brave so you wouldn't get in trouble?

Tommy: Yeah.

If Cattanach didn't get an answer she liked from Tommy, she had no problem restating it. If kids are re-asked a question, they will often think their first answer was wrong and then change it to please the asker. If an adult answered in court, and then was subsequently asked that question again by the same attorney, it would have been met with the objection "asked and answered." The kids in this trial were not given that option. And there were no objections from Eric.

Eric asked Tommy a few questions about things he did at my day care. He again asked Tommy who his friends were, and Emma was the only name he could remember. Tommy said he liked going to Lynn's.

Tina Reese followed as the next witness. Cattanach asked about Peter.

Tina: Peter has special needs. He has language delays and trouble with communication. He has anxiety, and a lot of things, actually.
Cattanach: Did Peter on occasion go to Lynn's house?
Tina: He was there all day the first week in July when our nanny was on vacation. Then he was there on September 22, 2008, in the afternoon.

Cattanach asked her what prompted her to remove Tommy from my day care. She said that I had called her and asked if she knew if anything was going on since I had kids drop out of my care. She then said she called Holly Jeter, who relayed Annie's story to her. "She said Lynn had banged Cody's head against the wall, I believe, while she was changing his diaper, and another incident, another incident somewhere else. There were two incidents in the one day."

That sure sounded like a practiced, concerted effort by Tina to get out the two-incident claim, again referencing a vague occurrence "somewhere else." That would not have been a naturally flowing conversation with Holly at the point they had spoken. I suspect, in the preparation for her testimony, Cattanach had wanted Tina to make sure to mention the second incident.

Cattanach: Is this the first that you ever heard of any sort of injury to Cody?

Tina: Well, I had asked Tommy previously, like I would ask all my kids at any day care or any situation, if Lynn ever yelled at them or hurt them, and he said only Cody. I asked him to describe that. It looked like . . . (indicating) she was consoling him. I thought he meant she was patting his back.

It appeared that Tina Reese had a light bulb moment here when she demonstrated the maneuver Tommy referred to—me patting Cody's back, not hitting him. It was obvious that Cattanach didn't appreciate hearing that it was a comforting gesture.

Cattanach: So this was in response to you asking if Lynn has ever hurt you, no, only Cody.

Tina: Yes.

Cattanach: Did you have occasion to see Cody at the day care when you were dropping or picking Tommy up?

Tina: Cody arrived around the same time we arrived every day, so I saw him most mornings.

Cattanach: Could you describe your observations of Cody?

Tina: Cody was hysterical a lot of the time when he would arrive. If he was there before us, he would be sitting by himself, quietly sobbing, or just really inside of himself.

Cattanach: Did you ever have occasion to watch Lynn's interactions with Cody?

Tina: Yeah, during drop off. Most of the time she would put him with the toys or books or something. One time he was crying and he had been there before we arrived and he was sitting on the floor and she leaned down and patted her hand on his arm and said "Stop crying," and he tried very hard to stop crying.

Cattanach: Did you have another conversation with Lynn on Sept. 22?

Tina: I did. Lynn was pretty distraught, and seemed agitated about the kids that had dropped out and how she wasn't getting a lot of information from the parents. The she started to tell me about how Cody throws up all the time, and she said she had been telling him not to throw up too much because now the kids were chanting "Don't throw up."

These were major exaggerations. I never said that Cody would throw up; it was spitting-up, a major distinction, since throwing-up kids were sick and would need to go home. And what was with her claim that I said the other kids were chanting "Don't throw up." The most I did was sigh and say, "Oh no, Cody, no spitting up." Yes, some of the kids did start to say that too, but Tina made it sound like they were all chanting in the style of "Attica! Attica!" I expected her to claim that the kids were banging their sippy cups on the table and stamping their feet as well.

Tina: I think she was describing a day being too rough with Cody when he had thrown up.
Cattanach: She was telling you that she was too rough with Cody when he threw up on the day Annie was there?
Tina: I believe that was the day she was describing.
Cattanach: Do you remember her telling you anything about her health or pain level the day that Annie was there?
Tina: Yes, she said she had a migraine that day, and had considered sending all the kids home but thought she could get through it.

More exaggerations. I have never referred to my headache that day as a migraine, as, thankfully, I don't get those. It was just a bad headache. However, it seems to have turned into fodder for why I beat Cody that day. And Tina's claims that I admitted I was too rough with Cody? I admitted I was likely rougher verbally (regrettably I used the term "rougher" for lack of a better word—the thesaurus in my brain was not functioning during this stressful period) with him than the other kids. One only has to know my soft-spoken

212

nature and personality to understand that my "rougher verbally" tone is akin to most other people's normal tone. I told Tina that, after his spitting-up issue that day, I pulled his chair away quickly from the table, and I wondered if that was what had upset Annie. Now that turned into me confessing that I was too rough with him.

Cattanach: After Lynn admitted being rough with Cody, what was going through your head?

Tina: I was thinking that this whole thing didn't make sense. Why would you yell at a child for throwing up, to the point of having the other kids chanting "Stop throwing up?" I would have pulled Tommy out of there for just that. I was nauseous. It didn't click together, didn't make any sense.

Cattanach: Did you have occasion to talk with your children after receiving this news?

Tina: Yes, initially they were having trouble answering. They were just denying things. They were okay. Then Tommy said he wanted to invite Lynn when we were having people over for brunch. I said, "Oh really." He said, "But she can't hurt Cody."

Cattanach: Did he ever say anything about having to be brave to you?

Tina: Yeah, we were driving on the road that passes Lynn's neighborhood and he started talking about the other kids, and I assured him that no kids went there anymore. He said he remembered his friend Emma and that he and Emma had to be brave together. I said, "Why would you have to be brave?" He said, "Not to cry."

These statements from Tina Reese almost made me laugh. It was obvious that Tommy had been swayed by her; her surprised reaction to his natural, innocent request to invite me to a party prompted him to qualify his statement. Speaking of oneself as brave is unnatural; that is something that someone tells you, and if a child hears it enough he will start to attribute that trait to himself. Tommy and Emma never had a reason to cry at my house. How much discussion had Tina had with Tommy about Cody and me, and was she telling him he had been brave? Even if discussions were on a subtle level, it seemed like it was enough to prejudice Tommy.

Cattanach: What did you observe during Peter's interview with Detective Johnson?

Tina: Peter got a very concerned look on his face and nodded to the question of if he had seen Lynn hurt Cody, but then shook his head that she had not hurt Peter or Tommy.

Cattanach: Did you see Peter physically show what he had seen Lynn do to Cody?

Tina: He banged his duck's head against the wall. He put his hand on the duck's head and pushed it against the wall.

Again, how ridiculous that Cattanach kept bringing up Peter and his non-existent memory of Cody. With his need for leading questions, how else would he demonstrate head banging with his duck?

Eric took over. He asked Tina Reese to clarify how much Peter was in my care. She admitted that it was only three-and-a-half days.

Eric: Before removing Tommy from Lynn's care around September 22, 2008, before then had you any urge at all to remove him from Lynn's day care?

Tina: Yes.

Eric: But you did not? You were concerned before September 22 about his welfare, and still kept him there?

Tina: I know I couldn't put my finger on anything and he had great friendships with the other kids there. That's why we decided to keep him there. I had removed him for the summer since I wanted him to be home with his brother with a nanny.

Eric: And then in the fall you sent him back to Lynn's.

Tina: Yes

Eric: You described Cody's demeanor as being something like hysterical. What did you mean by that?

Tina: He was screaming. He didn't want to be there and Lynn would pull him, peel him from the parent. He would get there fine, and then start screaming when he realized his parents were going to leave.

Those were outright lies by Tina. Cody usually arrived by seven o'clock, at least fifteen minutes before anyone else; for her to see this "hysterical arrival" was impossible. Cody was never hysterical;

his crying was always a low key, whiny, cry-just-to-cry type of noise. That is one of the reasons why I would tell him to stop crying. If he had been crying due to pain or agony, I certainly would have comforted him. I did not want to reward him for whining, but when he stopped crying and started playing, I made sure to give him positive feedback.

For her to say that she had considered pulling Tommy out of my care before these allegations started is absolutely false. If she thought I was inappropriate with Cody or had any other concerns, why would she ask if Tommy could come back for both the half days in summer and then full-time in fall? She switched child care providers at the drop of a hat; if she suspected anything wrong, she certainly would have pulled Tommy from my care. She said she was glad I could take Tommy back in the fall after she had withdrawn him for the summer; she was worried that I had filled the spot. If not happy with my services, why would she suggest me keeping the four-year-olds for another year instead of sending them to preschool?

Eric: Did his hysteria continue or was it abated with Lynn's help? Did it diminish, do you know?
Tina: The hysteria diminished. I don't know if Lynn helped him. She didn't really comfort him.
Eric: Did you have experience with Cody as a caregiver?
Tina: No.

Eric: Do you know what worked with him and what didn't?

Tina: I do not.

Eric: Do you know anything about what worked with Cody and what didn't when care was being provided to him?

Tina: I do not.

This was the most aggressive I had seen Eric with a witness, both in tone and questions.

Tina Reese, with her lies and exaggerations, left the witness stand. I'm sure I glared at her on her way out; I felt like her pants should start on fire. I'm glad people in the courtroom couldn't read my thought bubbles. I was upset that Eric hadn't confronted her in more detail about keeping Tommy in my care if she thought I acted inappropriately.

Chapter 24

Still No Little Accusers

mma Byer was the next witness. This was the first time seeing my day care kids since September 2008. It broke my heart that I had been ripped from their lives.

Cattanach: Do you remember the names of kids who went to day care at Lynn's with you?

Emma: Cody and Miles and David.

Cattanach: Do you remember anybody being sad when they were at Lynn's?

Emma: No.

Cattanach: Do you remember anybody getting hurt at Lynn's?

Emma: I don't remember.

Cattanach: Do you remember telling your mom that you saw Cody getting his hair pulled by Lynn?

Emma: No.

Cattanach: Do you remember that happening?

Emma: No.

Cattanach: Do you remember ever showing your mom on a doll what you saw Lynn do to Cody?

Emma: No.

Cattanach gave up; it was clear she would not get anything from Emma. Eric asked her what kind of things she did at Lynn's. She stated that she remembered playing with the toys. She responded, when asked, that she liked it there.

Emma's mom, Jane, was next. She stated that Emma had started with me when she was about a year-and-a-half old.

Cattanach: Were you familiar with Cody Marshall?

Jane: Yes, I had seen him at day care there.

Cattanach: Can you describe your observations of Cody?

Jane: Initially he was a very happy boy who would run and give me hugs. But then he became a very quiet boy who seemed sad. He was never smiling, very quiet, his eyes looked sad.

Cattanach: Did you have occasion to see interactions between Cody and Lynn?

Jane: They would be mainly at drop-off or pick-up times, so Cody would be quietly playing by himself or with other kids there. At the time, there wasn't a lot of direct interaction between Lynn and Cody.

Cattanach: At some point, did you have a conversation about abuse at Lynn's day care with someone?

Jane: Yes, with Holly Jeter. Holly called me because of what happened at day care with her oldest daughter. Annie had told her that she saw Lynn pull Emma's hair in addition to some concerns about Cody.

Cattanach: At that time, did you do anything different for day care then?

Jane: No.

Cattanach: Did you have a conversation with Emma about anything that occurred at Lynn's?

Jane: Yes, after Holly contacted me I asked Emma whether or not Lynn had pulled her hair, and she said no. I asked if Lynn ever pulled Cody's hair, and she kind of knocked on her head, and then she showed me on a doll how Lynn would pull Cody's hair.

Cattanach: What word did Emma use to describe to you what she saw happening to Cody?

Jane: I think it was more that I asked her if Lynn pulled Cody's hair and she goes like this and she just showed it to me. Emma knocked on her own hair. She didn't pull her hair; she took one of her dolls and pulled her doll's hair later.

Eric began his cross-exam. "You were asked about Emma's response to a question concerning hair being pulled. Do you remember how you asked the question?"

Jane: I believe I asked her if Lynn pulled Cody's hair. Her response was to take her fist and knock it against her head, and later to pull the hair on her doll.

Eric: Before the investigation that resulted in this, you had been satisfied with Emma being in Lynn's day care?

Jane: Yes.

Eric: When you observed Cody there when you arrived or left, would you characterize his behavior as being hysterical?

Jane: No. He was always quiet.

Eric: Was he usually playing alone?

Jane: Most of the time.

Eric: Did you keep up to date through Emma as to what was going on each week? Did she talk about it?

Jane. Yes.

Cattanach had a redirect question about Cody. "When you would drop off Emma, did you have occasion to see the drop off of Cody Marshall by his family?"

Jane: Maybe a few times, but not that I remember.

Cattanach: Nothing specific about the drop-off or condition of Cody at drop off?

Jane: No, I don't think I crossed paths with his parents at all that often.

Jane was done. I appreciated her honest answers about not seeing Cody at drop off times or seeing him in hysterics. I could tell by Cattanach's line of questioning that she hoped Jane would corroborate Tina Reese's claim of hysterical drop-off times, but Jane had the integrity to tell the truth.

Next up was David Christie. Cattanach asked him some preliminary questions to see if he remembered going to day care at my house. He stated that he remembered Cody, Emma, and Miles.

Cattanach: Do you remember any of the kids being sad at Lynn's?
David: No.

Why was Cattanach intent on asking all the kids if Cody was sad at day care? I never disputed that.

After each of the following suggestive questions by Cattanach, David answered negatively: Do you remember Cody crying? Do you remember Cody ever getting hurt? Do you remember talking to your mom and dad about something you saw happen to Cody? Have you ever seen a videotape of yourself talking about that? Do you remember telling your parents that you heard Lynn tell Cody to shut up? Do you remember telling your parents that Lynn would bonk Cody's head? Do you remember telling your parents that Cody doesn't stop crying at Lynn's?

Cattanach tried to hide her frustration with his negative responses. She asked for a sidebar. Again, it was out of my hearing. The defendant should hear these discussions.

We took a short break. I asked Eric about the last sidebar. He explained that because David had no recollection of anything, Cattanach would introduce the videotape his parents had made. I asked Eric how she could do that; it didn't meet the elements of Wisconsin statute 908.08, ensuring that videotaped statements of children are permitted only if safeguards are followed. Here, in David's video, no oath was given, or no affirmation that David understood the importance of telling the truth or that false statements were punishable. There was nothing to show that the time, content, and circumstances of the statement provided indicia of its trustworthiness. Eric said the judge allowed this recording as admissible as a statement of recent perception. This upset me. If David actually had information to share, he should have gone to Safe Harbor for a statement taken under the proper circumstances (although I hadn't been impressed with the Safe Harbor interviews, either).

David's dad, Mark Christie, was called as a witness after the break. Upon questioning about why they had pulled David out of my day care, he explained about his wife getting the information from Holly Jeter about what Annie claimed to see. Mark said they asked David the next morning about Cody, and David said that I would grab Cody's cheeks and mouth together and hit his head on the ground. Mark said he decided to videotape David's statements to document it.

Cattanach: Based up the information that your son provided you, what did you do?

Mark: We decided to pull him out of Lynn's care after that. It was an uncomfortable, awkward conversation with Lynn because I didn't want to go into specifics. Lynn pressed me on why we were pulling him out. I just said I thought it was an uncomfortable, bad situation, and we didn't want our son exposed to that. Lynn was upset. She continued to ask me questions about why we were pulling him out, trying to get specific answers. I didn't want to do that over the phone, or do any more than I had to.

Eric asked a few questions. "Until you heard about something concerning Cody, had you any intention of removing him from Lynn's day care?"

Mark: No.

Eric: Were you present when your son was interviewed by Detective Johnson?

Mark: Yes.

Eric: When he was asked if something happened in the day care center, do you remember him saying, "nothing, nothing, nothing?"

Mark: As I recall, he didn't remember much or didn't feel comfortable talking to the detective.

Eric: How long was that after you and your wife interviewed him?

Mark: Within a month, estimate two months.

Eric: When you saw Cody at the day care, would you characterize him as being hysterical?

Mark: No.

Again, there was no description of hysterical behavior by Cody. That interview with David and Detective Johnson was not a month or two after they interviewed him; it was six days later. On Thursday, September 18, he supposedly said all this stuff about Cody for the benefit of his parents, but less than a week later he tells Johnson that "nothing, nothing, nothing" happened at day care. Oh, that's right, according to Johnson, he was traumatized.

Bev Christie, David's mom, was the next and last witness for the day. She described her conversation with Holly Jeter about what Annie saw. Bev attempted to rationalize Annie's story. "Annie described to Holly the vantage point she was at, and, knowing the set-up, I knew that she was exactly in those places because you can't see in the bathroom from any other perspective. Annie was about seven at that time and very bright, articulate, smart, a very mature girl, and absolutely no question that what she was saying was what she observed."

How did this statement of Bev's go by with no objection from Eric? She couldn't testify about the veracity of another witness. Eric sat there taking it all in; I think a cardboard cutout of an attorney would have done a better job at this point.

Cattanach: When you videotaped David, what information did he provide?

Bev: It wasn't very much. As much as I can remember, he said Lynn pushed Cody's cheeks together. I didn't know what he was going to say. That's when we stopped and that was pretty much all that was said.

At this time, Cattanach played the homemade videotape of David. Again, I was struck by how much David acted for the camera, hamming it up. Leading questions were rampant, and if his parents didn't like a response, they asked him again or said, "No, no that."

Repeated questioning of children may cause them to change their answer, perceiving the recurring questions as a sign that they did not give the "correct" response. They want to please the adults asking the questions, and are especially susceptible to leading and suggestive questions. When an interviewer has a preconceived notion as to the truth of the matter being investigated, the questioning is conducted in a manner to extract statements that support these beliefs. As a result, evidence that could disprove the belief is never sought by the interviewer.

At one point Bob had told me that this videotape would not be admissible in court, yet here it was played and I didn't have an attorney fighting its admission.

After the tape finished playing, Cattanach had a few more questions for Bev. "Had you had occasion to view the play area in Lynn's day care?"

Bev: Yeah.
Cattanach: Where was the climber located at the time of August and September 2008?
Bev: It was in front of the bathroom door.

Cattanach showed Bev a photo. "Does this look familiar to you?"

Bev: Yes, that's the bathroom.
Cattanach: And in looking at the photo, is this the area where the climber was in August and September of 2008?
Bev: Directly outside of that door.
Cattanach: I'm going to give you a pointer. If you could indicate on the screen and describe where that climber was located.
Bev: This is inside the bathroom and like right out here, the wall is right here, so kind of against the wall right there.

Cattanach: So the area that Holly described to you that Annie saw, was this an area you knew?

Bev: Certainly, yes.

Cattanach: Did that vantage point seem consistent with being able to show what she described having seen?

Bev: Definitely, yes.

Well, there went Cattanach again, trying to get that climber right outside the bathroom. It was physically impossible. Now Bev lied about it being right outside the bathroom. She knew better. There was absolutely no room anywhere near the bathroom for the climber.

Eric asked her a few more questions about the vantage points. "You spoke of the bathroom in that play area. Have you been back in the bathroom?"

Bev: Yes.

Eric: It is accurate to say that, as you leave the bathroom, you would see the climber looking straight ahead from the bathroom door?

Bev: Yes.

Eric: Was it against the other wall?

Bev: It was like in the corner on the two walls.

Eric: When you speak of being able to see into the bathroom, did you place yourself where that climber was and try to look into the bathroom?

Bev: No, because I never went back there afterward.

Eric again referred to the picture of the bathroom that Cattanach had shown her. "Based on your familiarity with the area, was this view from someone standing in the bathroom door?"

Bev: That would be just outside the bathroom door, not in it.
Eric: Would you say immediately outside to be able to see that much of the changing table?
Bev: I don't know.

Well, at least Eric got Bev to change her story about the climber being right outside the bathroom. But why did she say that to Cattanach's questioning? She definitely knew the placement of that climbing structure was not right outside the bathroom.

Bev was dismissed as the last witness for the afternoon. The judge also dismissed the jury, with warnings not to discuss the case with anyone or do any research on it.

We remained behind for a few things to discuss. Cattanach said she had an issue to bring up regarding my witness, M.D. I had wanted M to testify that when she and her husband were going through a divorce, she was open with me in order to help her child. Cattanach argued that it had no relevance to the abuse in these cases.

Eric replied that it would be shown that the Marshalls were going through a divorce, but didn't let me know so I could help

Cody, who obviously was sad, withdrawn, and aloof during this time. The judge agreed that M's testimony would not be relevant to this case. Eric attempted another argument. "The premise is a day care provider should know what a child is going through so they can manage, redirect, teach, guide that child with the fact there's a divorce going on. In the Marshall case, she didn't know it. With M.D.'s child, she did, and was able to take steps." The judge didn't agree; whatever I did with another child had no bearing on Cody. I was disappointed, but not surprised.

I was stunned and upset that Cattanach said she planned to bring up marital issues that occurred between Ki and me to explain to the jury why I was "stressed" and how that was relevant to my reckless behavior. Yes, Ki and I had some issues in our marriage (how many couples don't?) during the summer of 2006 but they resolved. Regardless, that period was after the May 2006 bruises to Miles that I never saw or caused, and well before any alleged abuse to Cody in 2008. This was pure conjecture by Cattanach, but she was desperate to give a reason for my alleged lashing-out at kids. She said it was fair game for her to bring up my marital issues if we were going to confront the Marshalls about theirs. Judge Ehlke agreed, stating that if I testified, Cattanach would be able to cross-examine me about it because it would go to pressure I might have had, causing me to act in a certain way. BS, I wanted to shout! There was no pressure that caused me to harm any child. How unfair that Cattanach could use speculation to build her case.

We were done for the day. It had been exhausting to sit there and endure all the trash talk and lies about me. I was less than pleased with Eric's cross-exam performance. There were a few times when he did okay, but for the most part, he was non-confrontational and missed huge opportunities to catch the witnesses in lies or inconsistencies. I had not seen an aggressive defense, which would be crucial to prevailing at trial.

Here at trial, as in Johnson's interviews with them, no children except the Jeter kids claimed to ever see me harm Cody. But why were the parents able to speak for them? Wasn't that hearsay? There was not one hearsay objection from Eric. I couldn't fully introduce Dr. Andringa's professional medical report as it was considered hearsay, but the parents could say anything about what their kids supposedly told them at one time? Bob Burke had told me that hearsay would not be allowed—the kids would have to testify that they saw something. That sure is not how it ended up. I concluded that child abuse cases allow special rules that would not be permitted in other types of cases. Prosecution, one; defense, zero.

When I got home for the night, I checked my attendance records to see the times that Tommy and Cody arrived at my day care. Tina Reese could not have seen Cody in hysterics at his drop-off times. Tommy's arrival times varied from 7:15 to 9:15. Cody arrived at 7 a.m. almost every morning. Even on those days when Tommy was there right at 7:15, Joe Marshall was long gone. He never hung around—it was drop and go for him.

231

I also re-reviewed the reports of interviews that Holly Jeter or Annie gave to Detective Johnson. I wanted to see where this second incident of Cody's head banged on the "I can't remember which wall" originated. There was no reference by Annie or Holly anywhere in the reports that Annie saw more than one incident. Annie made some vague statements to Johnson about Cody being hurt more than once, but she didn't remember how many times. Was this more than one time at the diaper table? Or somewhere else? Johnson didn't pursue it since she wanted Safe Harbor interviews; we know what Annie said there. So where was the evidence for this second incident? What was the justification for its charge? I was upset that Eric gave no attempt to clarify it or challenge Annie with her inconsistent statements, especially after he informed me that he was aware of the change in the charges to reflect this supposed second incident.

Chapter 25

The Marshalls' Testimony

*D*ay two of the trial started with Cody. Joe and Maria were allowed to be in the courtroom; with the other children, the parents were not in attendance. Cody bounded right up into the witness stand. He certainly exhibited no "basket case" behavior. Cattanach asked him to state his name, but he shook his head. He did not respond to any of her questions. He was intent on playing with the microphone; tapping it with his fingers to hear the sound it made. As with Peter, Cattanach attempted to conceal her annoyance, but it was obvious she was not happy with Cody. Her patience was being tested; I was not impressed with her rapport with young children.

"Can you not play with the microphone and can you talk into it? Can you say 'hi'?" He still would not respond. She asked him if he would like his mom to be with him, so Maria came up to sit next to him. He gave a few one-word responses to Cattanach's further questions. When asked if he remembered going to Lynn's day care, he shook his head no.

233

Cattanach asked if he saw me in the courtroom and he didn't respond. She then went over to stand by me and asked if he knew me; he still gave no response or sign of recognition. She tried to ask him if he ever had any owies or bumps on his forehead or injuries to his ear. He shook his head. She wasn't going to get her desired answers from him; he only wanted to play with the microphone. Finally, when asked his age, Cody said, "four." Cattanach followed up with, "When's your birthday?" He did not respond to that, but did say "all mine" when asked if he got a lot of presents for his birthday.

Eric didn't see any point to cross-examine him. Cody left the stand and his dad, Joe Marshall was next. Cattanach asked Joe about injuries to Cody. "During Cody's stay at Lynn's, did something start happening?"

Joe: Yes, I would notice bruises on his forehead. I would notice them when I would pick him up, and they had not been there in the morning. They were always on the right side of his forehead. I would say it happened every couple of weeks or so. We had known Lynn for years and I didn't think anything about it.

Cattanach: In March of 2008, did Cody have a significant injury when you picked him up from day care?

Joe: Yeah. There were weird dots behind his ear. We took him to the doctor for that.

234

Cattanach: Do you recall anything specific happening on August 27, 2008 because it was your son Steven's birthday?

Joe: Yes, it was his 10th birthday and we took him to a water park. We all three dropped him off at day care. And when we picked him up, he had a bruise. I believe at that time it was a bruise to the head again, and a mark on the back of his neck.

Here was that imaginary injury again. If all three of them had dropped off Cody that morning, only Maria actually accompanied him into the day care. I find it hard to believe that Steven waited in the car; it was his birthday and I know he would have wanted to tell me about it. Joe was the only one who arrived at pick-up time; again, I expected Steven to come and tell me about his day.

Cattanach: Are you and Maria currently divorced?

Joe: Yes. It became final on May 13th of last year.

Cattanach: When did this divorce start?

Joe: August 11·2008 is pretty much the exact day it started.

Cattanach: Prior to that, was there talk of divorce or anything like that?

Joe: None.

That August 11 date corresponded with the episode of Cody not being picked up from my day care due to miscommunication among his parents, and the subsequent revelation by Joe of things not going well at home. It is hard for me to believe his story about no trouble brewing before that. There were times prior to that when they revealed a lack of communication, specifically with regard to picking up Cody at my house.

Cattanach: Did you notice any behavioral differences after Cody was removed from Lynn's day care?

Joe: He was biting his nails when he was going to Lynn's. Three or four weeks later, when he left her day care, he quit biting his nails.

Cattanach: Did you ever talk with Cody about the injuries?

Joe: I really didn't. He started saying "No Lynn's" before we took him out of there, and I didn't understand why.

This was the first I heard of any nail biting. Cody never did that at my house; had I observed nail biting, I would have worked with him to curtail it. Since it only happened at home, that seemed like more of a symptom of trouble at home. If Cody said that he didn't want to go to my house, why didn't Joe ever talk to me about it? How do you defend the things that come up at trial that you never heard before?

Eric began his cross-exam. "Mr. Marshall, you were saying that the injuries to Cody's head were usually on the forehead. Is that accurate?"

Joe: Yes, always on the right hand side.

Eric: Your son Steven is 11, right? Do you remember visiting a physician named Landry and speaking to him about the roughhousing between the boys?

Joe: Yes.

Eric: Do you remember saying to the physician that some of the bruises on Cody were just normally gotten in play with his brother?

Joe: We thought that might have been a possibility.

Eric: Did you and your wife share the duties of dropping off and picking up Cody from Lynn's house?

Joe: Yeah, we shared them, but I did it for the most part.

Eric: Do you remember any times when there was miscommunication between the two of you and Cody wasn't picked up when he might have been?

Joe: It might have happened. If it did, it wasn't very often.

Eric: It sounds like you were suggesting that there were times when Cody didn't want to go to Lynn's.

Joe: Yeah, there were times.

Eric: Did you talk to him about what he did there?

Joe: You know, he was only there up until he was two years old, so I don't recall.

Eric: Do you remember going over photos that Lynn gave you so you had some idea of what he had been doing in Lynn's day care?

Joe: Sure. Yes.

Eric: Is it accurate to say that, until the final episodes, you weren't planning to take him out of Lynn's day care?

Joe: No, we were not planning on taking him.

Eric: Did Steven attend the day care in August for a couple of times?

Joe: I believe so. I don't recall the reason why.

Eric: Are there times when anyone in the family, since this happened, tells Cody that if he doesn't behave, that he'll have to go to Lynn's again?

Joe: (indignantly) No.

Eric: That's never happened?

Joe: No.

Cattanach's re-direct questioning focused on the March visit to Dr. Landry. "Why did you go to the doctor?"

Joe responded. "Well, we didn't know what it was. It was weird looking. I was not aware of that type of mark behind an ear before, so I was concerned."

Joe admitted that Cody was only age two when he left my care, so he didn't talk to him about what went on, most likely due to Cody's lack of verbal skills. Detective Johnson, in her interview with Cody, made it seem like he was the world's best storyteller. Yet, in court, a year-and-a-half later, Cody couldn't say more than a two-word sentence.

Maria Marshall was next up. Would her testimony match that of the preliminary hearing over a year ago?

Cattanach: At some point, did you notice any injury to Cody that caused you concern?

Maria: Yes. On March 10, 2008. He had a large goose egg on his head, and his ear was bruised on the inside of the ear as well as behind the ear, and there were red dots on the lobe and up the ear. We took him to the doctor the next day.

Cattanach: Can you tell us more about what you observed to Cody's ear?

Maria: The bruising, there was bruising inside the ear as well as behind it, and there were red dots on his lobe and up the side of his ear, the cartilage.

Joe said there were weird dots behind the ear. Maria said there were bruises on the inside and behind the ear, as well as red dots on the lobe and up the ear, and a goose egg on his head.Dr. Landry's report mentions nothing about a goose egg. His report only references the auricle having some small superficial ecchymotic areas, nothing about any other bruise on or behind the ear. In fact, Dr. Landry said there was no evidence of hematoma, and he was less concerned about these superficial ecchymosis as opposed to a larger hematoma. His report references that Cody was rubbing his ear at day care, which I told Maria. What version is more likely — Dr. Landry's report, or the Marshall's trial testimony with obviously exaggerated and embellished injuries?

Cattanach: After that March incident, did other injuries show up on Cody?

Maria: Yes, one in particular was August 27th. That date sticks in my mind because it was Steven's birthday. Cody's injury was again a large goose egg on his head, and the skin on the back of his head was scuffed, I guess you would say, and red.

Cattanach: Did you ask Lynn about those injuries?

Maria: Not at that time.

Cattanach: After the August 27th injuries, did you observe any other injuries to your son?

Maria: Yes, specifically September 17. Again he had a goose egg on his head, bruising behind his ear, and a scrape behind his ear.

Maria's preliminary hearing testimony had been: "*On August 27 he had a lump on his head, bruising behind the ear; and a lump on the back of his head where there was also some skin scuffed off.*"

At least for this trial testimony, the bruising behind the ear disappeared for August 27. If she had been truthful, all injuries would have disappeared. He had had nothing besides an initial redness from contact with the ladder. If injuries had shown up later, I would have noted that. The pizza week photos confirm that there were no injuries to his face.

Her preliminary hearing testimony regarding September 17 was similar to the current trial testimony. "*He had a lump on the top of his head, a goose egg, and he had some bruising and some scratching behind his ear."*

Cattanach: Did you have a conversation with Lynn about what happened to your son on September 17th?
Maria: Yes. She said she didn't know.

Well, there was another lie. I had told Joe about the bump into the door because it happened a few minutes before he arrived. The next day I talked to Maria about it, and that's when she mentioned the crud behind his ear. Now that crud turned into a bruise and scratching.

Cattanach then asked Maria about hearing Annie's allegations.

Maria: On September 19th, Holly told me that she had some disturbing news about Cody, and that Annie had observed Lynn hitting his head on the wall.
Cattanach: And this is the day that you had observed that Cody had injuries?
Maria: Yes.
Cattanach: Prior to September 19th, had Holly called to share that information with you?
Maria: No.
Cattanach: Did you have any idea about the abuse?
Maria: No.

This last line of questioning was bizarre. Cattanach permitted Maria to say that Holly failed in her responsibility to report child abuse. That has been one of my major issues from the start—if Holly was concerned about Annie's allegations, why didn't she do something right away? Oh, yeah, according to her testimony, it was selfishly wanting to get Miles settled in his new preschool. Had it ever dawned on the Marshalls about Holly's negligent action in this regard?

Cattanach: During your drop-off or pick-up experiences at Lynn's, can you recall anything about Cody's demeanor?
Maria: On the way to Lynn's, he would say "No Lynn's." And he would cry.

Joe had made some of these same claims about Cody not wanting to go to my house. If this was true, why wasn't I informed of that? Every child has days when they don't want to go to day care or school, like we have days we don't want to go to work. However, if it was more than that occasional complaint, as both Joe and Maria now made it seem, why wouldn't they have dealt with that?

Cattanach: After the removal of Cody from Lynn's day care, did he go to another day care?

Maria: Yes. At the new place, the teachers commented that he was sweet and caring to all the other kids and he was the best helper they've ever had.

Cody was sweet and caring to all the kids at my house, too. He chose not to initiate play with them; once I helped him get involved with others, I observed those attributes. If Maria suggested that he had changed his demeanor at the new place, why did his teachers report that he was the best helper they've ever had? That would indicate that, as at my house, he was choosing to hang around the adults and do things for them. That is not giving credibility to the claim that his behavior changed dramatically once he was removed from my care.

Cattanach: Did you see any other changes regarding Cody after you removed him from Lynn's?
Maria: He stopped biting his fingernails. He had fewer temper tantrums. He had fewer incidents of hitting. He wasn't as angry outwardly.

Again with the story of the fingernail biting. I never observed Cody doing this. I helped him wash his hands many times throughout the day and never noticed any evidence of chewed-up nails. This was also the first I heard of temper tantrums or hitting behavior. Why didn't the Marshalls inform me of Cody's behavior? With Steven, I had heard every little detail of what he did. With Cody, nothing. The only thing I heard with regard to Cody's behavior were those few times when Maria told me he had acted up and they threatened him with me coming to make him be good.

During Eric's cross-exam of Maria, he asked about this issue. "Were there times during Cody's stay with Lynn that you might say to him that if he didn't behave, you'd take him to Lynn's and she could help him behave? Do you remember saying things like that?"

Maria stated, "I don't recall."

This response seemed like deliberate evasiveness. It sounded like she did not want to admit to engaging in such behavior with her son.

Eric continued. "You spoke of some of the injuries you saw on Cody. At one answer you said something about the back of his head, but your hand went more to your neck. Can you describe what you meant by the back of the head?" Maria indicated by pointing close to the base of her skull.

Eric: Just above where the neck starts?
Maria: Yes.
Eric: The other injuries were mostly to his forehead?
Maria: Yes.

Eric: Any to the back of his head other than the one that you've just described?

Maria: I don't believe so.

So I constantly banged the back of this poor child's head into walls, yet there was never a back of the head injury? Doesn't that say something?

Eric: When you were told that something happened to Cody, did you believe it?

Maria: I was told that there was a witness, yes. I believed that.

Eric: Was your divorce filed on October 8, 2008?

Maria: Yes.

Eric: Was August when you were first aware there may be a divorce coming?

Maria: Approximately.

Eric: I ask because that's only two months. Did you consider discussing this with Lynn as it might be something that would affect Cody's behavior?

Maria: No. I didn't consider it.

Cattanach had only brief re-direct questions, one in which I detected a hint of incredulity in her tone: "Opposing counsel keeps asking if you would threaten Cody to go to Lynn's when he would misbehave." I swear Cattanach's face showed bewilderment when Maria gave the same vague "I don't recall" response.

Chapter 26

Poor Attorney Performance

After a mid-morning break, Cathy Leaverton, the day care licensor, was called as a witness. Cattanach asked her about her visit with me on September 23, 2008. "I came because I had received a complaint, so I talked to her about how things were going, what kind of things had happened on this day of the complaint. She was identifying to me that a lot of the children were dropping out of her care. She had actually called me before I went out there to tell me that things were not going well and children were dropping out of her care. She didn't know why. She was visibly distraught about this. She thought the children were dropping out because of one child who was very sad and that it was bothersome to the other children. That child was Cody."

Cattanach: Did you ask her about Cody's head or specifics about a head injury?

Leaverton: I believe I did. I guess I don't remember the specifics of that. She showed me where the bathroom was, the diaper changing area.

Cattanach: When you were there, did she tell you anything that she had done the night before you came?

Leaverton: She had moved a piece of furniture. It's a piece of furniture that the children can walk up on. There are steps on it and they walk up to a loft area.

Cattanach: And Lynn told you that she moved that the night before?

Leaverton: She told me that she moved it. I don't know that I can say that she moved it the night before, but she moved it.

There was Cattanach, alluding that I moved the climber the night before Leaverton arrived, as if I tried to hide evidence. Cattanach was so desperate to prove that there was a view to the bathroom from the climber that she tried to influence her witness into saying I moved it before any investigation could take place. The September 19, 2008 "Talk like a Pirate Day" photo clearly shows that the climber was moved prior to me being aware of any child abuse allegations.

Cattanach: In regard to the climber, were you able to get into a position where the child would have been at the time of the abuse?

Leaverton: I was able to get into that corner, yes.

Cattanach: Did you go to that corner and take a look at the changing area from that corner?

Leaverton: I did.

Cattanach: What were you able to see?

Leaverton: You could see into part of the bathroom. The changing table is actually up near the door, the entrance to it, so you actually see more of the toilet, the shower, and part of the area of the changing table.

Wow—a huge lie! Leaverton never got off the chair when she came for that visit. I had invited her to check out the view, but she refused. She confirmed that with my investigator, Gwen Dunham, when Gwen met with her in the summer of 2009. (Gwen's report stated: *Leaverton said that she has no comment regarding whether a person would be able to see the bathroom changing table from the loft. She said that she didn't check it out; she only sat in the blue rocking chair.*)

Leaverton was willing to perjure herself. Why? What was the motivation to see me convicted?

Cattanach continued by asking Leaverton about my log book. "When looking through the log at the injury documentation, did you make any observations?"

Leaverton: Most of the entries are fairly brief. Usually there's just a little more detail as to what happened and what was done.

Oftentimes, you know, if a child gets an injury, it will say that they put ice on the injury or a parent was called. Details are also added as to where the injury took place, too.

Cattanach: Have you noticed, in your experience, documentation regarding head injuries?

Leaverton: Head injuries are taken more seriously, and usually the parent is called at that time.

Cattanach: It's not required, though?

Leaverton: It's not required, but it's more of a serious type of injury considered.

Cattanach tried to extract from Leaverton that I was less than thorough in my log book entries. Leaverton could not say I was, other than maybe being briefer in my entries than some other providers' log books she had reviewed.

I eagerly anticipated Eric's cross-exam. He asked about her view of the bathroom from the climber. "Are you saying that as you stood where you think the witness was, you could see the changing table in the bathroom?"

Leaverton: I could see part of it.

Eric: From that corner?

Leaverton: From that corner.

Eric: How much of it could you see?

Leaverton: Maybe a third.

Eric: And when you saw that third, you were standing near the back wall, the wall that's farthest from the bathroom; is that right?

Leaverton: I was standing in that corner, yeah.

Eric: In that corner. Was the climber there in the corner at the time?

Leaverton: No.

Eric: But you were standing by where the climber would have been?

Leaverton: Yes.

Okay, Eric, I thought. Time for the zinger where you ask her about Gwen's meeting with her and her admission that she never got off the blue chair. I wanted to see Leaverton squirm. All of a sudden, however, Eric switched topics. What? Was he not going to confront her about the interview with Gwen? What kind of attorney did I have? I spent a lot of money on fees for Gwen, and now Eric ignored a key factor of her investigation which would have exposed a lie by a State's witness.

Eric: You've spoken of the logbook. There are some rules attached to maintaining a log book, are there not?

Leaverton: Yes, there are.

Eric: Did you, in reviewing this log book, find any violation of the rules that are imposed on someone keeping that book?

Leaverton: No.

Eric: Are you suggesting in your answers to the DA that some of the entries are less complete than you think they should be?

Leaverton: I think they're just briefer than what I've seen in other centers.

Eric: Are they briefer than the instructions given to someone who keeps a logbook?

Leaverton: No.

Eric: In your opinion, do the instructions given to someone keeping a logbook suggest that they be brief?

Leaverton: I can't answer that.

Eric: All right. When you spoke with Lynn Moller on the day you went to visit her, did you describe the complaint that had been told to you?

Leaverton: I described a part of the complaint, but I did not describe where the complaint came from.

Cattanach presented a brief re-direct. "In the additional report, there were multiple abuse sightings by Annie, not just the one in the bathroom?"

Leaverton: Yes.

Cattanach: In the information that you shared with Lynn during the interview, you not only had the information that Annie had seen the one injury in the bathroom, there was another injury that Annie had seen somewhere else?

Leaverton: I think in the dining room area.

Cattanach: And in looking in that area, were you able to tell if Annie would have had a vantage point to see that injury?

Leaverton: She probably would have been. It was during a meal or a snack time. She probably would have been sitting there, too.

Why didn't Eric object to this response by Leaverton? It was obvious speculation. When Leaverton had her interview with me, I specifically asked if maybe Annie had seen me take Cody away from the table due to his spitting-up issue, and that is what she interpreted as abuse; Leaverton's answer to me was that this had nothing to do with anything in the kitchen. But now she changed her story, giving the prosecution fodder for that second charge, of which I had heard nothing until the start of trial yesterday.

My "favorite" detective was next up. Her testimony to Cattanach was similar to that of the preliminary hearing, where she magically got non-verbal Cody to open up and say things like, "Lynn wall, Lynn house" in a non-recorded, non-witnessed interview. Given her propensity for lying, I had a hard time believing anything she claimed.

As with Leaverton, the view from the corner into the bathroom suddenly became something that she checked. Yes, she had briefly looked into the bathroom on the day of the awful interrogation with me, but not back in the corner where the climber would have been. Now she claimed she went into the corner where the climber was and could miraculously see the changing area. Cattanach spent a great deal of time asking her about photos and the view into the bathroom. She tried to make Annie's climber claim credible. Johnson admitted that since the climber was not in the same place when she was there, her photos were taken "from standing outside of the bathroom approximately where we thought someone might be able to see if they were standing on that climber. I was trying to estimate, if I was on a climber, could I see into the bathroom and how far could I see."

Eric spent some time also questioning Johnson about her view and the photos. "You said that you stood where you thought the climber would be?"

Johnson: In the general area, yes.

Eric: And then from that corner of the room you looked into the bathroom?

Johnson: Yes.

Eric: Are you saying that, as you looked into the bathroom, you could see at least some of the changing pad?

Johnson: Yes.

Eric: Did you have someone standing in the bathroom so you could see how much of them you could see?

Johnson: No.

Eric showed Johnson a photo taken from farther back in which only the doorway of the bathroom was visible. "You stood in this spot and made this view; you saw what this shows?"

Johnson: Yes.

Eric: And you're saying that when you stood in the corner where the climber had been, you could see most of what this photo shows?

Johnson: Yes.

Eric: This photo shows some sort of small structure to the left. Do you see that? It looks like a wooden structure.

He tried to get Johnson to admit that all you could see from that view was the doorway. She hemmed and hawed and delayed answering; it was obvious she knew what he was asking but didn't want to admit it. I could hear the collective thoughts from my gallery chanting, "Admit it's the doorway!" Finally, grudgingly, Johnson said, "That would be the doorway."

Eric confirmed, "So that's the doorway to the bathroom?" "I believe so, yes." Cattanach, deflated, had no re-direct. Her lead detective admitted that the view was nonexistent.

The last witness for the morning was Dr. Marc Bellazzinni. He was the ER doctor who saw Cody on September 22, 2008, after the abuse allegations rose. Cattanach asked him to describe what he observed. He admitted that he did not have an independent rec- ollection of treating Cody on that day; he just reviewed the report.

"I obtained the history from the parents of Cody Marshall, who stated they presented for evaluation of possible abuse. They presented specifically to see Child Protective Services, which were initially unavailable. It's a specialty area in the hospital, with Dr. Barbara Knox as its head. She was unavailable at that time. Cody was awake and alert, acting appropriately, and the only physical exam findings were a bruise to the right forehead and an abrasion behind his left ear. Otherwise, his exam was normal. I found no fractures or any such indications."

Cattanach, in a barely audible voice, asked if Cody had had a skeletal survey with normal results. Dr. Bellazinni confirmed that he had. I think her whisper-like question had to do with the fact that she wasn't happy about the normal results of the skeletal survey. I wondered why she even brought that up.

Eric had no significant follow-up questions for the doctor. I had wanted him to ask about the skeletal survey. Why was it obtained? How likely was a normal skeletal survey for a child who allegedly had his head banged consistently? Unfortunately, Eric didn't ask, again to my dismay. Referencing Dr. Barbara Knox's favorite phrase, I felt it was "gravely concerning" that I was accused of harming Cody when there was no evidence of abuse.

It was just before noon when this last witness finished, so the judge excused the jury for lunch. He indicated that after the lunch break he would ask me if I planned to testify. Eric and I had discussed this. Most defense attorneys avoid having their clients testify. The average person is no match for a shrewd prosecutor's cross-examination. Eric never expressed this concern with me, and I saw no reason for me not to testify. I had nothing to hide, and hoped to undo some of the damage from the police interrogation. I was now in a much better state of mind and aware of Johnson's lies and exaggerations.

Chapter 27

Gravely Concerning

*T*he lunch hour flew by, and once again we were back in the courtroom. Outside the presence of the jury, Judge Ehlke asked me if I would be testifying. He made it clear that I had a constitutional right to testify or not to testify. When I affirmed my intention, he clarified with Eric that I had made that choice knowingly, intelligently, and voluntarily.

Dr. Barbara Knox was the first witness of the afternoon. Remembering her vast and conceited introduction of herself from the preliminary hearing, I wondered if we would be given the honor of listening to that again. We were, with even more embellishments and a rather condescending attitude that her "old" curriculum vitae was presented as an exhibit. "It doesn't list many of my most current publications, a lot of talks. A lot of the most recent talks that I've done nationally, internationally, are not listed, nor is some of my current research. I've given multiple other presentations which are honestly too numerous to count." While her background and experience were worthy of being presented, her arrogance and superior attitude stood out. I wonder how the jury felt about her introduction; was this smugness as apparent to them?

Cattanach showed her the seven photos of the bruises to Miles' face. Knox's testimony was similar to that of the preliminary hearing. She said that any bruising in the scalp region or the cheek on a child was concerning. The photos she viewed of Miles gave her concern that these demonstrated a classic pattern type injury, consistent with adult inflicted fingertip contusion injury. As at the preliminary hearing, she threw out her favorite catch phrases: "gravely concerning," "adult inflicted," "consistent with abuse." "My findings are that this case was consistent with adult inflicted fingertip contusion injuries." Her written report was marked as an exhibit.

Since Dr. Andringa's report of May 15, 2006 was not available at the time of the preliminary hearing, Cattanach now asked her about it. "Since your report, have you viewed another doctor's report regarding an examination of Miles Jeter that occurred on May 15, 2006?"

Knox: Yes.
Cattanach: Anything regarding your review of that report which changed the opinions you authored in this case?
Knox: No.

Andringa, a respected Madison pediatrician, with many more years of experience than Knox, authored a medical report, full of glaring inconsistencies of dates and unseen bruises compared to parents' testimony. But Knox wouldn't back down on her diagnosis, for a child she never saw, and her opinion based only on photos. How biased toward the prosecution was that?

Cattanach proceeded with questions about ear injuries. "Doctor, can you tell us more about ear injuries and their significance as identifiers for abuse?"

"One of the things I always teach is that any time you see ear bruising it is concerning and you at least have to think about the possibility of abuse as being one of the causative mechanisms for a bruise. The bottom line is I teach everyone that when you see ear bruising, think about the possibility of abuse in these cases because many times it is traumatic abusive etiology that causes that bruise."

Cattanach presented Dr. Landry's March 11, 2008 medical report regarding Cody's visit about the ear tugging and small pin-prick dots on his ear. She threw Knox's favorite word back at her: "In looking at this report, was there anything *concerning* to you?"

Knox: There was. He said the left auricle has evidence of some small superficial ecchymotic areas with a few petechia. He sees bruising, bruises to the ear, but no evidence of hematoma. He was looking to see if it was something that required surgical intervention that night. He did not see it, but clearly noted bruising to the ear in this record.

Cattanach: When you say ecchymotic area, noted some petechia, does that raise concerns with you?

Knox: It does. As I educate everyone, this would be concerning to me for the possibility of abuse. I would want a lot more information on this case, and I would want it investigated as to why this child has this bruise. I would want to have some trauma mechanism presented to me to see if it was consistent with that or not. So this would be concerning for the possibility of abuse to me.

So again, Knox editorialized on a report made by another respected, experienced local pediatrician. If this report was beneficial to the prosecution, why wasn't Dr. Landry called as a witness? I figured Cattanach didn't want him as a trial witness since he wouldn't confirm abuse for the March 11 visit. Absent him, this report was stipulated, likely so Knox could spin it to give a "concerning for abuse" impression.

Her version of the report made it seem like Cody had huge bruises all over his ear, when in fact Dr. Landry's description was "some small superficial ecchymotic areas with a few petechia." Dr. Landry went on to state, "My impression is that Cody has sustained a mild contusion to this ear. His parents report that he plays quite rough with his brother and is very active." That seemed to provide the "trauma mechanism" Knox sought.

Cattanach turned her focus to Cody's ER visit on September 22, 2008. Again, Knox was allowed to comment on a child she had not seen.

"This photo of Cody shows a superficial abrasion behind the ear. I was asked my opinion, and said that was non-specific in nature. Again, I'm looking for bruises behind the ear. I couldn't one hundred percent state if this was a rash or superficial abrasion by looking at a picture. It's not any injury that specifically has to be caused by abuse."

Cattanach really wanted to attribute that abrasion to abuse. "Doesn't have to be caused by abuse, but can be caused by abuse?"

"Yes, yes."

Knox confirmed that she could not sufficiently form an opinion regarding Cody in the September 2008 findings, and she couldn't conclude that it was abuse. However, she kowtowed to Cattanach's questioning that it could be caused by abuse, thereby again giving deference to the prosecution.

Eric took his turn with Knox for cross-exam. "In all your work with all the photos we have seen, you were observing photographs rather than the patient."

Knox: Correct.

Eric: Is that less preferable to a diagnostician?

Knox: Anytime I have the opportunity to see a patient in person, that is always the most preferable. However, it is not uncommon in my role as medical director of the Child Protection Program that I am asked to evaluate a case based upon photos or medical records.

Eric: Is the conclusion reached one in which you have more faith if you examined the patient personally?

Knox: I always like to see the patient because I feel that it allows me the best forum to objectively assess a case, but a good chunk of my practice is assessing cases based upon medical record assessment and photos, documentation review, and I feel equally confident on those cases or else I don't make a statement on them. One example might be Cody. When I see a photo that is not of diagnostic quality for me, I don't make a one hundred percent statement on anything.

Eric asked her if she could date bruises. Bob had asked her the same question at the preliminary hearing. Her response was consistent, stating that one can't be accurate on dating bruises. "I don't date bruises at all, and the literature supports that."

Eric: When you examined the photos of Miles, were you told that whatever appeared on those photos had not been there on the morning of the day the photos are dated?

Knox: Yes.

Eric: Did the report from Dr. Andringa suggest that at least one parent thought there were marks on his face before that day?

Knox: Yes, it suggested that there was the possibility of some marks. However, Dr. Andringa did not make that conclusion.

Eric: When you reached the conclusion based on your examination of the photographic images, did you assume that the photos accurately reflected what was photographed without manipulation?

Knox: The photos that are presented to me come from law enforcement, so I only make my statements off of what I am viewing on the photos. I look to them to determine if there is any manipulation of the photograph. The photos of Miles were brought in to me by law enforcement, so I expect law enforcement is going to look at the authenticity of the photos. I simply make a statement if I see concern for injury or not.

I had wondered all along about the authenticity of these Miles photos. How do we know they were what they seemed to be? All I know from police reports is that Holly emailed them to Detective Johnson. I didn't want to think that they were altered or fabricated, but given the major discrepancies between these pictures and the alleged dates of injury, my mind sure wandered to the possibility. There were also gaps in the sequence numbers of the photos submitted for evidence, with some missing photos. What did those missing photos show? Or not show?

I wondered, as an experiment, if Knox was given a random set of photos to comment on, would she make a finding of child abuse? I would have liked to present her with some true photos of abuse, and then some photo-shopped ones. Would she be able to give a proper diagnosis based only on photos? With the ease and prevalence of photo-altering capabilities, how could one know if a photo was a true depiction? Eric had asked, at jury selection, if people were aware of how photos could be altered; every potential jury member responded affirmatively. I had hoped he would pursue that at trial, but, as in many other strategic methods, he disappointed me by failing to follow-up on that subject. Nor had he asked Holly or Detective Johnson at trial about the authenticity of the Miles photos.

Eric had no further questions. Cattanach asked Knox if the report from Dr. Andringa had some identification issues that differed from the visual documentation that she saw (again, only via photos). "In my medical opinion, I did not feel that he [Dr. Andringa] was seeing what I was seeing the next day and these pictures were reportedly taken after the child was picked up from day care. If he were to see [what I saw], though I can't speak for Dr. Andringa, I certainly know him. I know his practice. I believe he would have reported it as a concern for abuse."

Cattanach: Do you have any opinion or speculations in regard to that?
Knox: Yes. I believe that Dr. Andringa was not viewing the contusion or bruising injury that I was viewing the next day off the photo documentation. I do believe it was not present at the point that he saw this child.
Cattanach: Dr. Andringa being unable to date the injury, is it possible there was bruising on the cheek when he saw Miles the first

day and then the next day when those photos are taken, the additional injuries that are caused?

Knox: Absolutely. It takes time for some bruising to come out. It's very common to see bruising come out over a period of time.

Cattanach was allowed to speculate that Miles had bruising on the cheek on Monday the 15th, and then the next day got more injuries. But while Dr. Andringa said he saw a little bit of discoloration on the cheek which might be a bruise, he didn't give a definitive diagnosis of bruising, and clearly said there was no other bruising anywhere on the face.

Knox was excused as a witness, after Cattanach confirmed with her that any of Miles' previous medical procedures would have no bearing on her diagnosis of adult inflicted fingertip contusion injury.

Information in Dr. Andringa's report that was in my favor and raised reasonable doubt was not allowed, as it was considered hearsay. Eric confronted Holly about the bruises being present for three or four days, but she didn't recall saying that. Because of the hearsay ruling, he was not able to follow up and ask Holly why she would have said it. Why would it be on the doctor report if not true? Holly went to the doctor with a worry about bruises around the ear and scalp, saying they had been noticeable for the last three to four days. The doctor couldn't verify her complaint other than a bit of discoloration on the cheek, but the next day those bruises mysteriously appear. Dr. Andringa wanted Miles to return if things were not better. Why did Holly not go back with the new bruises she was concerned about enough to photograph on the 16th? None of this made any sense. Knox essentially discredited Andringa's report by saying it would be normal for bruises to show up later.

Was Holly prophetic about these bruises? Did she want them to appear? Was there some type of factitious syndrome at play here? I can't get over the fact that she went to the doctor a day before they appeared. Something was not right, and it had nothing to do with any alleged abuse I inflicted upon Miles.

I had a poor impression of Dr. Knox. Her role in my case was less as a medical professional and more like a law enforcement official. Her sole purpose was to find child abuse. She doubted both Dr. Andringa and Dr. Landry's reports; she made it clear that her opinion of abuse for children she never saw overruled their non-abuse diagnoses.

Chapter 28

My Turn

inally, Cattanach announced that the State rested. That was a relief. I was tired of hearing all the bad, untrue things about me. I was concerned that irreparable damage had been done. With the exception of a few questions, I had not been pleased with Eric's cross-examination of anyone. We did not have much of an upcoming defense to present. How do you prove that I didn't do anything? I hoped my testimony could help, but was still afraid of how Cattanach could twist it.

My investigator, Gwen Dunham, was the first witness that Eric called. She had been to my house to take photos and videos of the day care rooms. She did a good job explaining where she was standing when she took the photos, most of which focused on the bathroom and the view from the climber. Yes, there was a straight-line view into the bathroom, but the countertop with the diaper changing pad on it was impossible to see; especially given Annie's testimony that she was on the stairs of the climber, even farther out.

Cattanach couldn't come up with any relevant cross-exam questions; obviously there was absolutely no way anyone could see the changing area from the climber.

Gwen was dismissed as a witness. However, Eric had missed questioning her about one major event — her July 2009 interview with the day care licensor, Cathy Leaverton. Leaverton had admitted to Gwen that she never got off the blue chair to check any view into the bathroom. Eric had not confronted Leaverton about this during her testimony, which upset me. It angered me more when Eric did not ask Gwen about it. Turns out that he knew nothing about that meeting between Gwen and Leaverton. Bob had arranged that meeting, but the report was in the file and Eric should have been aware of it. This was similar to him not knowing about Holly Jeter's preliminary hearing testimony that vastly differed from her trial story. There is no strategic reason for a lawyer not to study all of the pretrial materials. He could have obliterated both Holly and Leaverton. Regrettably, Eric missed key details, devastating my defense.

I was the next witness. Upon my approach to be sworn, I told myself to breathe, relax, and be myself. Eric began his direct examination with general questions about my background and family. He then focused on my early childhood education and experience, leading up to my time as a family child care provider in my home. He asked about the state requirements for obtaining and keeping a day care license, including required paperwork, record keeping, continuing education, and the medical logbook. Regarding the log-book, he asked if I was required to record instances of kids throwing up. I replied that it wasn't required, but I often did it. I know he asked this due to Cody's instances of spitting up, where I tried to find a pattern and therefore had started recording the occurrences.

Eric then said he wanted to ask some questions about the phys-ical layout of my facility. In preparation for this line of questioning, Ki had prepared a labeled diagram of the day care space, and we had it enlarged for use in court. It wasn't precisely to scale but it was close. It was drawn to depict the period of August 27-28, 2008, when Annie attended. Eric asked me to give a description of the area to go along with the visual. He then presented photos that Gwen had taken and asked me expound on what they showed. We spent a lot of time on the photos showing the view from the climber to the bathroom. No matter which photo was presented and from whatever angle, there was no view to be found from the climber to the changing table.

Eric's questions were presented in a low-key manner, and it was easy to answer them. I actually enjoyed talking about my day care program, facility, and the kids I loved. However, I knew the questioning line would take a painful direction, as I had to address events leading to the child abuse charges.

Eric: On May 16, 2006, the charge involves Miles. Were there any entries in your log book concerning injuries it is said that he suffered?

Lynn: No, there's nothing in my logbook. I did not notice any bruises. I would have logged it in my book that either he had arrived with a bruise like that or he had received them in my care.

Eric: On August 27, 2008, regarding Cody, what happened to him and is there a log entry to show it?

Lynn: In the afternoon outside play time, he slipped down the ladder of the play structure as he was climbing up. I didn't actually see it. I just know that I saw him on the ground, and he was holding the left side of his face. So I asked him if he needed an ice pack for that; he said yes.

Eric: On September 17, there's another notation about Cody suffering injury. Was there a log entry for that?

Lynn: Yes. On that day, he tripped on the rug right by the door as we were heading outside. The door was open and he clunked his head into that, on the upper right of his forehead.

Eric: Now I'd like to ask you some questions about statements you made when you were questioned by detectives. Do you remember saying something to the effect of maybe you were doing these things and didn't know it?

Lynn: Something like that. The interview that I had with the detectives was just awful. Detective Johnson grilled and grilled and grilled me and she told me all of the children were saying things about me. She said all the kids were saying I was mean, was banging Cody's head on the wall, I was pulling his hair. It just broke my heart to hear that. I started going numb. I was in shock to hear all these accusations against me. My soul was ripped out from me upon hearing that.

Eric: Did you think that you might be doing this if they were telling you that you were?

Lynn: I mumbled something like I didn't remember doing any of this, but if I did, it's scary that I don't remember. I don't really know what I was saying to the detective.

Eric: Do you remember saying to them you might have been too rough with Cody?

Lynn: I believe I used that term when I was describing how I needed to get him away from the kitchen table after he spit up.

Eric asked me if Cody had changed from when he first started with me. I explained that around the spring of 2008 he changed from a happy, smiling child to one who was sullen, quiet, and cried easily. I said I was worried about autism, as that is often manifested by a change in a young child's demeanor and behavior. I explained that I didn't want to scare his parents with that possible diagnosis, so I thought I'd monitor him a bit more. I described my strategies for dealing with his behavior and helping him interact with the other kids.

Eric: You heard some testimony about his reluctance to come to day care and his wanting to stay with his parents. Did you see some of that?

Lynn: A lot of kids just don't want to say goodbye to their parents in the morning. They get clingy, may sometimes cry. Everybody goes through phases. Cody would usually have a little crying period. Dad was usually the one who dropped him off, so for his dad's benefit he would cry. Once dad was gone, he knew crying would get him nowhere, so he stopped within a few minutes.

Eric: You said when Cody spit up at the table, you had to do something. Describe again how you managed that.

Lynn: My first concern was to make sure that he was okay, which he was. He wasn't vomiting. It wasn't throwing up. It was either a gag reflex or something not sitting right from the food he ate. I didn't know what was causing it; I was trying to figure that out. But I had to get him away from the table and clean up the table so none of the other kids touched bodily fluids. I disinfected it as much as I could with the other kids there. Then I would clean him up.

Eric: You've heard some testimony about having a headache on one of the days.

Lynn: Yes. That was on August 27, the first day Annie was here. It was a bad headache. I knew I could make it through the day, but at some of the quiet times I put my head down for a few minutes. That helped, but it was an all-day headache which is part of the reason I remember August 27 so well.

Eric ended by clarifying that, since all of this happened and the kids left my care, I hadn't done any more day care. I said yes, and that there had been a huge void in my life.

My heart sped up as Cattanach took over for cross-exam. She started out with the large room diagram. "Is this the position that everything was in on August and September of 2008?"

"For August it was," I answered. "For the second week in September I changed the position of the climber." I explained how I had to move the climber due to the new TV set up. I discussed how the climber could change into four different configurations; the climber was in the corner in an L-shape when Annie attended.

Cattanach spent a lot of time asking about the furniture and accessories in the day care room and their placement. She was determined to get the climber into a position where Annie's claim of seeing the diaper changing area was possible. I chuckled to myself at this zeal, knowing there was no way possible, no matter where that climber was, to see what Annie claimed. "Have you ever had the L-shaped moved over like that so that the stairs are coming forward toward the bath?"

I knew what she was trying to do. By having the climber in a configuration where the stairs were coming straight out toward the bathroom, she thought Annie's view would be possible. I said I had not had the climber in that position since there wasn't enough room there.

I then had to suppress a laugh when she threw out a photo showing the climber with the stairs coming straight out.

However, that photo was from early 2006, prior to our basement being fully finished, when the day care space was upstairs in our home. I told her so; it was obvious I was telling the truth as the paint color in this photo was different from the basement paint, and Miles was shown in the photo as much younger. She clearly didn't expect that response and became visibly flustered, quickly withdrawing the photo and that line of questioning. Did she think this photo would be the smoking gun showing Annie's view was possible? Cattanach had never been in my home; she only relied on photos and testimony from others as to the arrangement of my day care space. Nonetheless, she sure tried to place the climber into a position where she thought Annie's claim could be true. I wish I had been assertive enough at this time to call her on that.

Cattanach switched her questioning to the Miles bruises. "You have no recollection of Miles having those injuries or talking to his parents about them?"

"No."

Cattanach: In talking with a number of the parents, and Cathy Leaverton specifically, and Tina Reese, you told them that you were too rough with Cody; is that true?

Lynn: I meant when I was hearing all these people say these terrible things about what I was doing with Cody, I was racking my brain trying to think what I could have done to cause that impression. The only thing I could think that I did improper was when I moved him from his chair after his spitting-up issues; how the kids perceived me being too rough with him when pulling him away from the table. If I used the word "rough," I meant when I firmly and quickly pulled him away from the table.

Cattanach kept coming back to my "rough" term and how I told that to many people. She also said I admitted, in the detective interview, to get frustrated with Cody. I tried to clarify that I was frustrated with the spitting up and behavior change issues with him, and bothered by the parents' lack of concern. She kept asking about the responses I gave to Detective Johnson. That interrogation was not something I wanted to relive, and I couldn't give an accurate answer to everything I had said at the time. She hinted that it

276

was strange that I couldn't spit out verbatim the answers I gave a year-and-a-half ago. She started quoting from the interview transcript and asking me to confirm that I had made these incriminating statements. She made a big deal out of me not outright denying any abuse but rather trying to come up with explanations as to what I thought the kids were seeing.

Lynn: I'm not denying that injuries happened at my place. There was never any abuse that I did. After hearing everything Detective Johnson was throwing at me, I didn't know what to say.
Cattanach: You could have said I didn't hurt the children.
Lynn: I said I never intentionally hurt a child.
Cattanach: Intentionally.

Cattanach kept hammering home that "intentionally" word. I thought that was an element of what I was charged with (causing bruises to a face or banging a child's head into the wall sure sound like intentional acts to me), so I wanted to make it clear that I did not intentionally ever harm a child. Had I ever unintentionally harmed a child? Harmed is too harsh a word, but, in over twenty-five years, of course there have been incidents. I stuck a child with a diaper pin. I have tripped over children, or they have tripped over me. I have backed into kids standing behind me and stepped on feet. I clipped finger or toenails too deep. Of course, I've always felt bad about those few instances. So I really couldn't say I had never hurt a child, but I could honestly deny intentional harm.

Cattanach: Did Detective Johnson show you some photos?

Lynn: She showed me a series of photos of Miles with bruises.

Cattanach: Do you recall her asking for an explanation for these injuries?

I looked directly at Detective Johnson at the prosecutor's table when I answered, "I recall her asking outright, 'What did you do to Miles?'" Johnson sheepishly nodded her head. "Johnson told me that those bruises were reported to have occurred in my care. As a general statement, I said if I'm doing this, I shouldn't be working with kids. I meant that in general, as if someone was doing it, they shouldn't be working with children."

Cattanach was critical of me for not making any outright denials of abuse during that interview. However, any attempts I had made to deny allegations were brushed off by Johnson; she would quickly change the direction of her questioning any time I said "no" or gave a direct denial. Johnson had bombarded me with "all the kids are saying this" falsehoods, putting me in the terrible position of trying to make explanations. How could I defend myself upon hearing such shocking claims, from children that I loved as my own?

As promised, Cattanach brought up the subject of my marriage. "Between 2006 and 2008, you had some domestic problems of your own; is that true?"

She made it sound like it was an ongoing problem for two years in this same period as all the abuse allegations, when in fact it was a short time in summer of 2006, after the alleged Miles bruises and well before any allegations regarding Cody. "My husband and I had some issues the summer of 2006, which we worked out and resolved." She tried to get me to say I was under stress during this period; I didn't fall for her manipulation of the facts.

Cattanach was finally done with her cross-exam. Her attempt to get the climber in a position to match Annie's claim had failed. I felt good about that. However, she tried to nail me on the statements I made in the interview. I always felt that would be my undoing, and I had an uneasy feeling about it still. I knew she was a shrewd prosecutor with persuasive powers who could hang me with the quotes from the interview.

Eric had a few re-direct questions for me, mostly to confirm statements made by Detective Johnson in the interview. "Do you remember the detective saying things like, 'I have all these little kids pretty much telling me the same story? You bang his head against the wall, you're mean, and you do things to them.'"

"I remember that," I replied.

Eric continued. "Do you remember them saying they're looking for an explanation as to why, quote, 'you're beating the crap out of the kids?' Do you remember them saying, 'unless there's a confession to something, we're going to have to come away from here thinking that beatings are going on here on a daily basis?'"

Although I didn't remember everything from the horrid experience, those statements were seared in my mind. I could see that Eric closed with those statements to drive home the fact that Johnson was relentless in her quest for explanations, and I had succumbed to the pressure.

Darlene was the last witness. Eric only asked her if she subbed for me on occasion, and what type of equipment I had. She was prohibited from giving any character testimony about me. She was angry about her limited role as a defense witness; there were many things she wanted to say regarding me and my role as a child care provider.

The trial was over. All evidence had been presented. Only closing arguments remained, which were scheduled for the next morning.

Eric and I shared a few thoughts before leaving for the day. He was on his way to prepare his closing statement. I trusted him to develop a convincing argument. Eric was lax in much of his defense, failing to seize upon witnesses' stories or inconsistent accounts of events; hopefully by now he realized that and would bring it up in closing. I knew that Cattanach could easily spin things her way.

Chapter 29

Closing Statements

*T*he morning of Thursday, March 4, 2010, arrived. I am amazed I had slept at all. The fate of the rest of my life would likely be determined today by the jury verdict. If found guilty, would I be immediately taken to jail? Eric assured me there would be a sentencing hearing first, but I had no confidence in anything regarding the court system. With a heavy heart, I left for the courthouse, wondering if I would ever come back home. After all, I faced a potential fourteen years in prison.

I still had a courtroom full of supporters, for which I was grateful. They knew I was anxious and nervous, and tried their best to reassure me. I appreciated that, but felt that the black cloud hanging over my head was getting darker by the minute.

Judge Ehlke asked counsel if they had any last minute items to discuss. After a brief dialogue about exhibits and jury instructions, the jury filed in.

Ehlke began the jury instructions as he did the trial, with a list of the four counts of which I was charged. He reminded the jury that the defendant was not required to prove innocence. "The law presumes every person charged with the commission of an offense to be innocent. The burden of establishing every fact necessary to constitute guilt is upon the State. Before you can return a verdict of guilty, the evidence must satisfy you beyond a reasonable doubt that the defendant is guilty. If you can reconcile the evidence upon any reasonable hypothesis consistent with the defendant's innocence, you should do so and return a verdict of not guilty. The term 'reasonable doubt' means a doubt based upon reason and common sense. It is a doubt for which a reason can be given, arising from a fair and rational consideration of the evidence or lack of evidence. While it is your duty to give the defendant the benefit of every reasonable doubt, you are not to search for doubt. You are to search for the truth."

I thought the reasonable doubt description and instruction was good. However, Ehlke then threw in the last phrase about not searching for doubt but searching for the truth. That seemed strange—didn't that lower the State's burden of proof? The reasonable doubt standard is constitutionally guaranteed, but this extra language seemed to diminish that standard by suggesting that doubt be ignored in favor of a search for supposed truth. Why couldn't the jurors just be told to give me the benefit of every reasonable doubt (of which there was plenty)?

Ehlke clarified that remarks of the attorneys were not evidence. "If the remark suggested certain facts not in evidence, disregard the suggestion. Consider carefully the closing arguments of the attorneys, but their arguments, conclusions, and opinions are not evidence. Draw your own conclusions from evidence and decide upon your verdict according to the evidence."

The jury did not have their notebooks during closing arguments. That was good; I knew Cattanach could exaggerate and twist things, as well as speculate, and I didn't want the jury to be able to take notes on those types of inaccurate statements.

Cattanach's closing argument was awful. It seemed to go on forever. She regaled the jury with her rampant speculation, implying that I was taking stress in my life out on the children. She stated that I was frazzled from having the day care in my home and not having any escape from it.

She still tried her darndest to prove there was a view into the bathroom. The moving of the climber due to the TV placement became something I did to hide the "view."

I wanted to laugh at some of her actions during this closing statement. She demonstrated her theory on how I changed diapers: I wasn't standing directly at the diaper table but instead was standing back and sticking my head out of the bathroom door to check on the other kids at the same time. Apparently, that allowed me to change Cody's diaper while simultaneously banging his head on the wall and giving Annie a view to that, all the while paying attention to the kids in the other room. I would have had to have an eight-foot rubber neck in order to do what she described. Did she not realize how ridiculous she sounded? It was Saturday Night Live-esque. She took a small baby doll and pounded it on the jury bar, insinuating that's how I harmed the children, even though the smallest child I had in care weighed well over thirty pounds. "Abuse, abuse, abuse!" she chanted. She referred to the "poor" children and the "hell" they were going through. I almost felt at any time she would break into Billy Flynn's character from the musical *Chicago* and belt out *Razzle Dazzle*.

Eric's closing argument was weak. He talked about my nice day care setting, good toys, and projects. That should not have been the focus. He never presented the forty-pound bag of salt analogy to counter Cattanach's absurd demonstration of pounding the small doll on the jury bar.

Eric presented his "spark and wildfire" analogy. He reminded the jury that Annie admitted to being on the climber stairs when she claimed to have seen the abuse. He told the jurors to closely analyze the photos of the day care.

He gave what I thought was a half-hearted attempt to discredit Holly and her inconsistent stories about the facial bruises to Miles. He did a better job pointing out that the abuse Cody was alleged to have suffered was never substantiated by any medical professional.

Eric's closing line was, "Your task is to separate allegations that Lynn Moller's an imperfect day care provider from allegations that she committed crimes against children, and the standard is reasonable doubt."

Because the prosecution had the burden of proof, Cattanach had the chance of rebuttal. She chided Eric for failing to defend the second incident that Annie claimed. The proper context in which I described myself as being "rough" or "frustrated" with Cody was ignored; she dwelled on my admission of those terms. She seized upon my phrasing that I never intentionally harmed children, rather than denying abuse. Again, how could what I was charged with be anything less than deliberate? How does one unintentionally bang heads into a wall? Cattanach claimed my acts were reckless. "You don't have to find she did it intentionally. That's not what this is. It's reckless abuse. Her conduct is reckless. Shaking a child, pounding a child's head, it's reckless and it caused injury. You don't have to find that she intended to do it." Yet, her final words were, "Please find the defendant guilty of intentionally causing the fingertip contusions to Miles' head. Please find the defendant guilty of abusing Cody repeatedly." She was talking out of both sides of her mouth—one minute I was accused of reckless acts and then the next minute it was intentional.

Cattanach's words were the last that the jury heard before deliberating. It became apparent to me that a trial is not about finding the truth or justice, but rather who can put on the best show. Cattanach was a master storyteller; my attorney, not so much.

Hearing Cattanach's closing statement felt like a coffin being nailed shut with me in it. Her words were devastating to my defense. I felt vulnerable sitting there. I did not feel my attorney was passionate about my defense. As many people would say to me after the trial, "I don't have a law degree, but I could have done a better job."

Closing arguments ended just before lunch. A meal was ordered for the jurors, who would then begin deliberations. We were told we could wait at the courthouse, or leave if reachable by phone and could be back within ten minutes. Sometimes the jurors had questions that would require all parties to come back to the courtroom before the verdict was rendered. Many of my supporters went out for lunch and then came back to wait with me. I could not eat a thing.

One area that I kept mulling over was how the jury, in their deliberations, would know which charges went with which day or alleged injury. Judge Ehlke had given the four counts and the dates I was charged with in the jury instructions, but there was not a clear outline of what went with what. My attorney especially, in his closing statement, should have given a definite accounting of the dates and charges and compared them to what was presented in trial. For instance, count one, August 27, should have been labeled "Annie's X-ray vision view into the bathroom changing area." Okay, it wouldn't really have been called that, but the jury needed to know that was what started everything, and all the other counts were built on that. I was certain the jury would acquit me on that first count, as, despite Cattanach's attempts otherwise, our defense did prove that Annie's claimed view was impossible. But I sure wish Eric would have spent more time emphasizing that and how everything else was built and dependent upon that shaky foundation. He should have pounded home the fact that the base was weak and would not support the addition of the subsequent charges.

Chapter 30

The Verdict

*S*hortly after deliberations began, we received word that the jury had some questions. All parties convened back in the courtroom to discuss these, outside the presence of the jury. The first question was, "Before Lynn Moller was interviewed by Detective Johnson, was she told she didn't have to talk to her or that she could have someone there, like an attorney?"

There was some debate between the parties on how to answer this. They decided on the wishy-washy statement that "the evidence properly before you is that which was presented here in court."

The second jury question was, "Will the jury have access to the transcript of Julie Johnson's interview with Lynn Moller?" After discussion, Judge Ehlke said the answer to that would be, "You will not be provided with a copy of the transcript as that was not introduced as evidence." I hoped these questions meant that the jury was considering the interview as a coercive tactic by Johnson.

The last question confirmed my earlier concern that the jury did not know which count went with which date. "Counts one and two are both for August 27, 2008, but do not indicate which incident is which. Please clarify whether count one was the incident in the bathroom at the changing table." So, going into deliberations, the jury admitted that they were not clear on what charge was for what date. How was that fair, for either side? Even Judge Ehlke, on hearing this jury question, said, "This is one I thought they might ask. I anticipated they might ask this question."

Well, Judge, if you had anticipated this, why didn't you more clearly delineate the charges during jury instructions? In response to their query, the jury was told that yes, count one was the incident referring to the bathroom changing table.

I suspected, that, based on his lack of defense, my attorney wasn't even clear on all the charges and their corresponding dates. I would later have this suspicion confirmed.

The afternoon dragged on. I paced the courthouse halls, went outside for a walk, tried to read the paper, or talk with family and friends, but my mind was a million miles away. I did not have a good feeling. At 5:25 p.m. we were notified that the jury had another question, so we gathered back in the courtroom. Judge Ehlke read the question: "We have reached a unanimous decision on three of the four counts, but are still divided on count number four. Can you give us guidance on the procedure?" Discussion among the judge and attorneys resulted in a direction to the jury to keep deliberating.

I was nervous after hearing this last jury question. The first three counts had been decided. I figured that if I was found not guilty on all of those, there would be no way I could be guilty of the fourth one. However, if I was found guilty on any or all of the first three, it would be harder to decide that last count, which seemed to be happening. I expressed this concern to my friends and family who were still waiting with me, and they reluctantly agreed.

I felt the world closing in on me now. My dad, bless his heart, gathered everyone, and assured me that whatever happened, I had everyone's unwavering support, love, and belief in my innocence, and we would get through this. I certainly appreciated the kind words, but inside I was still riddled with anxiety.

Finally, at 6:55 p.m., the bailiff appeared to tell us that there was a verdict. I sauntered nervously into the courtroom. The die was cast, there's no turning back, what would be would be, and other defeatist idioms danced through my head. Before the jury came in, Judge Ehlke admonished everyone that there were to be no outbursts. "None of us know what the verdict is. I remind everyone this is a courtroom, so act accordingly." Never in the two-and-a-half days of trial had anyone in my audience done anything to cause a problem, but I suppose the judge had to give that warning anyway.

The jury panel entered the courtroom. The jury foreman passed the verdicts to the bailiff, who gave them to the judge to read. Unlike all courtroom television shows I had ever seen, the judge did not ask me to stand while the verdicts were pronounced. That was good, as my rubber legs likely would not have supported me.

My hopes soared when I was found not guilty of the first charge—the one based on Annie's X-ray vision. The jurors obviously realized her claim of seeing in the bathroom was impossible.

Those same hopes were instantly dashed, however, when guilty verdicts were revealed for the other three charges. I broke down in tears and collapsed into Eric. It was even more heartbreaking to see tears from my family and friends, especially my sons. Judge Ehlke declared that there would be a sentencing hearing in two months. I could go home, but the freedom which all my life I had taken for granted now felt as weak as a thin rubber band stretching toward the sentencing hearing and the murky future beyond.

Chapter 31

Pre-Sentence Investigation

I was up most of that night, trying to process what had happened. Family members and friends not in attendance at the time of the verdict needed to be notified. I was on autopilot in contacting them—emotionless and zombie-like. Once the initial shock wore off and the fog lifted from my brain, I thought about all that had transpired in the trial. I had always believed that Annie's initial allegation (count one) would have to be proven in order to make counts two, three, and four stick. How did this house of cards remain standing once the base was pulled? We presented a solid defense to count one, acknowledged by the jury with the not-guilty finding. Did they expect as strong a defense to all the charges? Were the jurors confused about the subsequent charges and dates, as I believed?

Family and friends were much more critical of Eric's performance than I was. They urged me to appeal the conviction. I was fairly certain that I would seek an appeal, but I couldn't dwell on that right now.

I had three guilty verdicts and needed to focus on the upcoming sentencing hearing. As part of the process, a pre-sentence investigation (PSI) had been ordered by Judge Ehlke. Its function was to provide the judge with sufficient information so he could sentence me consistent with the factors required under Wisconsin law: the gravity of the offense, the need to protect the public, and the character of the offender.

I was assigned to a department of corrections probation and parole agent, Marjorie McGraw, who called me a few days after the trial. She explained that she was a neutral party who would examine the case from the perspective of both the "victims" and myself in order to make a sentencing recommendation to the judge. She sent me some paperwork to fill out.

I worked hard on this assignment. The first parts where I discussed my family and background were easy to write. Then came the tough part—composing my version of the offense. It was painful to relive everything as I wrote about it, but I wanted to be thorough about what I experienced. I included specific ways my attorney had disappointed me and doomed my defense, and included information that for whatever reason was not allowed in the trial. I ended my statement by reaffirming my innocence and that I would not show remorse or accept responsibility for harming the children.

Several days after submitting my report, I met with McGraw. What an unpleasant person. She was rude and nasty to me, and asked me to explain my crime. When I told her I didn't do anything, she said she didn't believe that. "The jury found you guilty and there is evidence of you harming the children." So much for considering my side. I left her office in tears and went straight to Eric's office to report her offensive treatment. He said that, while I did still have to meet with her, I did not have to speak to her regarding the offense. I met with her one more time; she was cold to me and just asked which friends and family members she should call.

My sons and Ki met with her. I told my boys they did not need to, but they were adamant about doing so. I was proud of them. I warned them that McGraw was an unlikable figure, but they assured me they could handle her. She asked them if they had ever seen me act inappropriately or violently with a day care child, to which they both responded negatively. Aaron told her, "She is the nicest person I have ever known, and I am not just saying that because she is my mom. She would never do anything like this." Evan stated, "She's an angel. To accuse her of this is wrong; she would never hurt a child. The system doesn't work."

Ki's visit with McGraw had him running through a list of trial errors, and referencing the hysteria that ensued after Annie's first allegation. "They [parents] did not think with calm, normal heads. If one thing doesn't work, does everything else?" He finished his meeting with McGraw by commenting on the possible sentence. "She has already been penalized. She can never work with kids again. Prison would serve absolutely no purpose. You don't need to protect the community from her. She is more of an asset to the community."

McGraw conducted phone interviews with my siblings, dad, friends, and former day care parents. She asked many of them if I could have snapped or if I ever said I wanted out of the child care field; no one could verify those concepts. In mid-April, Eric called me to say that the PSI was completed. McGraw had recommended probation, which was a relief, but she also wanted a six-month jail term imposed as a condition of that probation. My heart dropped. The judge did not have to abide by McGraw's recommendation, but I knew that it would carry a great deal of weight in his ultimate decision. Combined with the nasty remarks I anticipated Cattanach making at the sentencing hearing, I feared the jail sentence was inevitable. Eric sent me a copy of the final PSI, which made for interesting reading. The comments from all my supporters were included, as well as statements from the "victims."

Many of the victim statements were laughable for their unreasonableness. The Jeters claimed they installed a home security system since they were worried about my family retaliating. "We don't let our children play outside unattended. We are afraid for their safety. We believe that Lynn or her family will abduct Annie or Miles and do the unthinkable." How ridiculous was that?

Holly stated that this had been stressful on her family and on her marriage. "We've had arguments over it." I found that quite telling. Seems they hadn't been on the same page through this ordeal. I am positive Holly pushed this along. She had the audacity to tell McGraw that I was a person in crisis and needed help.

Holly also claimed that Miles had a regression in his toilet training toward the end of his time with me. I don't know what she insinuated with this false claim; Miles was nowhere near ready for toilet training when he was with me. Holly had no problem lying to McGraw, an agent of the state. Did she not realize that I was given Miles' medical records in discovery, including documentation that Miles was not toilet trained even a year after leaving my care?

The day care families complained to McGraw that I would not take the plea deal and made them go to trial. Maria Marshall said, "The woman had a chance to take the plea bargain. She had a chance not to put the kids on the stand. She still maintains her innocence even after the trial." Holly Jeter stated, "She was given three chances for a plea bargain to get out of it. Instead she put everyone through a trial." Mark Christie's comment was, "She didn't take the plea. All seven families were put through the court proceedings and jury trial. She knew the kids would have to testify."

Wasn't it my right as an accused to have a trial? They were the ones making me go to court with the false allegations—the burden of proof was on them. Obviously, they had all been told that I was given plea deal opportunities. Did they ever stop to think about why I didn't take the deal? I would have been crazy not to take it if I was guilty; it was essentially a "Get Out of Jail Free" card. Wouldn't you want the person who cared for your child to fight vigorously to prove her innocence? Did these parents think I wanted to spend tens of thousands of dollars on legal fees when, if guilty, I could have taken the deal with no need to pay a lawyer?

Mark Christie, in his interview with McGraw, droned on about how, when he told me that David was leaving my care, my only concern was to get the payment owed me. "To me, it was like she was less concerned of the reason and more concerned about money," he complained. I had tried to get specific information from Mark, but he would not elaborate. He claimed to McGraw that he told me why he pulled David from my care. No, he had not done that, and he admitted as much in his trial testimony: "*It was an uncomfortable, awkward conversation with Lynn because I didn't want to go into specifics. Lynn pressed me on why we were pulling him out. I just said I thought it was a bad situation, and we didn't want our son exposed to that. Lynn was upset. She continued to ask me questions about why we were pulling him out, trying to get specific answers. I didn't want to do that over the phone, or do any more than I had to.*" Had he had been honest with me, I would have acknowledged that he had a legitimate concern and dealt with that; the payment issue would not have been an issue at that time.

Did these parents need to justify the accusations and convictions by making up and exaggerating their claims to McGraw? Tina Reese stated that she saw me on her street the weekend after the trial. "She turned around in the middle of the street when she saw us outside. I don't remember seeing her on our street before. This heightened our awareness of safety. We never felt this way before." The weekend after the trial, I was upset and didn't want to leave my house. Why would I have gone on her street?

Reese also complained to McGraw about the effect the trial had on her kids and how their behavior changed. "The trial was a difficult time. The kids were out of sorts for a while. Tommy is now in therapy to help with trusting adults and caregivers. He has hit a teacher and has acted out. One time he had such a temper tantrum and wouldn't come out of it. She [Lynn] definitely hurt him. Not sure if it was physically or emotionally. I wish she would just tell us what happened so we could deal with it. She won't admit to anything."

How strange that all of Tommy's problems started after leaving my care. He was a sweet, social, cooperative, polite child while in my day care. If he was affected by me, wouldn't his acting-up behavior have manifested while in my care? Tina Reese had even asked me if I would consider keeping the kids for another year; she never would have made that request if Tommy exhibited these troubling behaviors while in my care.

What was with all the lying—before, during, and after the trial? If it wasn't an outright lie, like Reese claiming she saw Cody upset at every morning drop-off, it was a lie by omission, such as Mark Christie and Holly Jeter not telling me the real reasons for pulling their kids. Had they been truthful, I would have invited them to come to the day care space and check out Annie's story for themselves. Even the jury discounted her initial claim.

McGraw's interview with Detective Johnson had Johnson calling the case a slam dunk. "She is not innocent. If I ever have doubts, I don't send it to the DA. It's my job to be a fact finder and I believe we found the facts in this case. People don't admit to something they didn't do. It's a definite no if you didn't do it. She didn't say, 'My God I didn't do it.' She would say it's not intentional. I think she was under a lot of stress and she lost it."

Johnson failed to mention her misleading and deceptive interview tactics to McGraw. How does Johnson's theory of me being under stress and losing it explain all these ongoing episodes of alleged abuse? Stress may cause someone to lash out once or twice, but continuing abusive behavior diminishes the stress factor and turns it into acting intentionally. Again, everything I was charged with was intentional; I don't care if the charge was listed as reckless.

I never admitted to anything. I may have made some feeble statements when overwhelmed by the detectives' lies about all the kids claiming abuse, but I never outright gave a confession or admission that I harmed any kids. Her claim of people not admitting to something they didn't do was a blatant lie. It's well documented that innocent people do confess to crimes they didn't commit, especially if they're subjected to psychologically coercive interrogation tactics.

McGraw even got Dr. Barbara Knox to add her two cents. Knox maintained she was very fair in her assessment, since she couldn't make any statements about the injuries to Cody. Her trial testimony regarding that was, *"I won't say anything to a reasonable degree of medical certainty because the quality of the photo was too blurry, but what I did see in this area was of concern to me for the possibility of a bruise and that when asked when I saw these types of bruises, it would be in fingertip contusion bruises where kids are pulled hard by their ear."* If she couldn't make a certain diagnosis, why didn't she stop talking after her comment about the blurry photos? By adding the next phrase, she was able to insert her opinion that there was the concern for abuse. That abated any "fair assessment" claim.

Knox admitted to McGraw that she had never met any of the children, parents, or the defendant in person. How could she make accurate diagnoses if she never saw the kids? I'll never understand that. I would at least have had some respect for her if she gave the caveat in her testimony that she never saw any of the kids involved in my case and she based her diagnosis on "questionable" photos or other doctors' reports. She only saw these photos and reports after allegations of abuse, not before.

Knox stated that her role in my case was very limited. That is incorrect. Her comments on Miles' "injuries" at the preliminary hearing convinced the judge to have the case proceed to trial: *"The testimony of Dr. Knox is pretty strong evidence that this injury was caused by an adult-sized hand. I don't have any difficulty finding probable cause in this matter."* In addition, Knox's favorite catch phrases at trial likely sealed the conviction on the Miles count.

By virtue of her position, Knox was biased against me. I am glad her position as a child abuse specialist exists. I have no sympathy toward anyone who harms a child, and I am sure she has seen some sad and horrific cases. Accusations involving child abuse must be investigated, but investigators do no favors by creating victims where none exist. Knox's preconceptions that abuse had occurred helped convict me of a crime that never happened.

The last part of the PSI consisted of McGraw's recommendation. She considered my lack of remorse or acceptance of responsibility as huge factors in her decision. "Moller needs to stop pointing fingers and look in the mirror and attempt to correct her behavior which begins with taking responsibility. It is troubling that Moller has stood by her denial in this case. Moller had something going on in her life to cause her to act the way she did to those children. This behavior is out of Moller's character and hard to understand. The truth is, only Moller can help us understand why she acted the way she did, but she is unwilling to give an explanation. Moller owes it to the families to admit her wrongdoing, but no one can force her to do that and she will have to face the consequences for that decision. I do not believe this is a prison case. Ms. Moller has no criminal background and is not a threat to the public. Community supervision is appropriate. I had no intention of requesting jail time along with probation, but due to Moller's lack of responsibility and lack of remorse, I feel a short term of jail is justified."

I wonder what went on in my life to make me "act the way I did to those children." I had a good paying job I loved, a dream day care space, wonderful home and family—would I jeopardize all that to bang kids' heads on the wall? That seemed to be the theory.

I had been in touch with Bob, my first attorney, after the trial. He was aware of the verdict, and expressed regret in the outcome. I told him about the discovery of Dr. Andringa's report. He was upset about that and said that was mishandled. I do believe he would have fought to get that admitted. Bob said that he would try to make an appearance at my sentencing hearing. I appreciated his support.

I thought long and hard about pursuing an appeal. After the sentencing hearing, there would only be twenty days to file an appeal, so a decision had to be made quickly. I knew it was a long shot to prevail on appeal. The Wisconsin Court of Appeals, on average, reversed the criminal conviction in only two percent of the appeals brought before it. It gave great deference to trial court results. The appeal process would also be an expensive and time-consuming endeavor. Nevertheless, I was innocent and this affected the rest of my life. If I didn't go for the appeal, I would regret it down the line.

Financially, though, I didn't know how I would afford another attorney for the appeal process. Legal costs up to this point, combined with my lack of income for almost two years, resulted in the depletion of our savings and retirement accounts, maxed out credit cards, and struggles to provide for my family, Yet, I was not considered "destitute" enough to qualify for a public defender. My dad and grandma generously offered to help; they were in agreement that it was important to try all avenues to clear my name.

Upon recommendation of my friend Rima, I contacted Attorney Tracey Wood for appellate consultation. Tracey had a reputation as one of the best criminal defense attorneys in Madison. She was sympathetic about the outcome of my trial, stating that I had the bad luck to get Cattanach, the pariah of the district attorney's office, as the prosecutor. I immediately regretted not having Tracey for my trial attorney. Tracey informed me that the Court of Appeals was an error-correcting court, but only a showing of prejudicial errors made at the trial level would give me a minuscule hope of reversal. I was aware of this and gave her a list of the flawed trial and pre-trial events. Tracey's first order of business was to order all the transcripts from the case. After review of those, she would be better able to make a determination on appealable issues.

I also felt I had a strong argument for a claim of ineffective assistance of counsel, since Eric's performance at trial fell below the standard guaranteed me by the Sixth Amendment. Eric was a wonderful person, and an experienced attorney, but he was not up to speed on my case. I realize he was put in a bad position, coming into this case late, but that didn't excuse his lack of preparation. He should have insisted on postponing the trial. I wanted the trial over, but I would rather have had a fully prepared attorney. Eric had a duty to zealously represent me, and he failed in that respect. He missed key aspects of things to defend and critical questions to ask, and overlooked crucial elements of proceedings that had occurred before his involvement. Eric, with his grandfatherly nature, did not perform well in confronting the witnesses or standing up to the aggressive tactics by the prosecution.

I informed Eric of my decision to appeal, including the ineffective assistance claim. He told me to do whatever I needed to; he was not offended. He said that he had learned a lesson—he would never again take over a case from another attorney. That was of little solace to me. But he was still my attorney, and, with McGraw's recommendation to the judge looming, Eric and I strategized for the upcoming sentencing hearing. I hoped that McGraw's jail suggestion would be mitigated by the testimony of my family, friends, day care families, and other child care providers. Those who couldn't testify had provided letters to McGraw and/or the judge. Deep down, however, I had feeling that the sentence was already cast in stone.

Out of curiosity, I called Dr. Andringa's clinic on the off-chance that I could learn when Holly Jeter had made the appointment for Miles for those May 2006 bruises. I didn't know if clinics kept that type of information, and, if they did, I suspected privacy issues would prevent them from sharing the information with me. Thus, I was surprised when I was told that the appointment was made at 4:30 on May 15. My attendance records showed that Holly picked up Miles after 4:30 on that date. She called the doctor's office prior to arriving at my house; obviously, she had knowledge of the bruises being present on Monday. I wish I had the foresight to make this inquiry prior to the trial, as it would have given us even more ammunition with which to impeach Holly about the timeline of Miles' bruises. But, again, we only received Dr. Andringa's report five days before trial, not giving us time to take advantage of it.

Chapter 32

The Sentencing Hearing

he sentencing hearing was held on the afternoon of May 6, 2010. My family and I made yet another trek to my least favorite building in Madison. The lobby outside of the courtroom swarmed with my friends and relatives. Many were there to testify on my behalf, and others were there to observe and be there for me. My heart swelled at this show of support and I became teary-eyed. I gathered everyone together before heading into the courtroom to profess my gratitude for their steadfast support, despite my felony convictions and all the terrible things they had heard about me.

I noticed the arrival of Tina Reese; she tried to slink by my group to make her way into the courtroom. Entering the courtroom, I saw that Marty and Holly Jeter were seated in the first row of the gallery, accompanied by Mark Kerman. Reese took her place next to them. The Marshalls were not in attendance. My group took up the rest of the available seating, with my brothers and good friends sitting right behind my antagonists. I took my usual place with Eric at the defendant's table, while Cattanach, Detective Johnson, and

Marge McGraw sat at the prosecution's table. There was no way that McGraw was the neutral party she claimed to be; sitting there next to Cattanach was an obvious testament to that.

Cattanach began by asking the judge that any testimony on my behalf address only sentencing factors, character of the defendant, and gravity of the offense. "Those are the things that you should be considering rather than their belief of her guilt or innocence, their belief of the evidence at trial, their belief of your performance, my performance, or Attorney Schulenburg's performance, treatment by the detective, that sort of thing."

Judge Ehlke agreed with her. "We're here at a sentencing and the purpose of the sentencing is to provide the court with as much information as possible to make determinations about those factors which are relevant to sentencing. We had a jury trial and the jury returned a verdict, so I agree that those types of things you're talking about, Ms. Cattanach, are not the subject of proper discourse here."

I swear I could hear collective groans from the gallery. "There goes what I want to say" is what most people were thinking. I know everyone wanted to comment on the mistakes made in the trial. From Cattanach's list about what to not allow people to speak of, she sure seemed aware of the problematic areas from this case.

She then said the State would offer no witnesses. What, none of those parents had the guts to get up and talk? That said a lot to me.

We proceeded with my witnesses. Fifteen family members, friends, day care colleagues, and former day care parents all pleaded for a lenient sentence. It was humbling to hear all the kind words said about me, but, as I glanced at the judge, it was apparent he was not paying attention. I suspect he had already made his mind up about the sentence, and listening to my supporters was just a legal requirement to fulfill. My friend Lynn said to me after the hearing, "I felt like he wasn't paying any attention to me. I had to use his title at the end to make sure he looked at me and acknowledged that I was speaking."

Cattanach gave her statement after all my witnesses were done. I felt like I was reliving her awful closing argument. "She had an opportunity to accept responsibility. She wanted a trial. She had a trial and she was found guilty of three of the four offenses. I don't believe the fact that she had a trial should be held against her, but her denial or any form of acceptance of responsibility should be held against her. I think that's what makes her even more of a danger because she will not accept responsibility for the actions.

"Regarding the character of the defendant, she accepts no responsibility. She has no remorse. She blames everyone else. She blames Annie, who just reported what she saw, she blames the police for their brutality, hostility, and basically the way she describes it, you'd think Detective Johnson pistol whipped her to get her to make the statements that she says."

She had no right to comment on my feelings about that interview. That was a subjective experience, and I did feel whipped. Maybe someone like Cattanach, with her domineering personality, would have told those detectives where to go, but that was not in my nature to do so.

Cattanach continued. "I think jail time is appropriate, warranted, and necessary because until there is acceptance, until there is remorse, she is a danger to the community." She argued for ten months of jail time, four years of probation, and no Huber (Wisconsin's work release) for the jail time. "If she is given Huber, we all know she will immediately be given home detention. I think to impress upon the defendant the severity of these offenses, to make her understand what she did was horrendous, Huber is not appropriate.

"What I found disturbing is that these parents are putting themselves through absolute torture saying 'I should have known better.' Some of the parents go on to say that 'I feel like a terrible parent and this stays with me. I should have known.'"

All these parents never knowing anything was wrong? That's because nothing was. Would they all have been in la-la land if abuse occurred? They all arrived and picked up at different times of the day. I welcomed drop-in visits, and there was actually a licensing requirement that permitted parents to visit and observe my program's operations at any time during open hours. I had older kids in attendance who surely would have said if something was amiss, including Cody's older brother, Steven. In addition to licensing visits, I had the food program staff that made unannounced visits. Miles had a physical therapist who worked with him once a week at my house. David had a speech therapist who made a couple visits at my house. My own family was in and out during day care hours. Had I been such a habitual child abuser, it would have been impossible for abusive behavior to go unnoticed with all the people coming and going. Someone's radar would have been up if only through gut instincts; one's body can pick up bad vibrations. In my many years of providing child care, a majority of the parents had told me their gut feelings played a big part in their decision to enroll their kids with me. That would work the same way if something was not right. There was no inner antennae rising with any of the parents because there was nothing of concern.

At trial, Tina Reese attempted to say that she had had the urge to remove Tommy before all these accusations came out, claiming that she couldn't put her finger on anything. Sorry, but actions speak louder than words. If she had any concerns, she never would have asked if Tommy could re-enroll for the fall, or if I would consider keeping him for another year beyond that.

Cattanach blathered on, referring to the hell that Cody went through every day from February to September 2008. Her exaggerations and lies emerged again—now it was February? Every day? That child would be dead if I did what she claimed for that length of time. She alleged that, since Miles' facial injuries were from 2006, more than two years of abuse occurred. Yet no one knew?

Eric argued for a term of probation only, citing no need to protect the community from me. I was pleased when he brought up as ridiculous the Jeters' fear that I planned to abduct Annie and Miles and do the unthinkable. When talking about the need for punishment, Eric stated that there seemed to be an inappropriate revenge factor by the parents in their requests for jail time. He gave an accurate description of how I already was punished—loss of income, respect, labeled a maltreater, and the loss of career and the chance to care for kids in the future. "That is substantial punishment by itself. To be deprived of that forever means that you're reminded every time you see a child that you can no longer do that." He acknowledged sadness and loss and unhappiness on the other side with the parents involved, but argued that that doesn't provide a need to lock someone up. "In summary, Your Honor, there should be some reason to impose jail, some reason linked to the public or to the person who needs it. In this case I don't see the reason, and I ask that the court impose no jail at all."

Again, Cattanach had the last word. "I believe incarceration is warranted to impress upon the defendant the severity because she does not understand how she has impacted each of these children, their families, and the rest of their lives. It is severe in nature and jail time is appropriate, and I also would ask that that jail time be forthwith." I'm sure that forthwith request was thrown in for spite.

She wanted to see me hauled off to jail right at the end of this hearing in front of my friends and family.

Judge Ehlke spoke about his response to letters he received or the PSI interviews where my supporters claimed that I had poor legal representation. "In many of the materials supplied, there are comments about Mr. Schulenburg, and how the jury verdict would have been different with a different attorney. I categorically reject those claims. Based on my observations, this case was very well tried on both sides. There's nothing about the record which should undercut anyone's confidence in the jury's verdict. In this case, the jury deliberated thoroughly based on a full and fair presentation of the evidence. The jury has spoken, and the jury found Ms. Moller guilty. This is an established fact in these proceedings, and any claim by Ms. Moller or others is notwithstanding. I think Ms. Moller's inability to come to terms with what happened is significant here. Despite the defendant's and others' protestations to the contrary, in my view the facts of this case are indisputable.

"When Annie reports what she saw, she was six years old, old enough to understand what she was observing, and I understand the questions about angles and so on, but she is reporting that she's seeing things. She had no reason to make up anything about Cody. I don't think it's coincidence that two years earlier, Miles' parents had taken pictures of bruising on his face. To me, that's indisputable proof and the jury found that as well. The photo evidence is indisputable. The photograph was taken. Dr. Knox testified that the injuries were consistent with adult inflicted fingertip contusion injury."

Ehlke sure liked the term "indisputable." And, um, Judge? Were you at the same trial? Do you remember that I was not found guilty on all counts? Didn't Annie admit upon questioning that she only heard something?

Eric: Could you see his head bump against the wall?
*Annie: **No.***
Eric: But you heard something thinking that it was?
Annie: Yes.

Ehlke continued. "I do believe the PSI writer had it about right in the recommendation. It's obviously a probation case, but I do believe some amount of jail time is appropriate. I think the gravity of the offense is high. We have three felony convictions. I think that Ms. Moller's failure to express remorse is also significant. And I think in this case, deterrence to others in the child care industry is a factor to be considered."

He placed me on probation for three years, with the six months of jail time as a condition of that probation. He did not follow Cattanach's recommendation for no Huber, meaning that I would be eligible for the electronic monitoring/home detention program. Other conditions of the probation were to have no contact with any of the victims or their families, or with Dr. Knox, and not to care for any children under the age of twelve. Fortunately, he clarified that that did not apply to my family members or relatives.

He said the State would have ninety days to submit any proposed restitution order. I could imagine the bogus claim that would come in for this.

The jail time was not ordered forthwith, much to Cattanach's disappointment, I'm sure. The jail sentence was set to begin in two months on July 5.

Ehlke ended the hearing by asking me if I understood about the appeal notice and emphasized that I only had twenty days to file the notice of appeal. He wished me good luck. I wasn't sure how to take that.

I thought about the statement Ehlke had made at the beginning of the hearing: *"We're here at a sentencing and the purpose of the sentencing is to provide the court with as much information as possible to make determinations about those factors which are relevant to sentencing."* Hardly. He had his mind made up before even entering the courtroom. This was clear from his noticeable lack of attention to my witnesses. It was a waste of time for my friends and family to testify. I greatly appreciated their efforts and bravery in coming forth to speak on my behalf, but it meant nothing to the judge. Their words fell on deaf ears.

I had already resigned myself to the jail aspect, somewhat comforted knowing that it would be home detention. Mainly I was relieved that there was no prison sentence. I found it amusing that the jail time was ordered partly as a deterrent to other potential "head-banging child care providers." My supporters, however, were more distraught than I was, some to the point of tears. My mellow, easy-going Uncle Don, a pastor, was so upset that he triggered a bailiff escort from the courtroom when he yelled, "This is ridiculous! This is a kangaroo court!"

I assured everyone that I would be okay, and announced that I would appeal the convictions. Over the next week, I wrote thank you notes to those who had attended or testified at this hearing.

Two weeks after the sentencing hearing, I received a letter from a local attorney. "Holly and Marty Jeter, parents of Miles, have sought my assistance in seeking compensation for Miles for the injuries and damages which he sustained on or about May 16, 2006, while he was under your care. Please forward this letter immediately to the insurance company that provided insurance coverage to you in May 2006, and ask them to contact me."

Well, the Jeters wasted no time trying to get money. What injuries and damages were there, anyway? I wondered if an underlying motivation for the abuse allegations against me was the possibility of a monetary payoff. After all, Holly also had a pending claim for compensation through the National Vaccine Injury Compensation Program.

I gave the letter to my insurer, American Family. Never was I so glad that my insurance company denied a claim.

While I had accepted the conditional jail term imposed by the judge, I didn't want to have to serve that until my appeal was decided, in my optimistic hope that I would prevail. Eric filed a motion to stay the sentence, in order to provide a temporary suspension of the sentence while the appeal was pending. Eric timed this motion so the hearing would be held while Cattanach was out on maternity leave, hinting that we had a much better chance of a favorable response to our motion with a different prosecutor. On June 24, 2010, which would be my last in-person meeting with Eric, we attended the hearing to address the stay. Deputy DA Judy Schwaemle appeared for the State. Detective Johnson sat next to her. Why did she need to be there? Would I never be free of that dreadful woman?

Schwaemle gave no objection to our motion. Judge Ehlke ordered the stay, and cancelled the July 5 jail start date.

I had met Schwaemle earlier at a pre-trial hearing when she filled in, and I was impressed with her. She was a prosecutor, but at least she demonstrated compassion and consideration for me as a human being, something I had never felt with Cattanach or Mades in the role. Prosecutors are the most powerful officials in the criminal justice system with vast, seemingly unlimited resources. I could never buy their complaints that they were underfunded and understaffed. My experience with Cattanach showed that winning a case was far more important than seeking justice. In theory, I appreciate the role of prosecutors in our adversarial justice system, and there are those who handle their work with honesty and integrity. I was not fortunate enough to land one of those prosecutors. I could not respect the liberties Cattanach took with her speculations and conjectures, especially rampant in her closing argument, and, as I would learn, in her sidebars with the judge. Her improper and misleading statements were treated as evidence in summation to the jury. Her nasty tone and references to the "poor children" and the "hell" they were going through made me seem a monster. Her misquotes of my statements condemned me. I recalled Cattanach's other cases, reinforcing my belief that the power she wielded in her prosecutorial position led to a win-at-all-costs attitude.

Cattanach's dramatic, over-the-top, closing argument became one of my family's favorite things to parody—acting out her speculations such as how I banged heads or how I would change diapers. We rarely referred to her by her proper name in our household; similar to the Harry Potter stories with "He Who Must Not Be Named." This was a coping mechanism akin to gallows humor, allowing us to deflect discomfort from a painful situation. Had Cattanach shown veracity in her prosecution of me, our criticism and disrespect of her would not have been justified.

In early August, 2010, Eric forwarded a letter to me from Mark Kerman. It was a claim for restitution from the Marshalls. I recalled at the sentencing hearing that the DA's office had ninety days to submit a claim. Kerman acknowledged in his letter that this case was under appeal, but he wanted to get the claim in within that ninety-day period. I couldn't believe the bogus claim that appeared. Kerman's letter gave a breakdown of amounts the Marshalls demanded (since the Marshalls were now divorced, the amounts were divided among them):

Lost wages for medical appointments, counseling, establishing new child care: $2,253
Medical bills beyond insurance: $460
Prepaid costs of child care: $5,880

The total was close to $9,000. What the heck was "pre-paid costs of child care?" No documentation was included with this restitution demand. Eric immediately objected to this and requested a hearing. The burden of demonstrating the amount of loss would be on the Marshalls, and detailed documentation for their claim would be required. Judge Ehlke stayed the restitution issue until a decision on the appeal was made. As with the Jeters, again I thought, was the pursuit of the child abuse charges by the Marshalls seen as a potential way to get money?

Chapter 33

Reading Transcripts

*T*he court reporters had sixty days from the date of the sentencing hearing to prepare and make available the transcripts from all the court proceedings. There had been four different court reporters for my trial and pre-trial proceedings. By the end of summer 2010, three of the four reporters had submitted their transcripts. I retrieved copies of these from Tracey. While I did not want to relive the trial, I was anxious to read these transcripts, especially the sidebars with the judge in which I was not included. I suspected a lot went on in those to which I would not agree or be pleased. This suspicion was confirmed right away when I read the transcript of the sidebars that occurred during Eric's cross-exam of Holly Jeter. The first sidebar took place after Eric asked Jeter about Miles' medical issues and her theory that they were linked to vaccinations:

Eric: What were Miles' medical issues then?
Holly: After his six-month immunizations, he was paralyzed from the waist down. To this date it's a spinal cord injury of which they

don't know the cause. So he had brain swelling, had the decom-
pression surgery, so I was always overly careful with him.
Eric: So you link that to the vaccination?
Holly: Yes. That's still a question. Yes.
Eric: Have you taken some action about that to try to recover for it?
Holly: Not so much to recover, but to get answers.
Eric: What was that action you took?
Cattanach: Objection. May we approach?

Sidebar conversation:

Cattanach: Your Honor, after the bruising came to light, further
medical research and expertise was sought, and they say it could
be very likely that this was caused by abuse and consistent with an
abuse sort of thing his spinal injury was. The line of questioning this
is going down, her response is going to be it was linked to abuse,
and he was in Lynn's care. I don't think Attorney Schulenburg
wants this door open.
Eric: Not knowing where that door is going, I'll withdraw
the question.

What the hell?
Cattanach's statement was a blatant lie to Eric and to the judge.
She blamed Miles' medical condition on me! Where was this evi-
dence she mentioned—the medical research and expertise? If she

had this, why wasn't I charged with causing his medical condition? If I was charged with a felony for causing a bruise on his face, I certainly would be charged with causing a major spinal injury. Miles had a documented medical condition with no link or suspicion to an abusive etiology. Cattanach's claim in this sidebar was a brazen attempt to pull the wool over both Eric's and the judge's eyes, and it worked. She succeeded in preventing Eric from questioning Holly Jeter any further about his medical condition.

In this sidebar, Cattanach speculated that Holly would respond to Eric's line of questioning by linking Miles' medical condition to abuse. There is no way Holly would have done that. The medical reports from Miles' myriad of medical professionals would have been thrown in her face with not one mention of an abuse concern. Even when directly asked on a questionnaire during Miles' 2009 hospitalization, when abuse charges were pending against me, she denied that any violence or abuse had affected anyone in her family. The claim submitted to NVICP had no allusion to abuse. Holly also maintained an active presence on Facebook in which she confirmed Miles' Chiari diagnosis, shared her concern about vaccinations, and promoted Chiari support groups.

I was irate when I read this portion of the transcript. Connecting Miles' condition to abuse was a deliberate, malicious lie by Cattanach. She stepped way over the line. Isn't that prosecutorial misconduct? Witnesses in a trial are sworn to tell the truth; obviously, this same concept does not apply to a prosecutor. My already low opinion of her bottomed out after reading this exchange. Eric went along with her, never bothering to fill me in on what transpired in that sidebar. Had I been privy to that conversation, I would have demanded that that "door open" and Cattanach be accountable for her statement. A lot of good it did me now, five months after trial.

The next sidebar happened after Eric showed Holly Jeter the May 15, 2006 Dr. Andringa report.

Sidebar conversation:

Eric: I seek its admission, it's a recorded recollection under 908.03(5). I've shown when it was recorded, that it was contemporaneous with the event, and I don't believe it has to be produced by the person whose recollection is being recorded.

Cattanach: I'd object to foundation. She did not offer the report, she's not saying that some of the stuff is untrue, it's hearsay stated by the doctor in there that is not admissible. I don't believe the document should come in.

Eric: I agree that the statements by the physician are not admissible. I can produce for the Wisconsin Code of Evidence a case that says it doesn't have to be prepared by her, it can be prepared by someone else. I agree, though, that his statements are not.

Cattanach: It has to be accurate. There is no accuracy to it. She's already said that she does not recall making that statement, therefore that statement does not come in.

Judge: Right. I think on the current record it's not admissible, the foundation's not there. If you called Dr. Andringa or someone from his staff you can get this in; it's a matter of it's a statement made for purposes of treatment. But I don't think it can go in the way it's being attempted to go in here.

Had I heard the judge's edict for not allowing the report, I would have insisted that Eric get on the phone to Dr. Andringa's office to get someone to admit that report. All Eric did, however, when I asked him about the report, was tell me that it wasn't allowed because it was hearsay.

I found fault with all Cattanach's arguments for not allowing the report. She objected to foundation, saying Holly Jeter did not offer the report. Well, yes she did, by asking for the medical records for court proceedings. She ordered and permitted the medical records to be released to the Dane County DA and Madison Police Department, thereby making them discovery documents.

Cattanach claimed that the report had no accuracy. Why wouldn't it be accurate? The doctor dictated his notes shortly after the appointment, while fresh in his mind. Why would he include things that were not accurate? Which is more likely, a doctor's report or a forgotten memory from a parent who now sees this report conflicting with the story she told?

Reading these accounts of the sidebars upset me. Again, defendants should be able to hear the sidebars. Now I was even more frustrated with Eric's trial performance.

Autumn arrived, and the fourth court reporter's transcripts were still outstanding. Tracey couldn't start on the appeal until all of these were available. In the meantime, Ki and I became aware of other local and national day care child abuse cases.

A prior local case that always bothered me was that of Audrey Edmunds, a day care provider from Waunakee, Wisconsin, who, in 1995, had a baby die after being in her care. I remember hearing the news stories when this happened. She was charged with first-degree reckless homicide; the cause of death was determined to be Shaken Baby Syndrome. A Dane County jury found her guilty and she was sentenced to eighteen years in prison. She served eleven of those years before the Wisconsin Innocence Project successfully appealed her conviction based on new medical research casting doubt on SBS. I followed that case from the start, always believing it was flawed. I met with Audrey at a signing event for her book, *It Happened to Audrey: A Terrifying Journey from Loving Mom to Accused Baby Killer.* She was no more capable of harming a child than I was, and we connected on our shared experiences. I am proud to call her a good friend now. Although her experience was far worse than mine, I found many parallels in our cases. I am glad that she penned her story; she has motivated me to do the same. Her book should be required reading for everyone, but especially educators, parents of young children, and anyone working in the criminal justice field.

The desire to convict someone accused of child abuse is emotionally and politically overwhelming. The hysterical epidemics of the McMartin Preschool case and other day care scandals resulted in millions of taxpayer dollars spent on those lawsuits, many of which resulted in no convictions. Countless lives were ruined in the process. (I highly recommend viewing the 1995 movie *Indictment: The McMartin Trial*.)

Even in my small corner of the world, there were other child care providers facing abuse allegations. Some of these were dismissed, but not before the providers had to close their businesses for weeks during the investigations, causing emotional turmoil and loss of income. When there were injuries to a child, why was it always the child care provider and not the parents or other parties suspected? Or, as in my case, why were there concerted efforts to create abuse when there was none?

Ki and I attended some court proceedings or parts of trials for other child abuse cases. I was curious to see how other prosecutors, defense attorneys, and judges performed. I admit I now had a natural bias against the prosecution side, but wanted to attempt to view other abuse cases objectively. This was not possible when I saw in these other cases, as in mine, much more favor bestowed upon the State's side. Dr. Knox was the go-to expert in most of these cases, again spewing her favorite catch-phrases: "gravely concerning" and "consistent with abuse."

During this time, I tried to figure out what I wanted to do for employment. I was fifty years old; starting a new career at this stage in my life seemed daunting. Hopes for resuming my child care career were dashed by the trial outcome. The "recalculating" message of the GPS system in my car echoed my feelings. Life had taken a wrong turn, and I needed a new route. With felony convictions, I was unsure if I could obtain any employment. Most job applications come with the dreaded "Have you ever been convicted of a crime?" question. Employers couldn't discriminate against an applicant if the conviction was not substantially related to the job, but I didn't figure there would be many good opportunities for a convicted child abuser.

I learned a great deal from my involuntary immersion into the legal system; could I use my terrible experience to help others in similar circumstances? My radar was on high alert for child abuse and wrongful conviction cases.

I looked into getting a paralegal degree. I checked out some programs at area colleges, and discovered that, since I already had a BS degree, I could obtain a paralegal certificate in a relatively short period. I obtained a student loan and made plans to start school in 2011.

Having made this decision, and knowing that my appeal could take years, I hoped that my family's life could get back on track.

The comfortable, ordinary life we had known and taken for granted was gone. Had the accusations and subsequent convictions only affected me, I could handle that, as bad as it was. However, I did not live in a bubble, and my entire family was sucked down the rabbit hole.

The strain of a false accusation and subsequent conviction had devastating effects on my family. My sons' faith in police and the criminal justice system was shattered. While we rallied and remained strong as a family, I know that hearing lies and terrible stories about their mom did irreparable harm to their psychological health. Their high school years would always be tarnished by our family crisis. They had even begun to wax nostalgic about pre-2008 years. How sad that they had to divide their short lives into before and after periods. Ki was devastated and took this ordeal personally as an attack on his family. He felt terrible that he couldn't protect or defend me against the phony abuse claims.

The outstanding court transcripts from my trial were finally ready at the end of April 2011, more than a year after my trial, and far past the court reporter's duty to serve them within sixty days. That was my first clue of the slowness of the appeal process, and how deadlines were arbitrary and easily extended. If I thought the regular trial procedure was slow as molasses, the appeals process would take that molasses and freeze it.

In this last batch of transcripts was the record from the February 24, 2010 motion hearing, held five days before the trial started. This is the hearing where that second charge supposedly was changed from the September 17, 2008 date to August 27, 2008; I only learned of it at the beginning of the trial and it seemed to magically correspond with Annie's disclosure of the second incident.

The transcript reads:

Judge: I think this is housekeeping, but we need to have a formal arraignment on the Amended Information on 09-CF-1330, which was granted before the original amendment, May 16, 2006, but appears in all other fashion to be the same. The Amended Information in 08-CF-2184 also appears to have the same charges as previously set forth.

Cattanach: It does, Your Honor. However, there is a date that's changed also to accurately reflect the child alleged by the state.

Judge: Right. Mr. Schulenburg, have you received a copy of those?

Eric: I have. We don't need to have it read aloud, plead not guilty to the charges.

So Eric had received a copy of the amendment, but never informed me? He waived the reading of it at that hearing, and the judge made no inquiry of me to confirm that I understood the amendment. The judge's "housekeeping" comment was way off-base, as this altered an entire element of the charge.

With no notice to me, wasn't I deprived of my Sixth Amendment right to be informed of the nature and cause of the accusation against me? I was prepared to defend two charges on the September 17 date. Here I was ambushed at trial when one of the charges was changed to the August 27 date, I had seen no evidence to validate the change, and Annie subsequently testified that there was a second incident. That changed the entire defense and gave me no opportunity to assist Eric in defending against that change in date. How was that fair to me? In this hearing, Cattanach claimed she amended the date to "accurately reflect the child alleged by the state." What did that even mean? She should have clarified exactly what changes she made. Did she take Annie's nonsensical Safe Harbor claim of Emma getting her head banged and change the child to Cody to strengthen her case? To what else would "accurately reflect the child" refer? After all, Annie's words in trial regarding the second Cody incident and her words in Safe Harbor regarding Emma are remarkably similar:

Annie's trial testimony regarding the second incident:

Cattanach: When you were there, did you ever see Cody get hurt another time?

Annie: Yes, umm, on the wall where she was banging his head on the wall, but not in the diaper station in the bathroom.

Annie's Safe Harbor testimony regarding Emma:

Simpson (interviewer): Did you ever see Lynn hurt anybody else?
Annie: Yeah, Emma. Lynn kind of banged her head on the wall, but
not in the bathroom. I don't know where it happened.

Again, I suspected that Cattanach knew we had a strong defense against Annie's X-ray vision, so she pulled this sly maneuver to add a second incident to bolster her case. She got the judge and Eric to blindly go along with her with no explanation required. She took advantage of Eric's gullibility and newness to the case. If Eric knew of this change, as he told me when I questioned it, where was his defense? There was none, a fact that Cattanach hammered home in her closing argument.

Chapter 34

Post-Conviction Motion

*W*ith all the transcripts finally available, I awaited contact from Tracey regarding the appeal. In early summer 2011, she let me know that she had found several appealable issues. I was not surprised. With her news, however, came the caveat that we faced an uphill battle; even with the appealable issues there was only a slim chance I would prevail. I still wanted to go for it, hoping that objective eyes would see all that went wrong and provide a remedy to correct the errors.

Due to substantial errors made by Eric in the trial, mostly due to lack of time to prepare and being unfamiliar with all aspects of the case, we decided to proceed first with a post-conviction motion at the circuit court level, claiming ineffective assistance of counsel. In order to succeed on an ineffective assistance of counsel claim, we would have to show: (1) that my lawyer committed errors so egregious that it was tantamount to no legal representation at all (known as the effectiveness prong), and (2) that but for the attorney's error(s) the result of the proceedings would have been different (known as the prejudice prong).

This was a high burden to meet, but, at times, I did feel like a cardboard cutout of Eric at trial would have been as effective. Had he been on top of things, I believe the outcome would have been different. The downside to proceeding with a motion back to the circuit court meant that it would again be Judge Ehlke at the helm, and at the sentencing hearing he stated unequivocally that he found no fault with Eric's defense. Hopefully, though, by having everything spelled out in a post-conviction brief, he would be forced to objectively look at errors and omissions and conclude that Eric had failed to offer effective representation.

Eric was cooperative with Tracey regarding the case and his involvement. He responded candidly to questions about aspects of his representation that we felt were ineffective; his answers were then included as stipulated facts submitted for the post-conviction motion. He agreed that he did not have enough time to prepare and would have certainly preferred a continuance, but did not request one because I did not want to delay the trial. He admitted that he did not have time to be as thorough as he would have liked, nor did he have the time to step back and consider the case as a whole before diving into the trial. He stated that it felt hurried and fleeting and he didn't like it. To this effect, Tracey would reference State v. Thiel, 264 Wis. 2d 571, 594, 665 N.W.2d 305 (2003) for its authority. This was a Wisconsin case with similar fact patterns regarding a change in counsel who proceeded, unprepared, with a scheduled trial. The Wisconsin Supreme Court ruled that "The defendant's demand for a speedy trial did not absolve counsel of the responsibility to be prepared for trial."

Eric responded to Tracey's query about the change in date for the second count. "I know that Lynn was upset by that and she expressed that to me. My response, based only on what I think I remember, is that the discovery materials somehow reflected the propriety of the change, and we were not surprised by the change in dates. But everything was a flurry of activity at that time; I was still trying to achieve a basic level of trial preparation."

So if Eric knew that the change was proper, where was his defense? Why didn't he inform me of the change? It certainly would have appeared to the jury that Annie's second accusation was conceded by the defense, as it went unchallenged. Eric was in no way prepared to meet or defend that second incident allegation.

The reason for no defense became painfully clear when I read his response to Tracey's question of why he didn't challenge Annie's second incident: "Isn't this the count on which we showed that she could not have seen what she related and therefore there was a verdict of not guilty?" Eric had absolutely no idea about the second charge, and was confused about which count led to the acquittal. Even at this point, after hearing the prosecution's story about the second incident, he was oblivious to that charge. How did I have effective counsel if he didn't even know what charges he was to defend?

Other responses Eric gave for what we thought were questionable trial tactics were quite vague and attributed to him not remembering. He didn't recall why there was no objection to the unredacted playing of the Safe Harbor recording regarding alleged abuse to Emma. "If Judge Ehlke had not yet ruled on this video and the other act it contained, I do not remember why I did not object." He didn't recall why he gave no challenge to the playing of David's video, when it clearly did not meet the statute requirements.

As to not confronting Cathy Leaverton about her contradictory statements at trial and with our private investigator, Eric said he didn't remember why he decided to not to ask the investigator to testify about the interview with Leaverton. I know we disproved Annie's bathroom view, but Leaverton still should have been confronted with her inconsistent stories and impeached as a witness. A secondary benefit of her impeachment would have been to show the jury that the State's witnesses were willing to lie.

When asked why there were no objections to the vast amount of hearsay regarding statements by the children that came in through the testimony of the parents, Eric stated that he concluded his string of objections would have been overruled and the importance of the statements underlined by the objections. After the fact, however, he admits the statements were clearly hearsay and deserved objections.

When questioned about Dr. Andringa's medical report, he replied, "I tried to introduce the report but it was rejected on hearsay grounds. I concluded that Dr. Andringa would have said something upon cross-examination that would have hurt us more than whatever good would have come from his direct testimony." I remember when I excitedly ran to his office upon discovery of the report, and was totally baffled with his unenthusiastic response. I don't know what he speculated the doctor would say, but he didn't need Dr. Andringa to testify in order to get the report admitted. He only would have needed to subpoena any medical records custodian at the clinic to establish foundation for admission of the report as an exception to the hearsay rules, according to Wis. Stat 908.03(6m).

Eric conceded his deficient performance in these areas. I could only hope that Judge Ehlke would come to the same conclusion.

Appeals are handled solely through briefing; there was no need for me to make appearances at the house of horrors known as the Dane County Courthouse. The waiting game began while the brief was prepared.

Interestingly, while reviewing Safe Harbor's website, I noticed that it now had revised information regarding the use of the child's recorded statement.

Current wording:

Safe Harbor provides a safe and friendly place for a child to talk about what has happened to them. Safe Harbor forensic interviewers are highly trained in best practice interviewing methods and understand child development. The forensic interview is video-recorded, so that the statement can be used in court. Unfortunately, children are still required to testify. However, the recording can reduce the amount of testifying time and the child's own words that are shown in the video have enormous impact on judges and juries.

Compare this to the original wording prior to my trial:

Safe Harbor provides a safe and friendly place for a child to talk about what has happened to them, so that hopefully the child will be interviewed only once. Safe Harbor brings professionals together from all the agencies involved with a case, and the child talks to a highly trained interviewer. The statement is recorded, and if charges are filed, the recorded statement may be used in court in place of the child's testimony.

Why the change? Was this to permit children to change their stories, as Annie had? The current wording of *"the child's own words that are shown in the video have enormous impact on judges and juries"* sure didn't work in my case, as Annie's trial testimony of two incidents was deemed accurate compared to her Safe Harbor

336

testimony where she only claimed one incident. What about inconsistencies? Are they addressed? They sure weren't in my case.

I started school for the paralegal program, and kept busy with my coursework. It had been thirty years since I was last in school, so I had to refresh my study habits. I especially related to the criminal law class. It was easy to do the assignments and tests since I had lived the criminal indictment process.

I also held a going-out-of-business-sale and sold or donated all my day care toys, equipment, and supplies. Seeing the materials leave my house was hard, as it hit home that I would never get my former life back. I prided myself on having had quality toys and equipment in my day care, and had invested tons of money in my business over the years, only to recoup garage sale prices. At least I knew that children in other programs would benefit from the equipment.

2012 arrived. I breezed through my schooling, and in March received my paralegal certificate; proudly carrying a 4.0 GPA. The best news was that I had also secured employment with a local insurance company.

In early June, Tracey submitted her brief for the post-conviction motion, asserting that both plain error and ineffective assistance of counsel justified reversal of my case and the granting of a new trial. I was pleased with her concluding remarks: "A prudent lawyer versed in the practice of criminal law would require more than six weeks to review all that had transpired in the case in the previous year-and-a-half along with the changes to the dates and other late developments. The pressure of a stressed client to get the case tried cannot be allowed to trump the lawyer's obligations to zealously represent the client at trial. Mr. Schulenburg is to be commended for conceding his deficient performance in these matters, as that is part of what we expect defense lawyers to do when they make significant erroneous decisions not strategically motivated in a client's defense. Had the proper objections and procedural rules been followed in this case, Ms. Moller stood a much greater chance of acquittal on all counts. By acquitting on the only seriously contested count, this jury demonstrated that it was prepared to accord Ms. Moller the presumption of innocence the law requires. There are serious questions about the integrity of the guilty verdicts in this case which would probably have been different had Mr. Schulenburg's performance been what is expected under the prevailing norms."

The State filed its response in opposition to my post-conviction motion at the end of July. The State's brief repeatedly argued that we waived many issues by failing to raise objections at trial. It also stated that the court should not believe Schulenburg's statements that he was not prepared for this trial and that he needed more time to prepare because he made those statements after the fact.

Tracey addressed the State's arguments in a reply brief. "The State's brief argues that the defense has waived many issues by failing to raise an objection at trial. This argument misses the point that in a motion hearing related to whether trial counsel was ineffective, the failure to object is the exact point of the proceedings and tends to favor a finding of ineffectiveness." She rebutted the State's claim that Eric made his admittance of trial unpreparedness after the fact. "He never in the underlying case said he was fully prepared, and the State points to no reason Schulenburg is not to be believed. The lack of preparation goes to each and every allegation in this motion. From failing to call witnesses, to confront witnesses, to being confused as to a second count of abuse against Cody, all are attributed to the simple problem that he did not have enough time. Counsel should have requested a continuance to be fully prepared in this case. The failure to do so led to the ineffectiveness discussed herein. Thus, Moller should be granted a new trial."

This reply brief was submitted August 7, 2012. I realized a favorable decision from Judge Ehlke was a long shot, already knowing that he felt I had received good representation. Therefore, it was upsetting, but not a shock, when, on November 6, 2012, he denied my motion for post-conviction relief. Ehlke stated that even if counsel's performance was deficient in any way, any prejudice was minimal and, in the totality of the circumstances and evidence, did not affect the outcome of my trial. The evidence against me was strong, he proclaimed, and supported the jury's guilty verdicts on the three counts of reckless child abuse. Again, I thought, what evidence?

It was infuriating to read his response to Eric not confronting Annie about the second incident claim. Instead of admitting that Eric did not understand that there were two incidents, Ehlke improperly credited Eric's failure to impeach Annie as a legitimate trial tactic. "Had counsel impeached Annie's testimony, he ran the risk of alienating the jury, which might have viewed this tactic as an unfair one to use against a seven-year-old girl. Accordingly, counsel's performance in this respect was objectively reasonable considering the special dangers inherent in attempting to impeach child witnesses."

Annie absolutely needed to be confronted about her inconsistent stories. She sparked this situation, and there were obvious concerns about her actual ability to see what she alleged. Given his mild manner and grandfatherly nature, Eric would have been gentle in his approach with Annie, had he actually been aware of and confronted her about her inconsistencies. There would have been no inciting this conjectured jury backlash.

As to our claim that Annie's Safe Harbor video should have been edited so the jury would not hear the portion regarding Emma getting her head banged, Ehlke said I was not prejudiced by that. "Annie admitted that she did not actually see Moller abuse Emma. Instead, she stated that she only saw Moller carry Emma into the playroom and then heard a noise. Notably, Annie could not explain why she thought that the noise meant that Emma's head was banged on the wall. Within the context of the entire video,

Annie's allegation was nothing more than a little girl's confusing assumption that a noise she heard that came from a room she could not see into was evidence of physical abuse."

It was vexing to compare Ehlke's statement about Annie's credibility at the sentencing hearing ("*When Annie reports what she saw, she was six years old, old enough to understand what she was observing, and I understand the questions about angles and so on, but she is reporting that she's seeing things. She had no reason to make up anything about Cody.*") with this appeal decision where he concedes that she was confused about something she heard but did not see. Two of three claims Annie made were not credible—her initial seeing into the diaper station in the bathroom and this claim of head banging to Emma—so what are the odds that the second incident in a place she can't remember actually occurred?

Tracey agreed that Ehlke's decision was not a big surprise, as trial courts are loathe to admit that they permitted a travesty of justice in their own courts. She indicated that the court simply said the pat answers to all challenges (not deficient, and even if deficient, not prejudicial) and ignored some of the bigger arguments in the briefs. Therefore, as expected, our next step was to the Wisconsin Court of Appeals, allowing us to challenge some of the court rulings that prejudiced me in the very beginning (such as the joinder issue). We could also appeal some of the stronger aspects of the ineffective counsel claims. This would then be out of Judge Ehlke's hands, onto a hopefully more objective panel of judges. The downside to this, of course, would be another delay to any finality for my case; this appeal step would likely take at least a year. But, other than additional attorney fees for this leg of the journey, I had nothing to lose. The black cloud had been hanging over my head for more than four years; another year or so would not matter much.

Chapter 35

Court of Appeals

*I*n April 2013, I gave a presentation at the annual University of Wisconsin-Whitewater Early Childhood Conference. I had almost yearly attended this conference during my career; it was a great way to get in-service/continuing education credits, and the various workshops on child development and curriculum always motivated me. I had submitted a proposal for a workshop entitled "It Can Happen to You—Allegations of Abuse in the Child Care Field." I was pleased when it was accepted. My goal was to explain what happened to me, and how easily it can happen to anyone, as well as give participants knowledge of what to do if faced with abuse allegations. In addition, I wanted others to learn from my mistakes, such as talking to the police, and not thinking I needed an attorney at the first hints of allegations. The importance of getting the word out to fellow child care providers pushed me to overcome my shyness and reluctance to speak publicly. If I could keep one person from going through what I endured, my ordeal may have had some benefit. My presentation was well received with positive feedback and many thanks for bringing this subject to others' attention.

Tracey submitted her brief to the Wisconsin Court of Appeals, District Four, on June 6, 2013. As indicated, she contested the joinder of the Cody and Miles charges, and once again raised the ineffective counsel claim, reiterating the points submitted to Ehlke in the post-conviction motion. The State, in its response brief, urged the Court of Appeals to affirm all prior decisions, saying that joinder was proper, and that I did not receive ineffective counsel. I noted that the author of the State's brief regurgitated Ehlke's responses in his "favorable-to-them" decision. Tracey's reply brief went in on October 23, 2013, and then it was another waiting game for a decision. Tracey had been candid with me all along that the chances for a reversal at this stage were slim, but I held out hope that the appeal judges, when presented with a factual record of events and relevant case law, would acknowledge the errors and mandate a new trial.

However, just as nothing went right for me all along, the Court of Appeal's decision, rendered on March 27, 2014, went against me. I was devastated and near tears. The appeal judges stated that any failures of trial counsel were either strategic and reasonable or not shown to prejudice my defense; therefore, I did not receive ineffective assistance of counsel. How could they call my attorney's actions strategic when he didn't even know the charges I faced?

Regarding joinder, the judges stated that the issue was forfeited since I didn't raise the concern of substantial prejudice at the circuit court level. What? The prejudice factor was indeed argued by Bob to both Judges Schwartz and Ehlke; it was that level of prejudice that made Bob object so vigorously to joinder. No waiver should have been presumed by these appeal judges; it wasn't even argued by the State. I read and re-read the decision. My initial sad reaction turned to anger.

Then I looked at the names of the three judges on the panel: Lundsten, Sherman, and Kloppenburg. Why did these names sound familiar to me? Turns out that two of the three, Lundsten and Kloppenburg, were parents of children I had in my classes at University Avenue Day Care. The good-bye card I received from the families was even signed by Judge Lundsten, thanking me for the good care I gave his son. I had no idea who appellate judges were; if I had, I would have requested that these two not be allowed to rule on my case.

Tracey immediately filed a Motion for Disqualification and Reconsideration. Given that my relationship with these judges was as a day care provider, and that my case dealt with child abuse in my role as a day care provider, Tracey argued that the prejudice to me was inherent in the nature of this case. She wrote, "It would be next to impossible for any parent whose children were cared for by Moller in a preschool or day care setting to not react with fear and horror in discovering that she had been convicted of physically abusing other children in her care in a similar situation. Any parent would be affected, and it is reasonable to assume that judges are not immune from such human emotions, especially in a case dealing with child abuse. Moller therefore requests this court permit a new panel of judges who did not have children in her preschool classes or under her care in day care to determine the validity of her appellate challenges.

"Moller also requests reconsideration of this court's decision, noting that the issue of prejudice to Moller in joining the cases was argued at length in the trial court. Additionally, Moller's counsel's errors cumulatively prejudiced her case."

It didn't take long for the Court of Appeals to deny this motion. "We conclude that disqualification is not warranted in this case. Neither Judge Lundsten nor Judge Kloppenburg has any recollection of Moller or whether she provided child care for any of their children. Additionally, neither judge has any recollection of a negative experience with any child care provider at UADC. Thus, when deciding this appeal, neither judge had any awareness that Moller might have had contact with his or her children in a day care setting. Accordingly, we determine that there is no reason that any judge on this panel could not act impartially.

"Moller also moves for reconsideration of our decision on the merits. Nothing in the material provided causes us to reconsider our decision."

Oh, well, it was worth a shot. My only remaining option now was the Wisconsin Supreme Court. Unlike the Court of Appeals, which takes all cases, the Supreme Court grants review of a case only when they feel special and important reasons are presented. I was well aware that the chances of the Supreme Court accepting my case were infinitesimal, but I remained determined to exhaust all avenues in my quest to seek justice.

Tracey submitted the Petition for Review to the Supreme Court in May 2014, requesting acceptance of my case to give clarification not only to my case but also to any future, similar cases. She wrote, in the preface, "This court should take this case because it involves significant questions of both constitutional and state law. Specifically, the Court of Appeals decision has sanctioned joinder in two non-sexual abuse cases occurring over twenty-seven months apart. There has been no published case to date finding that time frame to be short enough to permit joinder. Thus, a decision by this court will also serve to clarify the law in this regard, as the appeal decision conflicts with previous decisions both in federal and state court, where the permissible time frame between incidents sought to be joined was far less than twenty-seven months.

"Additionally, this case presents another significant question of constitutional law relating to the right to effective assistance of counsel. Specifically, this case deals with the question of how high a showing of prejudice needs to be to rise to the level of a finding of ineffective assistance of counsel. This case would also help to harmonize state law with respect to ineffective assistance of counsel claims, as previous cases have held that the types of errors in the instant case establish ineffective assistance."

While awaiting the Supreme Court decision, I presented another workshop at the Early Childhood Conference at UW-Stout, my alma mater. The school still had a strong Early Childhood Education program, so I was glad to be able to impart my knowledge to warn and protect my fellow early childhood educators. The session allotted seventy-five minutes; it could have easily been twice that long since the audience wanted to share stories or ask advice. I was, but shouldn't have been, surprised at how many people were affected by similar circumstances of children making false allegations. A common thought expressed by the participants was, "Do I need to get out of this career?" I felt bad, but all I could say was to be careful and aware. As at the Whitewater conference, I heavily stressed obtaining an attorney at any sign of trouble, and to *never talk to the police*.

Chapter 36

Jail

Knowing that the end of my appeal road approached, barring any Supreme Court decision miracle, and that I had been on borrowed time as far as serving my sentence, I used the summer of 2014 to prepare myself for the jail sentence. Chances were high that I would have home detention, but I would be limited in getting out and doing things that I had always taken for granted. I did some early Christmas shopping, took care of medical appointments, stocked up on household goods, and tried to do anything else I could think of to make it easier on my family and myself if I was under house arrest.

Sure enough, at the end of September I learned that my petition for review had been denied by the Supreme Court. Other than an initial shouting of an expletive, I was basically devoid of all emotion by this time regarding the case. It wasn't worth it to get upset anymore; I decided I would channel any negative feelings into chronicling my legal journey. This pending jail time would be another chapter in an increasingly long story. I thought it was unwise of the Supreme Court to refuse my case; whether or not they ruled in my favor, they could have made some precedential decisions regarding joinder and ineffective assistance of counsel issues. Without binding authority, these cloudy issues were likely to recur for some unfortunate defendant in the future.

I was able to pick my jail start date, so I chose October 27, 2014. I had been in contact with the representative at the sheriff's department who handled the Huber cases; she was quite nice and made sure I understood everything that needed to be done. Unfortunately, she said I was not eligible for the home detention/ electronic monitoring program due to the nature of my "crime." That surprised me, as that is what Judge Ehlke directed. Now it appeared that I would be released from jail for my normal work hours, but would have to return to the jail for nights and weekends. I was bummed, but chalked it up to another thing not going right in this whole mess.

However, no sooner did I get to jail, than someone talked to me about getting on the electronic monitoring program, stating that I did not belong in jail. Did one hand not know what the other was doing? After a short stint in jail, I was released for home detention. In the totality of the circumstances, being on the electronic monitoring program was not bad at all, other than having the ever-present appendage on my ankle. Besides going to work, I could attend medical appointments, get a monthly haircut, and go grocery shopping once a week. I never felt punished. In fact, since I had to relinquish many of the tasks and errands I normally did, it was almost like a mini-vacation. I wonder how the parents who demanded jail time for me, as well as Cattanach, would feel knowing that I was actually having a good time.

How was the short time I actually spent in the jail? I was surprisingly not nervous when I first reported, knowing that at least I would be out at work for most of the daytime hours. The jail unit was a large room with a series of bunk beds on one end and a common room on the other; no stereotypical individual cells with metal bars. There were about twenty other women in the unit, ranging from teenagers to sixty-year-olds. Most of them were in for OWI or drug-related offenses. They were all nice, and curious about why I was there; they expressed disbelief when I told them. I guess I didn't fit the typical inmate profile. I had a good rapport with them; they joked about which actors would portray them in the movie based on my story.

I did not observe any bad treatment by the jail staff, but some officers exhibited obvious "I'm better than you" and "Don't mess with me" attitudes. Other deputies, however, were nice, friendly, and respectful. The jail food was absolutely awful; fortunately, I did not have to rely on those meals.

I had expected jail to be a demeaning and humiliating experience. In those respects, my short stint there actually paled in comparison to all the other court proceedings I had endured.

351

Probation was no big deal. The worst part of it was voting ineligibility. In Wisconsin, felons can't vote until discharged from supervision (it is still incredible that the label "felon" applies to me). Cattanach, at the sentencing hearing, snidely reminded the judge to rescind my voting rights. Although the jail and probation time had been suspended during the long appeal process, my voting prohibition continued, essentially turning the three-year penalty into seven-and-a-half years. I missed key local, state, and national elections. Sorry, fellow Democrats.

With the appeal process over, the restitution issue resurfaced. Mark Kerman sent a letter to Tracey, explaining the amount sought: "The Marshalls paid Lynn Moller $5,880 for their son's last six months of childcare, during the time their son was abused. Seventy-five dollars was the pre-school deposit paid by the Marshalls for their son's childcare that followed his time with Lynn Moller."

So I abused Cody for six months? Since March 2008? That was not what I was charged with or convicted of. This went back to that time Cody had what I thought was an ear infection, and I suggested that he go to the doctor. At that doctor visit, tiny red marks were seen in his ear, and Dr. Landry opined that he likely had received a contusion to his ear from rough play with his brother. He was not concerned about the small bruises. Then Cattanach used this report as the springboard for Cody being abused. She exaggerated the claims in Dr. Landry's report to suit her speculative theory. The statement in her closing argument regarding this doctor report was inaccurate and misleading: *"Then all of sudden in March 2008 we've got doctors' records recording an ear injury with the red dots and the bruising. Dr. Knox says this is gravely concerning for abuse."*

There was absolutely nothing in Landry's report to corroborate Cattanach's or Knox's claim of "gravely concerning for abuse." Believing they could capitalize on it through a restitution claim, the Marshalls bought into that six-month period of alleged abuse. By doing so, however, they admitted that they were clueless and never suspected anything.

Now they wanted me to pay the seventy-five dollar deposit for the new pre-school. Why? They would have had to pay that at some point when he graduated from my care. Leaving my care abruptly didn't mean I was responsible for that charge.

I knew that I was entitled to a restitution hearing where the Marshalls would have to document their claim. Tracey proposed that I make a lower offer to the Marshalls to avoid the hearing; her suggested number was half of what they asked. I thought that amount was too high without making them prove their claim. If they didn't have proper documentation, wouldn't that be tantamount to lying to the court? However, I agreed that maybe we could make this issue go away with an out-of-court settlement. I was not admitting to any wrongdoing, but given the history of Judge Ehlke ruling against me, I didn't want to take a chance on him saying I needed to pay their entire phony claim. I (grudgingly) told Tracey I would give the Marshalls $2,000 ($1,000 each) to settle this. I was not at all surprised to hear that they accepted the offer. It was patently obvious by their immediate acceptance of my lowball offer that they had no basis for their restitution claim. They surely would have held out for their full amount if they believed their claim was justified or documented.

Chapter 37

Moving On

My life now is an interminable allusion to the "if onlys." If only I never let Annie come for those days. If only Holly Jeter had been truthful with me. If only I hadn't talked to the police. If only my first attorney, Bob, had remained on the case. If only I hired a more aggressive replacement attorney. On and on.

Friends and relatives frequently expressed admiration that I remained strong through this ordeal, doubting their abilities to do so if caught in similar circumstances. We underestimate our capacity to deal with adversity until it is thrust upon us. Everyone has a cross to bear; mine was legal. Bob Marley hit the nail on the head with his quote: "You never know how strong you are until being strong is your only choice." There were plenty of times when the defeatist attitude reared its head and I wanted to give up, or I wallowed in self-pity, but I pushed myself to keep going. I couldn't let the opponents drag me down without a fight, and I was determined to set a good example for my sons. Forced to grow beyond the person I was when this all started, I've emerged stronger and wiser.

But at what cost? The events since 2008 have consumed me. No matter how hard I try to banish them, thoughts about this time of tribulation haunt me daily. My physical and emotional reserves have been depleted. I wouldn't be surprised if ten years have been taken from my life. I still experience night terrors and mini panic attacks. The nightmare replays in my mind, along with punishing thoughts of what I should have done differently.

Countless times, I imagine a happier scenario where the prosecution's case was destroyed and the accusers exposed for their false stories, with me vindicated and returning to my beloved child care career. Once I snap out of my reverie, however, I am faced with the harsh reality of being a convicted felon with no future working with children.

The financial ramifications of this nightmare are staggering. Attorney fees, appeal fees, court costs, probation and jail costs, and loss of income have reached into the hundreds of thousands of dollars. Financial goals I had for the future are completely out of reach. The costs that I incurred don't even include the vast taxpayer resources wasted by pursuing my case.

I've been critical of the conduct of the professionals involved in this case—ADA Cattanach, Detective Johnson, Dr. Knox, and Cathy Leaverton. Since they acted in the scope of their jobs, their behavior was allowed and encouraged. I know I am not the only defendant to fall prey to questionable maneuvers by a prosecution team. Devious interrogation tactics by police paired with prosecutorial misdeeds of overcharging, mischaracterizing or manipulating evidence, and theatrical closing argument performances are justified as a means to an end, ensuring victory for their side. Such latitude would never be allowed in defense strategies. Can we trust the reliability of guilty verdicts in trials where dubious tactics were employed?

I think about McGraw's statement in the PSI: *"Moller needs to stop pointing fingers and look in the mirror and attempt to correct her behavior which begins with taking responsibility."* I've looked in the mirror, but all I see is someone who was caught up in a situation that quickly spun out of control.

The person who should take a good look in the mirror is Holly Jeter. As a teacher, mother, and human being, her actions in this affair were unconscionable. Lying to me about why she pulled Miles from my care; not checking the credibility of Annie's initial claim; making Annie and Miles continue to go to my house after Annie said something troubling, without bothering to investigate it; not reporting abuse to the proper authorities if she suspected it; only caring about getting her own kids out of a potential abusive situation but letting the others remain; telling different stories about when she noticed the bruises on Miles; the list goes on. How does she rationalize her actions? Do the other parents realize what she did, or did not do? As a teacher, does Holly realize how easily she could be swept up in a similar situation? Would she like to deal with someone who acted as she did?

For whatever reason, Annie felt the need to report abuse. I try not to blame her (she was six), but, subconsciously or not, I probably do. She was the catalyst for suspicion gone wildly out of control. No favors were done to Annie by blindly accepting her allegations and conflicting stories. The jury at least knew her initial claim was not possible. Her parents, the other parents, Detective Johnson, Cattanach, and even Judge Ehlke all gave too much power to Annie, making her a victim of power and lies, and contributing to the chain of events that has forever altered my life. Has she grown up thinking she's a hero for her role in all this? Is this something for which she is still praised? Does she have any idea of the impact of her accusations?

I feel sorry for the Marshalls. They were duped into believing that their son was abused. Never mind that no doctor gave that diagnosis. They obviously had some personal issues going on during this time; how much that clouded their judgment, I'll never know. Why didn't they ask me? Check it out for themselves? The ten-year relationship I had had with them was wiped out in a minute once they bought into Annie's story.

I acknowledge that this was an emotionally charged ordeal for the families. But why were they all quick to abandon me? That has been more devastating to me than the actual convictions, leaving a deep wound that will probably never heal. Are they actually convinced of my guilt? What did they think when the jury found Annie's initial claim not credible? Allegations of abuse need to be applied with common sense and judgment, not hysteria. Had clearer heads prevailed, this entire fiasco could have been avoided. The adults whose trust in me was broken only needed a simple investigation to realize the impossibility of Annie's claim.

The natural instinct of our society is to protect our children at all costs, and the legal system follows that inclination. However, in doing so, collateral damage is done to teachers, child care providers, coaches, and even parents wrongly accused of abuse. Every adult who works with children is at risk of having abuse allegations levied upon them.

Contrary to the constitutional assumption of innocence, guilty until proven innocent is the reality for those charged with crimes against children. It's hard to prove you're innocent when there was never a crime. Most people believe that if a defendant is in court, a crime was committed, a perception that stacks the deck immediately against the defendant. This belief also focuses on the connection between the crime and the defendant, rather than questioning if the crime actually occurred.

For many years, I belonged to a small support group of area family child care providers. I shared my experience with them from the start; they stood by me and provided emotional support, for which I am ever grateful. The members were well aware that it wouldn't take much for any one of them to get caught up in a similar situation. However, I received absolutely no advocacy from the state day care licensing department or other local child care associations. As a professional child care provider, I paid a fee to these organizations for licensing and memberships. They had no trouble taking my money, but quickly boarded the "guilty until proven innocent" bandwagon when the abuse allegations surfaced, in effect exiling me. I now exclude the local Wisconsin child care resource agency from my United Way contribution through work. I refuse to donate to the children's hospital as long as Dr. Barbara Knox works there. I roll my eyes when I hear fundraising requests for Safe Harbor. Any minuscule amounts I am capable of donating will not help anyone, but it's the principle of the thing. Future charitable contributions will be directed to innocence projects or other causes that advocate for the wrongly accused and convicted.

Life threw me a curve ball. Never in a million years did I anticipate being not only accused but also convicted of child abuse. I've been on a horrible journey through the darkest valley of my life. For the longest time I felt empty, a ghost of a person. I had put my heart and soul into my career. Working with kids, I knew who I was. Once that was taken away, I floundered. Now all I can do is move forward, admittedly nervous about the direction my life has taken and the uncertain road ahead, a far cry from my prior hopes, goals, and dreams.

By nature, I am not a resentful or bitter person, and I have a forgiving spirit. As this ordeal approaches the decade mark, however,

I frankly can't claim to not hold a grudge. I am only human, after all, and have been terribly hurt and affected by those I had trusted and considered an important part of my life. With time, I hope my heart heals, allowing me peace and acceptance. The legendary angel and devil, omnipresent on my shoulders, bicker over disparate wishes of forgiveness and karma. The prevailing character remains to be seen.

But for this awful experience, I likely would still hold my naïve belief that the criminal justice system works. I regret that this was the prerequisite to raise my awareness of wrongful convictions. As bad as it was, I know my situation is minor compared to others who've been wrongly accused, convicted, and incarcerated. My heart aches for those who lost, and continue to lose, years of their lives behind bars due to wrongful convictions. I've often been asked if I contacted the Innocence Project for help. While I would jump at any opportunity to clear my name, I would not burden the Innocence Project with my case. There are innocent folks languishing behind bars who are more deserving of the limited resources of the innocence organizations. Hats off to the hardworking attorneys and staff of such programs.

My personal library now contains too many books about false accusations and wrongful convictions. The nightmare comes alive in these narratives, as the writers detail their experiences with criminal justice system failings, mass hysteria, police and prosecutorial misconduct, and junk science. Reading these horror stories was agonizing, and I found myself agreeing with so much. "Yes, that's exactly what happens," or "That's how I felt," were sentiments I expressed while reading others' accounts. There is a shared connection among those with similar experiences. I never expected to be a member of this club. I hope no one else ever joins, but, unfortunately, that is an unrealistic dream.

My experience and awareness have spawned a commitment to help others avoid the same or worse fate. We all have to be aware of the workings and the pitfalls of our criminal justice system. This system is subject to human error and people do make mistakes. We can't accept all convictions at face value, and we must be concerned about those whose lives it deeply affects. Justice in the courts is not guaranteed.

Please believe me: what happened to me could easily happen to you, to your loved ones, to anyone. We are all just one Annie away from the nightmare of a wrongful conviction.

Acknowledgments

"When one door closes, another opens; but we often look so long and so regretfully upon the closed door that we do not see the one which has opened for us."

– Alexander Graham Bell

*U*ndeniably, I pine for my pre-2008 life. However, as Mr. Bell so aptly stated, the time has come for me to close that door and venture through the open one. Challenging circumstances have pointed me in a new direction, but I could not have made the leap without the support of so many people. Heartfelt appreciation is extended:

- To my forever friends, Kellylee, Jean, Mary, Lynn, Jan, Helen. You were there when I needed to laugh, cry, complain, or just melt down. Thank you for caring for me and my family when I couldn't. You embody the spirit of true friendship.

- To my friends and fellow child care providers, Rima, Darlene, Patti, Sharon. You truly define the "support" in support group. You have been a source of comfort and strength.

- To the unexpected connections I made via this journey. My life is now richer with you in it. Martha and Betsy, thank you for making my house arrest enjoyable (and for the euchre games!). Joan and Audrey, you inspire me. Mark, promoting my story on The Reporters Inc. motivated me to continue my writing. New friendships have developed through my classes and employment, proving that good can come from the bad.

- To all the considerate folks who wrote character refer-ences and letters of support, attended the trial or sentencing hearing, sent money, checked on me, and encouraged me to keep fighting. Those kind acts meant the world to me.

- To the day care families who avoided the hysteria and defended me. Your time with me is a cherished memory, and I couldn't be prouder of all my day care kids. Deb, your legal advice and advocacy on my behalf were priceless.

- To my relatives, far and near, who never once doubted my innocence and jumped in with both feet to support me. Aunt Sherry and (late) Uncle Wayne, Aunt Jane and Uncle Don,

Aunt Eleanor and Uncle David, Aunt Jeannette, (late) Aunt Mary Ann and Uncle Doug, cousins Jean, Fred and June, Larry and Colleen, my (late) grandmothers Marion and Dorothy, and many other extended family members provided emotional, psychological, and financial assistance.

• To the best siblings in the world, PJ, Andy, and Nikki, who never abandoned their big sister and delivered much needed comic relief. PJ, thank you for your journalistic skills, editing input, and title suggestions as I worked on this book.

• To my parents, Phil and (late) Marilyn, who raised me in a loving home and were strong role models. Mom, your inspirational spirit motivated me to keep fighting. Dad, you stood by me in every way possible. The world is a better place for having you in it.

• To my cherished sons, Evan and Aaron, who were involuntarily thrust into the midst of my trials and tribulations. You handled the situation maturely, beyond your young years, and I am so proud of you. You are the reason I stayed in the fight.

- Lastly, to my dear husband, Ki. You took this ordeal even harder than me. We've been on a roller coaster of ups and downs, loops and turns, and screams, cries, and laughs. It would have been easy for you to jump ship, but you stood by and never wavered in your belief in me. Your unique sense of humor pulled me through my darkest moments. Our plans have been altered, but we will embrace the future together, whatever it brings. Hawaii still beckons.

CPSIA information can be obtained
at www.ICGtesting.com
Printed in the USA
FFOW04n0533190218
45110942-45554FF

9 781545 602584